d:
Principles and Realities

Edited by
Margaret Boushel, Mary Fawcett and Julie Selwyn

b

**Blackwell
Science**

© 2000 by Blackwell Science Ltd, a Blackwell Publishing company
Editorial offices:
Blackwell Science Ltd, 9600 Garsington Road, Oxford OX4 2DQ, UK
   Tel: +44 (0)1865 776868
Blackwell Publishing Inc., 350 Main Street, Malden, MA 02148-5020, USA
   Tel: +1 781 388 8250
Blackwell Science Asia Pty Ltd, 550 Swanston Street, Carlton, Victoria 3053, Australia
   Tel: +61 (0)3 8359 1011

2004000717

First published 2000
Reprinted 2005

Library of Congress Cataloging-in-Publication Data
Boushel, Margaret
   Focus on early childhood: principles and realities/Margaret Boushel, Mary Fawcett, and Julie Selwyn.
      p. cm.
   Includes bibliographical references and index.
   ISBN 0-632-05157-4
   1. Child psychology — Research.   2. Child development — Research.   3. Child rearing.
   I. Fawcett, Mary, 1936–   II. Selwyn, Julie.   III. Title.

   BF722 .B68 2000
   305.23 — dc21   00-027797

ISBN 0-632-05157-4

A catalogue record for this title is available from the British Library

Set in 10/12pt Palatino
by DP Photosetting, Aylesbury, Bucks
Printed and bound in Great Britain
by Marston Book Services, Oxford

The publisher's policy is to use permanent paper from mills that operate a sustainable forestry policy, and which has been manufactured from pulp processed using acid-free and elementary chlorine-free practices. Furthermore, the publisher ensures that the text paper and cover board used have met acceptable environmental accreditation standards.

For further information on Blackwell Publishing, visit our website:
www.blackwellpublishing.com

Contents

List of Contributors

John Barrett has lectured and supervised research on Developmental Psychology in the Department of Experimental Psychology of the University of Bristol for over thirty years. He specialises in biopsychosocial and ecological approaches to lifespan development, and their applications in education and health. His publications include fetal and early childhood development, learning disability and conduct disorder.

Margaret Boushel is a lecturer in the School for Policy Studies at the University of Bristol, where she has been director of the BSc in early childhood studies and teaches on postgraduate and professional social work and child welfare programmes. She is a qualified barrister and social worker with many years' experience as a practitioner, manager and policy maker in local authority social work in Scotland and England. Since January 2000 she has been seconded by the university to become Programme Manager for the first Sure Start 'Trailblazer' project in Bristol.

Hilary Burgess is a lecturer in the School for Policy Studies at the University of Bristol. Her main interests are professional learning and development, family support, interprofessional work and community-based practice. She is also a non-executive director of Gloucestershire Royal NHS Trust, and combines commitments with caring for her children.

Mary Fawcett taught in nursery and infant schools in Scotland and England before working with communities and parents in the early days of the playgroup movement. She was a lecturer in the Universities of East Anglia (School of Education) and Bristol (School for Policy Studies). She initiated and then directed the BSc in early childhood studies, one of the first in the country, until her recent retirement. Her handbook *Learning Through Child Observation* was published in 1996.

Hilary Land is Professor of Family Policy and Child Welfare at the School for Policy Studies, University of Bristol. She has a long-standing interest in families and social policies which started in the 1960s when she worked on a national study of poverty with Peter Townsend and Brian Abel Smith. Current research interests include women returners to education and the labour market, day care policies, pensions, young people's transitions to adulthood. Her latest book *Lone Mothers in Twentieth Century*

Britain (OUP), with Kathleen Kiernan and Jane Lewis, was published in 1998.

Andrew Pollard is a professor at the Graduate School of Education, University of Bristol. Having taught in primary and middle schools, he specialised in teacher education and research, and has developed particular interests in pupil perspectives and the sociology of learning. Among his books are *The Social World of Children's Learning* and *Policy, Practice and Pupil Experience*.

Julie Selwyn is a lecturer in the School for Policy Studies at the University of Bristol. Her research interests are in the field of adoption and fostering and she is currently undertaking a project for the Department of Health examining the costs and outcomes of a sample of late placed adopted children. Before teaching she was a practising social worker working with children and families in a variety of settings.

Foreword

Olive Stephenson

The very word 'children' raises profound and complex emotions. Here are small, immature human beings, upon whom the future of man- and woman-kind literally depends. Society has a powerful interest in ensuring the survival of these children. Individually, all kinds of adults invest emotionally in children; passionate love and hope, dark fears and anxieties – all this and more is the everyday stuff of adult–child relationships. Furthermore, ambivalence is an essential element in the way adults relate to children for they pose a threat to us: they challenge our power; they may achieve where we have failed. The battle of the generations is mirrored in our greatest literature, as *King Lear* so vividly illustrates.

Such is the intensity of these emotions that they frequently reduce and distort the quality of public debate about 'the business' of childhood. Angry dogmatism is a feature of much media comment which feeds on people's raw feelings. Reactions to the James Bolger case illustrated such distortion with fearful clarity. Pity for the suffering of one small child led to the demonising of two small children and the strange idea of 'evil' as a freestanding element of some personalities.

So, we are in a muddle about children. This book, which is a thorough, scholarly and wide ranging discussion of many aspects of early childhood, is precisely what we need to improve understanding and awareness of early childhood's pathways towards adulthood and of the circumstances in which children grow up. It deals with development *per se*, but also with the social context and institutions in which children are reared. It is research-focused and offers a formidable body of evidence for statements and assertions. It draws from a wide variety of sources and theories and from a holistic understanding which is the product of interdisciplinary study.

This book should be read by those who work for and care for children and will be further enjoyed by many who would, in this context, describe themselves as interested 'lay' people. Not everybody will read each chapter with equal seriousness because there is comprehensive coverage of many issues. It is, however, most valuable to find, between the covers of one book, objective analysis of different critical determinants of children's development and well-being.

Because this book has potentially a very wide readership, it would be inappropriate to stress its value to one section of readers rather than another. But perhaps, given my own background, I may be allowed to stress that the readership should most definitely include social workers in child welfare who have not in recent years been well-served by social work education. They urgently need the knowledge and understanding which is to be found in these chapters.

In recent years, the study of early childhood has grown in popularity. This is to be warmly welcomed. This book will be recognised as a significant contribution to the literature.

Olive Stevenson
Professor Emeritus of Social Work Studies
University of Nottingham

Acknowledgements

For over seven years the University of Bristol has been successfully running one of the first degrees in early childhood studies in the UK. The three editors have been part of the teaching team from the start. Over the years many individuals have been involved: the students, colleagues within the university, the community and the voluntary sector as well as professionals in the many services involved with children and young families. We have been stimulated, challenged and informed, as well as supported by these people.

We particularly wish to thank Julia Jefferies, Dave Worth, Trevor Fawcett and Bill Selwyn for cover photography. Outside Bristol, Ann Robinson at the National Children's Bureau helped with the preschool statistics.

Finally we could not have managed without the support of our families who have accepted our absorption and occupation over several years, and to whom we dedicate this book.

Margaret Boushel, Mary Fawcett and Julie Selwyn

Introduction

Childhood can seem the simplest and most natural period in the human lifespan, but it is increasingly viewed as problematic. The stereotypical view of childhood, characterised as a time of innocence, dependence and vulnerability, is being challenged from several angles – among them important research studies and children's own changing behaviour.

Everyone who reads this book, and all those who wrote it, have once been children. We undoubtedly all retain memories from that time, some of which may be happy and some painful. How we understand childhood *now*, as adults at the beginning of the twenty-first century, is the result of myriad encounters with the concept of childhood through all kinds of social and cultural exchanges, such as the media, literature and film and our friends and community. Our own experiences set in a particular cultural context, time and place, therefore, are only a limited guide to the world of childhoods now.

Information, theoretical knowledge and research about children's lives and development are extremely diverse and scattered amongst a range of different academic and professional disciplines such as sociology, history, anthropology, medicine, education and social policy. There is still much to be learnt about how best to bring together this huge range of material and large diversity in approach. In writing this book we have found our own varied academic and professional backgrounds essential, inspirational and extremely challenging! We hope we will have some success in integrating the knowledge we have gained and in whetting the reader's appetite for further study.

Social construction of childhood

Humans all share a biological pattern through conception, infancy and growth to adulthood but the ways in which we make sense of this process are cultural and greatly influenced by our own experiences. Childhood as a cultural construction has in fact many variations – within each community, each generation and among children themselves. Childhood is constantly being constructed and reconstructed (Prout & James, 1997).

Thinking about childhood in this way raises several key issues. When childhood is viewed as social construction it appears not as a natural or universal period in human life, but rather as a variable cultural element within different societies. There are other cultural variables too, such as class, gender and ethnicity, which need to be taken into account along with childhood.

Significantly, children are viewed as active constructors not only of their own social lives, but also of the lives of those around them. Children may be said to 'bring their parents up' as well as being brought up themselves, because being a child is not just about passively receiving adults' teaching and directing, but also about having an active role in these interactions (Chapter 9).

In the past, children's voices were not usually heard and the impact of policies on them not properly considered. Newer studies of children, however, some based in the discipline of sociology, start from the perspective of taking seriously the world inhabited by children – their social relationships, their cultures and their view of adult demands. As yet, most of these studies concentrate on the world of the older child.

Until recently the study of young children and their development was dominated by another discipline, that of psychology. For many years it has provided a framework of explanation for the process of maturation, in particular emphasising the step-by-step growth and adjustment of the young 'incompetent' child on its way to 'rational' adulthood. Thus biology and psychology worked together to shape western thinking about child development. More than this, these two disciplines have under-pinned political decisions about education, welfare and social planning. A broader view has emerged more recently from the fascinating work of psychologists studying child development across cultures (Chapter 5).

The ecology of human development – 'the Russian doll'

Clearly we are all located in, and grew up within a culture and sub-culture that has shaped our thinking and behaviour patterns. A picture has now emerged which is much broader, more complex and inter-disciplinary. From this fresh perspective, biology and psychology, sociology, anthropology and history all come together to contribute to our understanding of child development.

Since his first full presentation of it in *The Ecology of Human Development* (1979), Bronfenbrenner's systems approach, which offers an efficient framework for analysing the complexities of the environment, has become the most influential approach in the developmental sciences. He sees the environment as a Russian doll, a series of environments nested one inside the other. Face-to-face environments, for example the home, the school, or the street, including the relationship behaviours found there, form the innermost systems, or 'microsystems'. The set of micro-systems which make up the child's immediate world interact with each other, and these interactions Bronfenbrenner calls the 'mesosystem'.

Environments of which the child has no direct experience but which have a profound indirect effect on her, for example a caregiver's place of work, are called 'exosystems'. Exosystem influences, such as working hours, distance of workplace from home, shift systems, relationships with mates and bosses, and the many other examples of occupational stress, have transformed the home as an environment for development. The encircling shell of wider cultural influences, including neighbourhood and national influences, which heavily influence the inner shells, is termed the 'macrosystem'. The different ways schooling is organised in different countries is one route by which macrosystems influence the child's microsystems; another is the way TV and other media transmit the macrosystem (and exosystem) influences into the microsystem of the home; yet another is the way cultural traditions in relationships between adults and children are passed on from generation to generation. Bronfenbrenner has added a further shell, the 'chronosystem', the time frame in which all events are located.

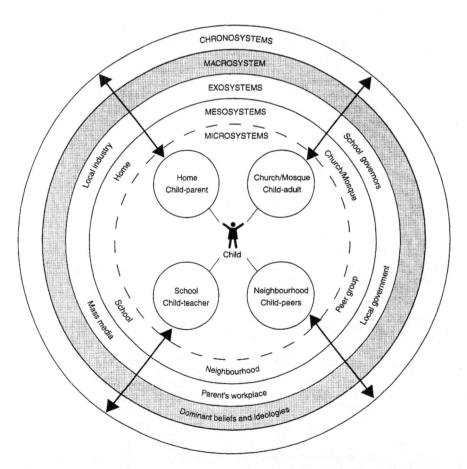

Fig. 1   Bronfenbrenner's ecological framework of human development.

A pathways approach

This book is an exploration of the ways in which we think about early childhood, the lived-in circumstances of young children's lives and the processes by which they develop. The idea of a 'pathways' approach constructed by Rutter (1989) influences many of our chapters.

Most important of all, it focuses on a lifespan perspective, in which human beings continue to develop, interacting with others in their social environment, throughout their lives (Erikson, 1963; Bronfenbrenner, 1979). Nevertheless, the timing of certain events within a lifespan is highly significant, especially in the early years. For example, lack of stimulation in the first year of life limits irreparably the neural connections in the developing brain (Chapter 3); and insecure attachments between very young children and their caretakers may have life-long consequences.

The pathway model demonstrates the possibility of both continuities and discontinuities as children develop through their experiences of families, peer friendships and activities, and schooling. While early patterns of behaviour may well carry forward into later life, they do not necessarily do so. Both good and bad experiences influence development and human beings are remarkable for their flexibility and ability to learn. The possibility of chain reactions can be seen through the analysis of longitudinal studies.

The common view of development as 'ladder-like' is not helpful and one of the advantages of a pathway model lies in its ability to incorporate the many different patterns of individual lives. Rutter's studies present evidence that successful coping with stressful circumstances can have protective benefits in the longer term. In addition, the ability to plan and take control, rather than to simply be swept along by events, is a valuable mode of behaviour.

Essentially this model extends Bronfenbrenner's ecological framework. It identifies the interactive nature of development, for example at the microsystem level, especially within the child's family (see Chapter 5). The microsystems of the preschool and then the school again have potential or limitations in leading to either enabling or restrictive pathways (Chapters 8 and 9).

International context

A landmark in global thinking about children occurred in 1989 when the General Assembly of the United Nations adopted the Convention on the Rights of the Child. Since then virtually every country has ratified it, making it the most widely adopted of all UN conventions.

Four key principles underlie the articles:

- Non-discrimination: the provision of equality of opportunity 'irrespective of the child's ... race, colour, sex, language, religion, political or other opinion, national, ethnic or social origin, property, disability, birth or other status' (Article 2).

- The best interests of the child, which is the phrase used to enjoin all those taking action on behalf of children to have their interests as their first consideration. In particular, this alters previous emphasis on the rights of parents (Article 3.1).
- The right to survival and development is fundamental. This article signals the need for preventive action across the full range of development, not just physical but also cognitive, social and emotional (Article 6).
- The views of the child: perhaps the most innovative aspect of the Convention is the right accorded to children to make known their views and wishes (Article 12).

Beyond the four key principles, the articles cover civil rights and freedoms, family environment and alternative care, education and cultural activities, 'special protection measures' which includes refugee children, armed conflicts, juvenile justice, as well as the deprivation of liberty, exploitation and issues concerning minority groups.

It is evident that while the Convention has become part of most states' rhetoric concerning children, in reality the underpinning values, the 'macrosystem' it espouses, have yet to permeate policy development in many areas. Many countries are constrained in their efforts to implement the Convention by poverty, international debt, wars and unrest. However, the United Kingdom too still has to come to terms with the letter and spirit of many of the requirements of the Convention. Many areas need more consideration, for example child poverty, the age of criminal responsibility, children's right to freedom from physical punishment and their right to be heard, and to participate, both in matters concerning their own life and as members of a democratic society (see Chapter 7). A monitoring programme is following up the UK's progress and in 1999 submitted its second report to the UN Committee on the Rights of the Child (Chapter 12).

The British context

For over 50 years the lives of children and their families in Britain have been lived in the context of the welfare state which covers employment policy, social security, education, health, housing and personal social services. In this time span, under the National Health Service, children's life chances and health have improved significantly. Theoretically there is a safety net for families who suffer unemployment or housing problems but we know all too well that relative poverty, especially for children, has increased in the last twenty years (Chapter 12). Women's lives and family structures are changing rapidly. These sociological transformations intricately affect children's lives and the implications will be evident in several chapters, especially Chapters 5 and 11. The central control of education for children of school age has undergone a sea change in the last fifteen years (Chapter 9), and now preschool services are also undergoing a transformation (Chapter 8). The government is optimistic about the impact of these changes but their consequences remain to be seen.

In some European countries – Norway, for example – the impact for children of national and local policies is scrutinised across all areas of state activity. However, so far this has not been the case in Britain and anomalies occur. Chapter 12 draws on European experience to suggest some alternative governmental approaches.

Children as actors

Throughout the book we will keep in mind the concept of the child as an active social constructor. There is still a brittle tension between the image of the child as incompetent, unformed, unknowing, dependent, in need of moulding by 'mature', knowledgeable adults and the image of the child as strong, competent, and an active agent in their own development. Adults still have enormous power over children's lives, and many feel threatened by changes in the status quo.

Chapter 2 draws on technological research which has revealed the earliest, self-directed competencies of the as yet unborn infant. Babies too have capacities we have failed to recognise in the past. The powerful drive to be a communicating, active member of whatever community we are born into is a major theme in the academic study of children (Bruner & Haste, 1987; Berk, 1998), yet in practice the world for young children tends not to reflect this (Chapters 8 and 9).

The themes of the social construction of childhood, the ecology of human development, children's rights, cultural diversity and the children's agency in their own lives will appear throughout the book, reminding us that childhood cannot be a separate, idyllic uncomplicated world. On the contrary, it is dynamic and socially complex and of fundamental importance to children and society. Our children now are our future.

Chapter 1
Historical Views of Childhood

Mary Fawcett

In 1991 the United Kingdom ratified the UN Convention on the Rights of the Child. It seems only obvious that children should have adequate food, clothing, protection, medical care, and appropriate education, but it is quite recently that safeguards, which still fail too often, have been put in place. Throughout most of history children have lacked these rights and have been at the mercy of adults with their inevitably greater power.

Opening with a historical chapter is justified because attitudes to children and childhood are constantly evolving, whether in the fields of child rearing in the home or in professional healthcare, work, welfare, and education. Knowledge of continuities and discontinuities with past ideas can lead to a better sense of perspective and balance in dealing with present challenges. It is a fascinating story, full of human interest, and it is, of course, the story of our own past. (Interviews with grandparents or other older members of the community about their childhoods of more than 50 years ago can be most revealing.)

In Britain, the gradual recognition of children's vulnerability and rights has led to protective legislation over a mere two hundred years. The balance between children's rights and responsibilities has changed dramatically in this period, as witnessed in adult expectations and in the organisation and control of children in private and public domains. This chapter offers a sketch of the major developments in the 'social construction' of childhood (defined in the Introduction) in families, in health and welfare, in work situations, and in school.

In order to follow this transformation of childhood, especially for the 'children of the poor' (Cunningham, 1991), three separate periods have been chosen. The first, around 1800, is characterised by the huge chasm between a new vision of the special quality of childhood associated with the ideologies of the Romantic movement, and the actual reality of life for the majority of children. The second, the mid-Victorian period from 1850 to 1880, is of special interest because it reflected society's growing recognition and concern for children's well-being, education and protection. The final period, 1918 to 1939, between the two World Wars, is significant for its focus on the early years – on mothering in the home and genuine child-centred policies in schooling. This chapter concentrates on children under ten in working-class families – both the very poor and the 'respectable' poor – rather than the privileged minority with their servants, nannies, governesses and private education. (See Gathorne-Hardy, 1972 for an account of the latter.)

Where children are concerned there are really two histories. On the one hand there is the adult construct, an idea of childhood, and on the other hand the real, lived experience of actual children. The academic debate about the concept of childhood was largely initiated by Philippe Ariès (1962) who argued that prior to the eighteenth century childhood was not perceived as a distinct period, children being seen instead as miniature adults subject to neglect and cruel treatment. His seminal book sparked off many other studies such as those of Lawrence Stone (1977) and Linda Pollock (1983, 1987). The range of literature continues to grow with Diana Gittins (1998) making a stimulating recent contribution.

Around 1800

'Heaven lies about us in our infancy' wrote Wordsworth (c. 1803), praising the idea of childhood as a special period of life, a time of happiness. He was not alone. Perhaps the most important influence around this time was the Swiss philosopher Jean-Jacques Rousseau who presented his famous ideas on education in the form of a novel, *Émile* (1762) – the story of the upbringing of Émile and his future partner Sophie. Rousseau in turn had been profoudly influenced by an earlier English writer, John Locke, whose book *Some Thoughts on Education* (1693) was frequently reprinted throughout the eighteenth century and translated into most European languages. Locke introduced the idea of the *tabula rasa* – or blank slate – to describe the condition of a newborn child's mind. Children, he believed, were born neither good nor essentially sinful (as Puritanism had taught), but ready to be formed by their experiences and education. Ideally children's minds should be filled with useful information and moral understanding through the guidance of wise adults, though young children should also be allowed to play (Hardyment, 1995).

Rousseau extended these ideas but with a slant of his own. Like Locke he opposed the widespread belief in 'original sin' which placed an obligation on parents to save their children from hellfire by instilling Christian principles. Instead he held that children were fundamentally good but corrupted by society. For Rousseau, civilisation served only to alienate human beings from the great teacher Nature. Hence he argued that, in childrearing, natural ways were always best. He condemned the fashionable wet-nursing of infants, saying that mothers should breast-feed their own offspring. Swaddling was also out: babies should be allowed freedom of movement from the start. Learning for Émile, the young boy, should be through play and practical experience, with formal school education delayed until he was twelve. Rousseau took a more sexist line with Sophie. The sole objective of her upbringing was to prepare her as a suitable wife for Émile. These were very radical ideas but they spread rapidly, especially to the middle classes. One notable example was the Rev. Patrick Brontë, who brought up Charlotte, Emily and Anne according to Rousseau's principles.

Rousseau and other radical thinkers like Thomas Paine (whose stirring defence of the French Revolution, *Rights of Man*, appeared in 1791-2) helped stimulate a wide debate on social equality which provoked expressions of opinion on all sides. Many feared that the doctrine of equality would lead to anarchy with the collapse of the age-old certainties of a patriarchal hierarchy. The idea that women too had 'rights' was ridiculed by one outspoken critic, Hannah More, who foresaw other consequences:

> 'It follows, according to the actual progression of human beings, that the next influx of that irradiation which our enlighteners are pouring on us, will illuminate the world with grave descants on the rights of youth, the rights of children, the rights of babies.'
>
> (More, 1801, in Walvin, 1982, p44)

In sharp contrast, Mary Wollstonecraft believed passionately in the rights of both men and women. In the *Vindication of the Rights of Women* (1792) she made the logical leap: extension of human rights implied not only ending male dominance over women but also improving the rights of children. Her vision of education prescribed the mixing of children from different social groups, an unheard-of innovation. She also wanted girls to be given a broader, more intellectual education, not limited to the study of trivialities – a point of view with which Hannah More also agreed.

Accompanying these thoughts about childhood came a new vision which increasingly emphasised the innocence and beauty of young children. Numerous examples can be found in the literature of Wordsworth and Blake, and in sentimental images of children in paintings and prints (Coveney, 1957; Steward, 1995).

The actuality of poor children's lives was in almost complete contrast with this image. Within the family high mortality rates, the dominating position of fathers, work expectations and discipline based on religious principles (Pinchbeck & Hewitt, 1973, Chapter XIII) all took their toll on the early years of a child's life. While the average household size (excluding servants) was not significantly different from now, and most families were nuclear rather than extended (Anderson, 1980), the statistical mean conceals the fact that some families were very large by today's standards. Moreover, the very high infant mortality rates and the frequent childbearing of women lacking reliable methods of birth control are hidden in statistical analysis (Porter, 1982).

For the new baby the first few years were usually very precarious. Cunningham estimates that one in four or five died in their first year (1995a, p90). Feeding, hygiene and poverty were principally to blame. The reality that fashionable families disapproved of breast-feeding had knock-on effects for children of the poor since the child of the wet nurse (inevitably from a poorer class) would be deprived of milk. If for any reason a mother could not feed her baby (nor find or afford a wet nurse) the chances of survival were low. The poor scientific knowledge about diet for babies and children to replace or follow breast-feeding is evident. In practice the aim was to have a substance which looked like milk, perhaps made by mixing uncooked flour and water (Hardyment, 1995; Soloman, 1995).

If there was little awareness of suitable feeding, the fundamentals of hygiene were even less well understood. All babies would be swaddled in bands of cloth. The notion underlying this strapping up of the limbs was that unless a baby's arms and legs were held firmly in place, they would grow misshapen. In practice such tight bands would have slowed the heart rate, keeping the infant quiet. Attached to a cradle board, the parcelled-up baby could be hung up on the wall, out of the way of dirt and draughts on the ground. The summer months were the most hazardous for babies when food-borne bacteria flourished. Infants and small children were at risk not only of bacterial infections like dysentery (safe water supplies and reliable sewerage being many decades off – Davidoff & Hall, 1987) but of common infectious diseases such as whooping cough, measles and scarlet fever, which at that time often proved fatal.

Medical help, though mostly beyond the purse of the poor, was often dubious in any case. It is true that published guidance for parents on medical matters and baby care had begun to appear (e.g. Cadogan, 1748; Buchan, 1796) which generally encouraged an approach as close to nature as possible (Hardyment, 1995). We can assume that the poor had little access to this literature. In any case, disease and epidemics hit all classes, though the poorest, because they lived in the most insanitary conditions, suffered worst.

The high incidence of child mortality is one of the major differences from our own period. Parents and other siblings often had to cope with bereavements, helped perhaps by the solace of religion. Similarly, many children had lost one of their parents before they reached adulthood (death in childbirth itself was not uncommon), but if one parent died the survivor would be likely to remarry (Cunningham, 1995a, p96).

Within the family, children were expected to defer to and obey adults. Wives too were subordinate, legally and otherwise. 'Obedient [especially middle class] females were type-cast as the guardian angels of family and virtue...' (Porter, 1982, p39). Among the working classes, however, women inevitably took a considerable share in breadwinning, assisting their husbands or taking employment on their own. But only when widowed did they enjoy specific rights. In addition, being a wife and mother might mean constant pregnancies. Women might well spend much of their life in a pregnant state and give birth to more than a dozen children.

Religious and moral beliefs strongly influenced views in bringing up children. Strong discipline served to control children, inculcate habits of deference to their betters and make them amenable to a life of work. Thus John Wesley's mother, Susanna, said of her babies that 'when turned a year old ... they were taught to fear the rod, and to cry softly' (Porter, 1982, p165). On the other hand family regimes were often less harsh than this suggests. Most parents wished to see their children happy (Pollock,

1987). Certainly there were serious cases of harm and assault, but society could not intervene and there were no laws to protect children within the home.

Illegitimacy was of course frowned on; 'the bastards of the poor were considered an affront to morality ' (Pinchbeck & Hewitt, 1973, p583). All the same, the numbers of children born out of wedlock increased greatly during the eighteenth century (Pinchbeck & Hewitt, 1973, p585). Children might be abandoned and infanticide was probably not uncommon. The first foundling hospital, Thomas Coram's in London established earlier in the eighteenth century, led eventually to others (Hardyment, 1995; Cunningham, 1995a, p95–6).

The socio-economic status of the family was critical to the quality of life a child under ten years old would experience. Among the working classes children were not just a useful pair of hands but were often economically crucial. More than this, they were thought of as an investment, an insurance policy to provide for their parents in old age. The middle classes too, not supported by family wealth, set great store on self-sufficiency (Davidoff & Hall, 1987). At this date – long before pensions, social security, or a National Health Service – support systems were limited to parish relief and sporadic charitable institutions.

In working-class families, children were expected to help out as soon as they were able. A three-year-old might be expected to undertake tasks like scaring birds off the crops. Tasks were usually highly gender differentiated and children in many labouring families would be engaged in local home industries, such as weaving, lace-making and basketry. Some perhaps gained early satisfaction from mastering skills but children were undeniably exploited, sometimes to the detriment of their health and education.

By 1800 the Industrial Revolution was already beginning to revolutionise many children's lives. Large movements in population brought children and their families off the land to new or expanded towns. Some were drawn into factories and mines at an early age, though the actual extent of child labour is debatable since the numbers and ages of children were inadequately recorded (Cunningham, 1991; Horn, 1994; Horrell & Humphries, 1995). The first significant piece of legislation dealing with children, the 1802 Health and Morals of Apprentices Act, covered children over ten, though its regulations on working hours and minimal education were inadequately enforced because of a lack of inspectors. But it did herald a series of nineteenth-century acts affecting children's welfare.

Though there would be no national education system until 1870, there was an increasing variety of schooling for the less well-off. A rough indication of educational provision can be gleaned from literacy rates (from signatures on marriage registers), but these rates vary from area to area and by gender. In an example from the East Riding of Yorkshire in 1801–1810, 64% of males and 43% of females could sign their names (Sanderson, 1983, pp14–15).

For the youngest there were dame schools (typically a small group of children in an ordinary house) which probably offered little more than custodial care. In some towns, charity schools provided a solid elementary education with an Anglican flavour for older children from respectable working-class families. Philanthropic and religious organisations were behind many educational initiatives. Among these were village schools and also the Sunday Schools which spread dramatically through the country from the 1780s, and kept many poor children occupied on the Sabbath through disciplined basic instruction (Walvin, 1982).

The early nineteenth century saw fresh efforts to promote elementary education. Monitorial schools spread rapidly since they allowed a single teacher aided by a team of child assistants to provide cheap instruction for hundreds of working-class youngsters in any convenient large hall. In general these schools took pupils from the age of seven, but the innovatory infant schools pioneered by Robert Owen (1771–1858) and Samuel Wilderspin (1792–1866) were designed for the younger age groups. Owen, drawing on his belief that early education would have long-term social benefits, set up the pioneering New Lanark school at his textile mill in 1816. Here children began school as soon as they could walk but the curriculum was designed to sustain their interest, permitting play, outdoor activity and story-telling but no corporal punishment (Spodek, 1973). Samuel Wilderspin was even more influential, helping to set up dozens of infant schools in London and across the country. Though his system was more instructional than Owen's, with much rote learning and repetition, his teachers also used practical demonstration and visual aids, and playground apparatus (Whitbread, 1975). For the majority of children, though, there was only a minimal amount of education in an overcrowded and generally harsh régime.

The mid-Victorian period 1850–1880

Mid-Victorian feelings about children, and about their upbringing, welfare and education, were greatly conditioned by the printed word and the massive increase in pictorial imagery in the popular press. The insights of Wordsworth, Coleridge and other writers into children's imaginative processes and self-development continued to influence attitudes, heightening the 'reverence towards the child' given currency by Rousseau (Hendrick, 1999). Dickens turned his spotlight on child exploitation, Charlotte Brontë in *Jane Eyre* (1848) drew attention to the psychological loneliness some youngsters experienced, and Charles Kingsley campaigned against the scandal of the climbing boys (child chimney sweeps) in *The Water-Babies* (1863). Evangelical tracts and moral tales spelled out the need to protect children on the streets and even in the home, and a number of writers published vivid exposés of the social conditions in which many children lived. Richard Oastler, for example, castigated the use of child labour in factories, and various official publications – such as the government report on the sanitary condition of London (1848–9) – gave further ammunition to the reformers. Mayhew's remarkable word portraits in *London Labour and the London Poor* likewise brought home to a wide public the vulnerable lives of the working classes (Quennell, 1969).

By the mid-nineteenth century, the cult of 'home sweet home' was triumphant, even among the working classes. 'The home came to be seen as a haven, a retreat from the capitalistically orientated competitive world' (Anderson, 1980, p33). This was above all the nest of family domesticity, focusing on the woman in charge of housekeeping and childrearing. The almost mystical role of the self-sacrificing wife and ideal mother–educator (Badinter, 1981) was frequently portrayed in art (Steward, 1995). But the stereotype of the Victorian mother was of a middle-class woman supervising servants and children in the family home. Most working-class women, on the other hand, were obliged to find employment (Tilly & Scott, 1987) and to depend on neighbours and older children – 'little mothers' – for help with housework and childcare (Davin, 1996). The reality of home life for the less well-off was far from sweet. Migrations of many families to urban conurbations in pursuit of work meant pressure for cheap, basic housing which rapidly degenerated into unhygienic, cramped and dirty slums. Fathers were still omnipotent with the right to administer 'reasonable correction' and the state was reluctant to step in between parent and child (Behlmer, 1982).

Mortality rates for young children continued to be worrying. In the year 1850, of infants aged 0–3, nearly 6.7% of boys and over 5.7% of girls died. For babies under one year the figure was worse, as high as 16.2% (Mitchell & Deane, 1962). Housing, proper sewerage systems and safe water supplies, though improving, were still inadequate. Advances in the field of statistics provided a much clearer understanding of children's physical and mental conditions. For example, the statistics for the causes of infant deaths in 1864 are illuminating – diarrhoea carried off 8.7%, whooping cough 3.1%, convulsions 18.4%, and violent deaths 1.5% (a figure including cases of homicide and accidental or negligent suffocation).

It was this last statistic, together with the many newspaper reports of infanticide, that created alarm about the 'slaughter of the innocents' in English cities. Behlmer shows that 'mid-Victorian infants clearly were more apt to be killed than all other age groups combined' (1982, p18). Children died not only within their own families. Those in the care of 'baby-farmers' (a type of fostering) were at much greater risk. The scandal of this particular form of childcare was the focus of public attention in 1868 when two doctors, pretending to be seeking a child nurse, tracked down many of the 333 people who responded to their advertisement. Articles based on their research in the *British Medical Journal* captured public attention and secured the involvement of the great reformer, the Earl of Shaftesbury (Behlmer, 1982). During the debate that ensued, a government committee drew up twenty recommendations that included the creation of a (non-capital) offence of infanticide, the compulsory registration of all births (not omitting still births), and the registration of foster-nurses who took in illegitimate children (Rose, 1991). The Infant Life Protection Society, founded in 1870, played an important part in the campaign, emphasising not only the physical safety of infants but also the well-being of children under ten in workhouses – of whom there were 51 939 in 1868, suffering with their parents the harsh regime imposed by the Poor Law legislation of 1834. However, the Infant Life Protection Act, eventually passed in 1872, still failed to live up to expectations (Behlmer, 1982, Chapter 2; Hendrick, 1999).

But children were exposed to other dangers, including abuse by callous adults in their own home and in schools, where excessive corporal punishment was not uncommon. Mundella's proposals for child protection in 1873 tried to reach 'tyrannical parents' by demanding the right to inspect any place where children lived. This was still in advance of public opinion but the 1889 Prevention of Cruelty to Children Act, later to be called the Children's Charter, proved to be the major turning point in legal and social attitudes regarding neglect and cruelty (Behlmer, 1982; Hendrick, 1999).

Legislation defining the relationship between the state and the individual continued to be implemented through the last decades of the nineteenth century; indeed, 52 Acts of Parliament affecting child welfare were passed between 1885 and 1913. Philanthropic societies concerned with children's welfare, such as the National Children's Home and Dr Barnardo's, had also been proliferating. Yet there was still much deprivation, malnutrition and disease. Reformers returned to the family as the source of protection, guidance, discipline and love for the child, but failing working-class families still faced having their children sent to reformatory schools. Child delinquency was much discussed. Children might be victims of circumstances in the eyes of some, but for others any precocious, streetwise youngster was an object of suspicion. The reformer Mary Carpenter objected to children who were 'independent, self-reliant, advanced in knowledge of evil but not of good, devoid of reverence for God or man, utterly destitute of any sound guiding principle of action', and unwilling to submit humbly to adult bidding (Hendrick, in Prout & James, 1997, p44).

The Industrial Revolution continued to bring countless people off the land and into manufacturing towns in search of work, among them many fleeing the great Irish famine of the late 1840s. To find young children employed in factories and mines is not surprising therefore, given that they had always been expected to participate in the family economy (Tilly & Scott, 1987). Furthermore children seemed especially suited to certain tasks – small enough to crawl between machines to clean them or along tunnels in mines, nimble-fingered enough for mill jobs and cheaper and more controllable than adult workers. The extent of child labour is hard to determine (Horrell & Humphries, 1995). While the Factory Act (1833) had prohibited the employment of children under nine in textile factories and limited the working day for older children (9–13) to nine hours, such legislation was often flouted, and quite young children did work in conditions harmful to their health and development. The drive for reform stemmed from the clash between a vision of childhood as a time of natural innocence, carefree and playful, and the reality of the factory child's existence. During the anti-slavery campaign of the early 1830s the comparison between slaves and employed children had already been made in Richard Oastler's famous letter to the *Leeds Mercury* about the woollen mills (1830).

> 'Thousands of little children, both male and female, *but principally female*, from seven to fourteen years of age, are daily *compelled* to labour from six o'clock in the morning to seven in the evening, with only – Britons, blush while you read it! – *with only thirty minutes allowed for eating and recreation*. . . . ye are slaves without the only comfort which the negro has. He knows it is his sordid, mercenary master's interest that he should live, be *strong* and *healthy*. Not so with you. Ye are doomed to labour from morning to night for one who cares not how soon your weak and tender frames are stretched to breaking!'
>
> (Cole & Filson, 1967, pp316–17)

A decade later another group of reformers argued that halting child labour was beneficial in economic terms – if children grew up healthy they would become more productive workers later on (Horn, 1994).

Evangelical religion too contributed, with leaders like the Earl of Shaftesbury playing a key role in reform movements to improve conditions of child chimney sweeps and mine workers. Shaftesbury believed that the state 'has an interest and a right to watch over and provide for the moral and physical well-being of her people' (Behlmer, 1982, p9). By 1875 the minimum age was ten for half-time and fourteen for full-time employment (Hendrick, 1999), and most young children were in school anyway.

The future education of many young children was to be influenced by a German schoolteacher, Friedrich Froebel (1782–1852). His vision of the ideal environment for children was a rural, natural one, conveying Rousseauesque ideas and symbolised in his word *kindergarten*, a garden for children. Froebel held that children would grow naturally in harmony with God and nature if given freedom to develop under the guidance of a woman teacher, 'the mother made conscious'. His ideas were fruitful in spreading private kindergartens in Britain, but they eventually had a wide influence on infant education more generally (Whitbread, 1975).

Many children still attended small dame schools and other private establishments but elementary education was now dominated by the large national and British schools. These were increasingly state subsidised since the grounding of children in the 3Rs (reading, writing and arithmetic) and inculcation of Christian precepts from an early age would, it was argued, have national benefits in producing an amenable, efficient workforce and in reducing criminality. In addition some of the most deprived children in society received a rudimentary education at so-called ragged schools, and in workhouse, prison and factory schools (Sanderson, 1983). Nevertheless, in 1870 almost 40% of children (3–12) were still not catered for, and school places were failing to keep up with rapidly rising urban populations (Sanderson, 1983; Horn, 1994, p59). Not all poor parents gave school the priority expected of them, seeing little point in education and resenting the 1d or 2d a week that schools cost when a child might be earning as much as 9d or 18d instead.

Forster's 1870 Elementary Education Act aimed to make education up to the age of ten compulsory, with state schools being built as necessary. School boards were established across the country, though only when fees were abolished in 1891 did education become truly universal. One effect was to bring to public attention the health and conditions of poorer children (Horn, 1994).

As regards the youngest children, several issues worried educationalists. Large numbers of two-, three- and four-year-olds now attended ordinary state and church schools for lack of any other public childcare for the children of working women. The proportion of two-year-olds soon declined, but numbers of three- and four-year-olds in schools continued to rise until, by 1900, 43% of this age group were attending (Whitbread, 1975). Many educationalists disagreed with the policy, believing that under-fives did not belong in crowded urban schools but ought to be at home with their mothers. Not only was the accommodation often unsuitable, the elementary school curriculum, driven by the 'payment by results' system, was hardly geared to the needs of small infants who underwent the same régime of rote learning as the older children, even if they escaped being examined. Concerns of this kind led to calls for state infant schools based on ideas from Pestalozzi (1745–1827) or Froebel, rather than rote learning. Private kindergartens attached to independent schools adopted the Froebelian approach with some success, but in the state sector the curriculum inevitably became watered down and debased. Indeed, the more active Froebel method was quite impractical given the huge class sizes and the fact that untrained teachers – often 'pupil teachers' no more than thirteen or fourteen years old themselves – might be in sole charge of 50–60 small children (Whitbread, 1975).

Between the Wars 1918–1939

Increasing European nationalism and the experience of war helped to change ideas about the relationship of the state and family. In Britain, the Boer War (1899–1902) and the First World War (1914–18) had revealed alarming levels of poor health amongst war recruits (Dwork, 1987; Davin, 1978). The large numbers of young men killed in battle reminded the nation of the need to breed new generations of soldiers to defend the Empire and workers to keep the economy strong in the face of foreign competition. But anxieties about improving the 'national stock' could easily lead to calls for a full-blown programme of eugenics (or selective breeding) – a principle that would tragically culminate in the Nazi policy of cleansing the nation by deliberately exterminating those not viewed as 'racially pure'.

Meanwhile new scientific data on human development were accumulating and beginning to filter into childrearing texts and other literature aimed at parents. Although Freud had in a sense 'destroyed ideas of the sexual innocence of childhood' (Cunningham, 1995a, p170), his impact on the flood of childrearing advice between the Wars seems to have been negligible (Hardyment, 1995). Other voices were more influential, such as the American doctor J.B. Watson who, claiming scientific authority for his principles, advocated 'sensible' ways of treating young children – for example 'Never hug and kiss them, never let them sit in your lap' (Cunningham, 1995a). But it was another behaviourist, Truby King, who was most listened to in the United Kingdom. Experiments on the scientific rearing of calves had convinced him that the same methods should be applied to humans. In particular, babies must be breast-fed at regular, fixed, four-hourly intervals, regardless of when they happened to cry (Hardyment, 1995). Countless families, but not the very poorest, took up the Truby King method and accepted his belief that lack of regularity might lead to 'hysteria, epilepsy and imbecility and also other forms of degeneracy' in adulthood (Urwin & Sharland, in Cooter, 1992).

Psychodynamic approaches to childrearing reached parents through Susan Isaacs' influential book *The Nursery Years* (1929). Her aim was to try to understand the child's own point of view and emotions – infant fears and jealousies, for example. This child-centred attitude contrasted strongly with the training regimes of the behaviourists, yet she had concerns in common with theirs, notably about children's mental health (Urwin & Sharland in Cooter, 1992). The importance of child development for social and political reasons was clear:

> ' "It needed the impetus of the Great War to make the country realise the value and importance of infant life", recorded Gwen St Aubyn in her encyclopediac *Family Book* (1935). "The neglected toddler in everyone's way is the material which becomes the disgruntled agitator, while the contented child is the pillar of the state".'
>
> (Quoted in Hardyment, 1995, p159)

In this political climate motherhood was seen as a duty and a destiny. According to a book on marriage for young women, the purpose of marriage was the reproduction of the race, the maintenance of social purity, and the mutual comfort and assistance of each married couple (Davin, 1978). In promoting the task of mothering there were prizes for 'bonny babies', a deluge of leaflets, and increasing numbers of health visitors, baby clinics and hygenic milk depots. Motherhood was expected to be full-time, with serious disapproval awaiting those who worked outside the home. Poorer working-class women eked out their limited resources by taking in 'homework', such as laundry, rather than going out to work. It was difficult anyway to find care for children because kindergartens and creches were objected to as 'infringing the maternalist principle' (Davin, 1978).

According to research in the 1930s, many working-class wives suffered frequent pregnancies and miscarriages, chronic ill health, inadequate diet and isolation. This research made explicit the link between poverty and health, a connection which tended not to be made at this time (Spring-Rice, 1939, reprinted 1981). The Depression and unemployment seriously affected the lives of a large proportion of the population, but as usual the burden of keeping families going rested on women (Davin, 1996).

One major influence on the lives of mothers at this period was the spread of contraception. The controversial influence of Marie Stopes and her book *Married Love* stimulated the growth of family planning clinics, especially in middle-class areas (Horn, 1995). Better-off families had markedly fewer children – to the dismay of those who felt that these were the very families who should be adding to the nation's stock.

Thanks to improved water-supplies and housing (many suburban estates were built in this period), immunisation, and better knowledge of hygiene and nutrition, the reduction in infant mortality had been dramatic. The nationally aggregated totals peaked in 1901 (16.1%) and by 1928 had declined to 6.6%. However, average mortality rates fail to give a full picture of the quality of life for British children. Improvement was patchy and for a substantial minority health and social problems remained, as the massive evacuation of children during the Second World War would strikingly reveal.

In the early 1920s between a quarter and a third of children starting school needed medical treatment, and though the local authorities had powers to provide services for young families – such as free ante- and post-natal clinics and health visiting – not all did so. Nevertheless health visitors were now part of the national scene. In schools there were free meals for those who 'needed' them – a judgment based on medical health or poverty – but in the financial crisis of 1931 it was announced that free meals were to be restricted even further. While surveys showed that up to half of the population were not receiving a proper diet and that a large proportion of these were children under fourteen, official reports painted a different picture, claiming that in some depressed areas not a single child suffered from bad nutrition (Hendrick, 1999).

A change in attitudes towards delinquency can be noted – from punishment and control towards prevention and treatment through the newly developed child guidance clinics. A greater understanding of children's minds emerged from three different sources: the British child study tradition, Viennese psychoanalysis, and American psychological medicine (Thom in Cooter, 1992). Nevertheless birching was still accepted, though used sparingly. Even some progressive reformers favoured corporal punishment in this period and the chief constables were much in favour of flogging children under sixteen years for any offence (Hendrick, 1999).

The employment of children under ten in Britain had technically ceased to be an issue, the 1933 Children and Young Persons Act having prohibited under-twelves from employment, except for light agricultural work within a family setting. However, the true picture of young children's employment was not acknowledged, as is still the case today.

As ever, there was great faith in the potential of education to change society. There was a new emphasis on the all-round development of the individual and a fresh interest in what were believed to be scientific approaches to pedagogy. During the inter-war period Summerhill, Dartington and other experimental schools were established (Selleck, 1972) and progressive educational thinking infiltrated even state school practice. Teachers, no longer pressured by the payment-by-results system and having to examine younger primary school children, were able to use more flexible and coherent teaching methods.

It was the schooling for children under seven which made the greatest strides. Two remarkable women, Margaret McMillan (1860–1931) and Maria Montessori (1870–1952), enlarged the debate about the education of young children, both of them drawing on Froebel's work. McMillan, a committed socialist concerned about the very poor health of many school children, aimed her campaign at political as well as medical and educational opinion, always emphasising the importance of an all-round approach to young children's physical and mental development. Her contemporary, the charismatic Maria Montessori, was similarly alive to the deprivations of urban childhood and the need for compensatory education. She too had faith in the potential of young children to thrive in a specially beneficial environment, notably the *casa dei bambini* through which she demonstrated her method of sensory learning (Whitbread, 1975).

Separate infant schools became common and by 1926 some 70% of five- to seven-year-olds attended such establishments. As the school-leaving age rose, there was less pressure for academic 3Rs work (reading, writing and arithmetic) in the first years at school, so the free-standing infant schools had the chance to develop a tradition of their own. The Hadow Committee Report on Nursery and Infant Schools (1933), much influenced by the psychologists Isaacs and Burt and by the practical pioneering work and teaching of Montessori and McMillan, became national policy for state nursery, infant and junior schools. This report advised thinking of education '...in terms of activity and experience rather than knowledge to be acquired and facts to be stored' (quoted in Whitbread, 1975, p96). For children under seven the secular curriculum would include play, handwork (creative art) and instruction in the three Rs (Whitbread, 1975). Whole-class instruction was avoided and the teaching of reading waited until the age of six, or earlier if the child was 'ready'. The curricula of the nursery and infant schools were envisaged as a continuum. So began a process which lead to international fame in the 1950s, '60s and '70s for the English nursery-infant school.

There was some new building of schools in the 1920s and early '30s, much of it based on McMillan's ideas of using gardens and the open air. In furnishing the classrooms, Montessori's small chairs and moveable tables (not fixed desks and rows) became the norm. However, the physical condition of the schools in the inter-war period deteriorated badly as funds dried up: contaminated water supplies, inadequate toilets, and dangerous playgrounds were not uncommon, potentially affecting children's health. None the less, a School Medical Service had been in place before World War I and medical inspections continued to be a regular event in school life. The purpose was deemed educational in that health problems which might hinder learning would be prevented, but the service was criticised for the brevity of the inspections and its narrow concentration on children's bodies rather than looking at their environmental context.

And now

The story of early childhood in Britain continues. We have seen how children's rights and responsibilities have changed over the last 200 years, but there are still anomalies and contradictions. Opinions differ about the degree to which children are 'clay to be moulded' or active constructors of their own knowledge. The employment of children, while not at present an overt issue, still goes on. Some children carry heavy responsibilities as carers within their own family and heavy demands are made on children in terms of school work. The tension between the rights of families and the rights of children continues, as can be seen in the Children Act 1989. The promised expansion of nursery schools in 1944 did not take place and early childhood provision largely stagnated until 1998. Childhood mortality in our society may be much reduced, but there has been an increase in certain chronic illnesses. While the welfare state, established after World War II, has produced support systems – for health, unemployment, old age, education and social services – and the population at large is more affluent, nevertheless, as the following chapters will show, the quality of children's lives in Britain still causes concern. A constant tension remains between the concept of the ideal childhood and the reality of the lived experience.

Chapter 2
Fetal Development

Julie Selwyn

We begin life as a single cell, smaller than the full stop at the end of this sentence. By the time we are born we have over two billion cells and weigh on average 3.5 kg. The development of the single cell into a baby is a fantastic process, one that is still not fully understood. For many years, the period before birth was a mystery and it is only recently that this area of human biology has begun to reveal its secrets. Perhaps one of the most exciting discoveries about this period of life is the extent to which the fetus is active in development and this is where this chapter will begin. Development occurs inside the womb, hidden and apparently protected from outside influences, but we are now discovering just how important and influential the external environment is to healthy development. What the mother feels, eats and breathes can all cross the placenta.

The particular ways we have of talking, writing and thinking about certain groups are known as discourses. These have an impact on parental expectations of what pregnancy and parenthood are going to be like. Motherhood is commonly discussed as though it involves only pleasurable feelings. When faced with the reality of pregnancy, many mothers have a mixture of feelings: disgust at changes in body shape, joy if the pregnancy is wanted, or terror at the forthcoming labour. In this chapter, we will look at three examples of procedures that challenge beliefs about parenting: abortion, infertility treatment and gene therapy. They provoke intense and sometimes violent reactions from society. Parents are affected by dominant discourses, by changes in their own physical and psychological health and changes in relationships with extended family and friends. In turn, fetal development is affected by these changes and by the wider environment. Understanding the interaction of these systems is important, as professionals involved at this point in development are often concerned with only one aspect. As we learn more about fetal development it is becoming clearer that professionals will have to be more aware of the impact of all these systems on the mother and the fetus to ensure better outcomes for all.

Development of the fetus

In the past scientists could only guess at how the fetus developed by examining animal fetuses, premature babies, aborted fetuses and listening to mothers' accounts of their pregnancies. It was believed that the fetus lived in a watery world, empty of stimulation, with the fetus playing no part in development. With the introduction of ultrasound in the 1970s, the fetus could be observed. Further understanding has come from the improved survival of very premature babies, developments in assisted reproduction, molecular biology and the new genetics (Nathanielsz, 1996). Life before birth is unique in many ways. The fetus is attached to the placenta which acts as the fetal lungs, digestive system, and kidneys. However, the fetus is active; practising breathing, swallowing amniotic fluid and eliminating waste products. The placenta is formed by the fetus *and* the mother and allows the mother's body to tolerate the presence of the fetus, which otherwise would be rejected as a foreign object. Messages are sent back and forth across the placenta from the fetus. Although much is known about these pathways much is still to be discovered. However, it is clear that for healthy development both the placenta and the fetus need to work together.

At birth, the placenta is no longer needed. It is the only major organ in the human body that is disposable. The ancient Pharaohs of Egypt worshipped the placenta and many cultures have customs and rituals around its disposal after birth. For example, traditional Filipino practice is for the father to stay during the birth as his role is to bury the placenta as fast as possible. The burying of the placenta is believed to end any problems the woman may be experiencing in labour. Other cultures believe the placenta is the newborn's twin, or is linked to reincarnation as it represents both the newborn's birth and rebirth (for an interesting discussion on the role of the placenta see Rice & Manderson, 1996). In Britain today the placenta remains rather mysterious. Some women cook and eat the placenta after birth, as it is highly nutritious. The placenta's full role in the developmental process remains to be understood, as does the effect on premature babies of its early loss. Special care baby units cannot recreate the properties of the placenta.

For nine months, the mother's body usually provides a protective and supportive environment for the growing fetus. It was believed that the fetus developed in a peaceful world but in fact, the uterus is a very noisy place. The fetus from 14–16 weeks hears the sound of her mother's lungs, the beat of her heart, food being digested and external sounds such as music and language. Movements begin around 7 weeks' gestation although most pregnant women do not report feeling movement until 16 weeks. The range of movements expands rapidly, so by 10 weeks the fetus can stretch, yawn and move the tongue. By 15 weeks, the fetus is moving 20 000 times a day and these movements are vital for healthy development. Each fetus has its own distinct pattern of movement and an individual daily routine of activity, rest, sleep, and wake cycles. Some patterns of movement continue when the baby is born. For example De Vries and colleagues (1984) describe a stretch yawn pattern at 10 weeks' gestation that can be seen in newborns and fetal thumb sucking which may continue for many years after birth. Other types of movement, for example, a scissoring and extension of the legs, are only seen during specific points in fetal development whereas other movements increase in intensity at various points, for example, breathing movements increase as the fetus develops.

The fetus has periods of rapid eye movement whilst asleep which in adults is associated with dreaming. This raises the interesting question of whether the fetus dreams and if so what about? As the fetus develops, all the muscles needed during the fetal period and after birth are exercised. The fetus practises breathing, sucking in about half a cup of amniotic fluid a day to exercise the developing lungs. This also provides practice in swallowing and is of nutritional value. However, if for any reason the fetus gets short of oxygen, it stops breathing, reverting back to the placenta. This has become known as the paradoxical response as it is the opposite of what the baby will have to do if short of oxygen when born. Outside the uterus the baby needs to breathe deeply, not stop breathing. This has raised the question of whether this response is implicated in sudden infant death syndrome. If a baby has a blocked nose or is short of oxygen, might she revert to her old habit of not breathing? Without the placenta, this has disastrous consequences (Nathanielsz, 1996).

It is not known how the senses operate, whether they operate in isolation or have more than one function. It may be, for example, that the senses are not clearly differentiated and that the fetus feels sounds through the skin. The fetus can perceive light through the abdominal wall and detect changes in the mother's bodily posture. It was believed by many cultures that a mother's likes and fears would be transmitted to the unborn child and consequently the child would be born with the same likes and fears. This has not been demonstrated but it is known that fetuses recognise the sound of familiar voices. A newborn baby recognises the mother's voice and that of any others who were heard regularly during pregnancy. This recognition helps the baby and carers bond after birth as the baby responds positively to familiar voices. De Casper and colleagues (1986, 1994) went further and asked a group of pregnant women to read aloud *The Cat in the Hat* by Dr Seuss twice a day for the last six weeks of pregnancy. Two or three days after birth, the babies were given dummies that were wired to record their rate of sucking. By changing their rate of sucking they could turn the story on and off. Half the babies had the familiar story read and changed the rate of sucking; the other babies heard an unfamiliar story and did not change their sucking rate. The researchers found that not only had the babies heard the story in the womb but their learning influenced the sorts of sounds they found rewarding.

These results were reported in the popular press and some psychologists have gone on to promote intensive learning programmes for fetuses. Cassettes (BabyPlus) are strapped to the pregnant mother's stomach with the aim of giving the newborn child a head start in life. Logan (1992) argues that by providing environmental enrichment fetal brain cells are stimulated, improving IQ scores, giving non-traumatised births, better health and ensuring that as babies, they reach developmental stages (e.g. walking) before the norm. Logan's results have been severely criticised for their methodological inadequacies but the pressure on mothers to have a 'clever' baby and give their baby the best start in life starts very early indeed! The belief that early intervention can affect developmental outcomes leads us on to thinking about the relative importance of a child's genetic inheritance and the influence of environmental factors.

Nature and nurture

The nature and nurture debate is one of the oldest debates in science. The debate has centred on whether a child's pattern of development is determined by their genetic heritage or whether it is shaped by experiences throughout life. Is it possible, for example, to change levels of intelligence or personality by events after birth or are these pre-determined? There is now widespread agreement that nature and nurture interact and the word nurture has been replaced by thinking more about the kinds of experiences children have. Today, the debates (Plomin, 1994) are about how much of children's genes contribute to their development and the relative importance of early versus later environmental effects.

There are periods in fetal development where, if organs are going to develop, they need beneficial stimuli. If an organ receives different stimuli, or if the stimulus is missing, the organ is permanently affected. It has been known for some time that diseases like rubella or rickets permanently influence the development of the fetus. The time at which events happen seems to be important. For example, the drug thalidomide only seems to have disastrous effects on the growing limbs when taken in the early part of pregnancy; if taken later there are no effects (Bee, 1995). Some researchers see the effect of early environmental experiences as 'programming' organs, of changing organs permanently and believe that it is these changes that determine poor outcomes later in life. The concept of critical or sensitive periods has its supporters and challengers. Development can also be seen as a pathway. In this model, people who are exposed to adverse circumstances early in life meet other experiences as they grow, which can amplify, maintain or reduce the previous adversity – what Rutter (1989) calls the 'chain of risk'. This debate can be illustrated by current research on the impact of diet on fetal development and the links with later ill health in adulthood.

The diversity of babies born after normal pregnancies is remarkable. Studying the birthweights of relatives and the effects of famine during World War II has led to the conclusion that the diversity is mainly due to the environment within the womb rather than the influence of genes (Barker, 1997). A combination of what the mother eats and the ability of the placenta to transfer the nutrients affects fetal nutrition. There are also profound differences depending on whether the mother herself is well nourished at the start of the pregnancy. The uterine environment is critical for the development of the brain, muscle and fat tissues. During the fetal period, there is rapid differentiation and multiplication of these cells. After birth, the cells continue to grow but the *total* number of cells is already established. In contrast, the cells of the liver, kidney and blood, for example, are renewed throughout the lifespan. The fetus adapts to lack of nutrition or oxygen by slowing the rate of cell division and it is claimed (Barker, 1992) that this permanently affects certain organs. In the early part of the twentieth century in Britain, low birthweight (as in fetal failure to grow rather than premature birth) was often the certified cause of death. Death rates varied considerably, being highest in northern industrial towns and poorer rural areas. This geographical pattern in death rates closely resembles today's patterns of high coronary heart disease and it was suggested that there was a link. Studies in Sheffield, India and the USA have confirmed the association between low birthweight and coronary heart disease, the development of hypertension, and non-insulin dependent diabetes (NIDD).

Barker and colleagues (1992, 1997) have attempted to explain the link. Those born in Hertfordshire between 1911 and 1930 were traced and a sample of 16 000 men and women was established (Barker, 1992). Studies of this cohort demonstrated that the male infants who were smallest at birth had a five times higher risk of having NIDD and hypertension than those whose birthweight was nearer the norm. Barker suggested that the fetal environment 'programmed' permanent changes in the hormonal, vascular and lipid responses. Although the mechanisms are not fully understood, lack of nutrition does result in fewer pancreatic cells and a reduced capacity to make insulin, with less ability as an adult to cope with obesity. It is also thought that the fetus responds to undernourishment by diverting oxygen from developing organs to protect the brain. This affects the growth of the liver, which regulates cholesterol and blood clotting, both of which are linked with the onset of heart disease.

A number of studies support the thesis that fetal growth and ageing are linked. Sayer and colleagues (1997) speculate that programming of a range of organs such as the eyes and skin are linked to changes in fetal cells in the womb and ask the question 'Is life span determined *in utero*?'. They argue that the fetal environment determines not just the likelihood of future cardiovascular disease but the ageing of eyes, ears, muscles and skin.

Those who view development as a pathway dispute the view that organs are permanently 'programmed' (see the *British Medical Bulletin*, 1997). There are other explanations for the results. Mothers may have over-compensated after the war by over-feeding their children and therefore the young men became obese. The effect of a lack of adequate nutrients also has different implications depending on which nutrients were missing and at what point and for how long in the pregnancy the deficits occurred. The effects of poor diet are very difficult to study as poor diet is often linked with other factors such as poor housing, poverty, poor education, and smoking. There are also differences between male and female patterns of ill health and the role of gender is still unclear. Low birthweight is seen by those supporting the pathway model as the first step in a chain of events that may eventually lead to ill health in adulthood. The pathway model sees the initial programming as correctable – it is the *accumulation* of adversity that increases the risk of ill health in adulthood.

Rutter (1989) argues that starting at a disadvantage makes it more likely that future environments also will not be supportive and will reinforce the early vulnerability. A start on the wrong foot makes it very difficult to get back on the right foot but it is still possible. In a British follow-up study (Wadsworth, 1991) of a cohort of births from 1946, raised blood pressure in adulthood was associated with low birthweight, poor growth and poor circumstances. However, those who later went on to higher education or training reduced their chances of obesity in middle life. Poor early life circumstances did carry a significant risk but were modified by educational attainment. Those who received higher education made changes in their lifestyle that protected them from the vulnerability of being born with a low birthweight. There is room within the pathway model for the concept of programming, but not *vice versa*.

The two models attract different audiences and there are few academic links. Barker's work attracts a medical audience whereas Rutter appeals more to psychologists and those with a social science background. They also generate different policy approaches. The first argues for massive investment during pregnancy and early childhood whereas the pathway model demands lifelong investment. Both models agree that low birthweight is an important indicator of the likelihood of infant mortality, increased risk of disability, and, as we have seen, makes the infant more vulnerable across the lifespan (Botting, 1996; Population Trends, 1998).

It is agreed that good nutrition during pregnancy is extremely important, especially for healthy fetal brain development (Barrett, 1999). The Department of Health (1994) has produced several reports outlining the amount of nutrients a pregnant woman needs but benefit levels are such that it is very difficult to meet these targets. Surveys (OPCS, 1991; Dallison & Lobstein, 1995) have found that most pregnant women on low incomes were below the nutrient recommendations and one in five of these frequently went hungry, as they did not have enough money to buy food. There are several different rates of benefits; for example, pregnant 16–17 year olds are only entitled to Income Support in the last 11 weeks of pregnancy. Yet pregnancy places additional demands on young teenagers whose own bodies are still growing and needing extra nutrients. State benefits for this group are very low and inadequate (Dallison & Lobstein, 1995). This is especially significant as Britain has the highest rate of teenage pregnancy in Europe.

We know little about the effect on the fetus of some substances, e.g. coffee, tea or herbal remedies, whereas other substances such as alcohol or cocaine have received far more attention. Although alcohol is the most commonly abused drug only about 2–3% of pregnant women are heavy drinkers and 0.5% of all newborns suffer from fetal alcohol syndrome. These babies are born small with smaller brains and continue to develop much more slowly than their peers. Mothers are often made to feel very guilty if they take any alcohol although some research suggest that small amounts of alcohol may in fact be beneficial (Passaro *et al.*, 1996).

Unlike the United States, 'crack babies' (babies who are addicted to crack cocaine at birth) are not born in substantial numbers in Britain. The effects of these substances are complex. Continuing research suggests that cocaine exposure alone is unlikely to cause persistent neurobehavioural problems. Chasanoff (1992) (whose early work was often cited as proof of the crack baby syndrome) has acknowledged that other environmental factors, especially poverty, may play a far more important role in the poor development of these children.

The powerful image of 'crack babies' grabbed the attention of the media and the public in the USA and was used by political parties for different ends. The right-wing politicians wanted severer punishments for drug offences and the left wanted more money for public welfare programmes. Research is showing that outcomes for these babies are far more complex than portrayed. The interaction of the ecological system determines the extent to which cocaine has a lasting effect on their development. 'Crack babies' are exposed to a host of risk factors before and after birth: other drugs, alcohol, poverty, poor nutrition, and often a chaotic and non-nurturing early environment.

We know more about the impact of smoking. Smoking is associated with low birthweight and mothers who smoke are more likely to continue feeling unwell, be admitted to hospital and to have urinary infections. Having a mother who smokes has an impact on more than just one generation. Recent evidence suggests that smoking affects the ovaries and the testes of the fetus. The total number of eggs in the ovaries is formed when the embryo is only eight weeks old. Smoking affects the condition of those eggs and therefore another generation when the fetus becomes a woman. If her own mother smoked, she will have a 68% greater chance of starting her periods early and a 27% greater chance of having a miscarriage. Boys are 42% more likely to have their testes in their abdomen (Golding, 1996). Smoking, diet, poverty, stress and drugs all have an adverse affect on the developing fetus. These factors tend not to operate in isolation but are connected with one another and their impact multiplies in effect.

Ethical, moral and cultural issues

The ethical and moral debates that occur around parenting and fetal life can be seen recurring throughout a child's development. The discourses around mothering and fathering and the way they have been constructed are powerful and important: Is having a child a selfish or a selfless act? Is mothering a wholly positive experience? Who should be mothers? Are fathers important? Does everyone have the right to have a child? Do children have rights and if so, at what point do they begin? What role should the state have?

Women are having children later than previous generations and an increasing number are making a decision to be childless by choice. However, it is still assumed that at some point in their lives women will become mothers. Phoenix *et al.* (1991) highlight how women continue to be defined by their biological functions regardless of whether they become mothers. Cultural evaluations of fertility and infertility are reflected in language – 'pregnant with hope', 'a barren land', a 'sterile environment', etc. Mothers are vilified if they are viewed as having had children at the wrong time (too old or too young), are not in a stable relationship (single parents), or have too many children or choose to have none at all. Society has a view about the optimum time and the characteristics of being a good mother. Fathering is less prescribed, with men in their sixties viewed sympathetically if they father children. Elliot (1996) comments on the changing patterns of parenthood with a half of all children born outside marriage and gay/lesbian parenthood more visible. Although there have been changes, Elliot (1996) draws attention to the continuities and to the resilience of traditional cultural patterns within our society, with marriage and parenthood still highly valued.

Babies bring a new status to men and women and carry powerful symbols. Parents can re-live their own childhood or try to ensure their child has a better start in life by putting perceived wrongs to right. It has been argued (Selwyn, 1996) that in an insecure world children represent achievement and creativity and give parents a genetic link to the future. Abortion therefore remains controversial and there have been 20 attempts to change the law since 1967. Around four million abortions have been carried out in England, Wales and Scotland since the introduction of legal abortion in 1968 and consequently a large number of women are affected directly and men indirectly by its impact. Yet it remains secretive. Northern Ireland and Eire in contrast have some of the most restrictive laws in the world. Abortion debates bring out the moral, political, social and religious arguments that centre on rights to life, the role of motherhood and the control of women's sexuality. The role of fathers in making abortion decisions has been under-researched. Yet men control and decide who can have an abortion. In an interesting analysis of abortion, Boyle (1997) looks at this gender imbalance and at how society primarily associates women with nurturing behaviour. Discourses around motherhood are predominantly positive; it is a desired state. Boyle argues that to maintain this view of motherhood women who want abortions have to be portrayed as selfish, morally deficient and sexually promiscuous. This discourse implies that the decision to become a mother will have no negative consequences. However, from mothers' own accounts (Green *et al.*, 1998) and from research (Phoenix *et al.*, 1991) we know that motherhood can bring negative as well as positive consequences. Niven's study (Boyle, 1997) of a group of women followed up four years after childbirth found that 15% were still reporting experiences associated with the birth: intrusive thoughts, flash backs and nightmares, symptoms similar to post-traumatic stress disorder.

It has been claimed that women have abortions for trivial reasons, but, at the same time, they are seriously damaged psychologically by the process. The weight of evidence is that legal abortion as a resolution to an unwanted pregnancy, particularly during the first three months, does not create long-term psychological problems and that the decision is not taken lightly (Adler, 1992 quoted in Boyle, 1997). The majority of women cope well with abortion, despite the secrecy that surrounds the procedure. Although the experience of having a late abortion or an abortion of a wanted pregnancy due to fetal abnormality may cause more distress for women, it does not necessarily mean a wrong decision. In a study of late abortions by Kolker & Burke (Boyle, 1997) women stated that they would make the same choice again in similar circumstances.

Poorer outcomes are more likely when women feel coerced into making the decision. Phoenix (1990) has commented on how black teenagers are referred in disproportionate numbers for abortion after the first antenatal visit, with black women's sexual behaviour judged more readily as promiscuous. Research looking at the outcomes for children who were born after abortion had been refused shows very poor social and psychological developmental outcomes for children (David, 1992 quoted in Boyle, 1997).

Challenges to the current position with regard to fetal rights and the effects on children's development have come from those concerned about the lack of state regulation in infertility treatment (Blyth, 1995). For those unable to have children, technology has moved quickly. It was only in 1978 that Steptoe and Edwards reported the birth of Louise Brown, the first child conceived by *in vitro* fertilisation (IVF). Since then thousands of children have been born by this method and there have been other rapid developments in the field of assisted reproduction. It is now possible to change the fertilised egg before implantation in the womb and to store an embryo in a frozen state to be implanted later, even after a parent's death. Conception no longer needs to involve sexual intercourse and the biological mother and father need not be the same as the genetic mother and father.

Increasing medical expertise and the status attached to motherhood have (Barron & Roberts, 1995), it is alleged, led to increasing consumerism where children are seen as commodities. Others, such as Campbell (1997), argue that the debates around new technologies mask a 'new kind of eugenics masquerading as moralism' where only some people are believed to be suitable as parents. The debates can be seen as driven by dominant discourses which express prejudice against those (e.g. lesbian mothers) who are not deemed by society to be suitable parents, rather than against those who can afford the anonymity of the infertility clinics.

There is little known about the outcomes for children born as the result of surrogacy arrangements. It is not known how children will feel about being created with the expressed purpose of being given away (Department of Health, Brazier report, 1998) but the outcomes may be very culturally specific. Treatments such as IVF involve anonymous donors so that children have no right to information about their genetic father or mother.

Do children have a right to know who their genetic parents are? Those against argue that anonymity is essential to protect the identities of the donors. Without this anonymity, the supply of donors would decrease. Those who argue for the child's right to know point to changes in the adoption law, where, since 1976, all adopted children, upon reaching 18 years of age, have had the right to information about their birth parents. This has occurred without distress to the majority of families involved. Adoption research has also shown that lack of knowledge about one's genetic heritage and birth parents can affect children's sense of self worth and development of identity. The children often have too many unanswered questions and a sense of not being complete (Triseliotis *et al.*, 1997). Children born as the result of donor-assisted conception are the only group who are denied access when reaching adulthood to official records about their genetic origins.

New technologies and knowledge have also raised issues about how much and what medical intervention there should be before birth and who should have the power to make these decisions. Should it be the professionals or parents? Of course, some new technologies might actually reduce intervention levels. For example, a technique involving a simple non-invasive procedure may soon remove the need for amniocentesis, as a way of screening for Down's syndrome. At present, many fetal abnormalities can be detected but few treated. The possibility of future gene treatment will spare parents the choice of abortion or giving birth to a child whose length and quality of life will be affected by a particular illness.

However, the new techniques might be used to foster a consumer attitude towards conception and children. There are two types of gene therapy (Sutton, 1995). Somatic gene therapy targets cells in specific organs and it is widely agreed that in principle it is not very different from conventional medicine as it targets only the individual. Germ line therapy, however, is intended to cure the individual and future generations by introducing new genetic material into cells. This latter therapy raises moral questions about the genetic manipulation of the cells of the embryo. Should fetuses that are unhealthy be discarded? Can parents give consent to treatment that will affect not only their own child, but also their grandchildren? Conversely, do they have the right to refuse treatment that will affect future generations?

Sutton (1995) argues that we are already in danger of moving to a society which has a eugenic outlook, one that only values 'perfect' human beings and which fails to respect the dignity of all human beings irrespective of whether they have a disability. Do we want a society that is free from inherited disease? The removal of the pain and suffering from the lives of children and their families would be welcomed, but how will this change the way society thinks about children and how will it affect views of disability?

The transition to parenthood

During pregnancy, parents become increasingly aware of the expectations and the responsibilities attached to parenting a child. Pregnancy and birth involve a major life transition; nothing will ever be the same again. A woman's status changes to that of a mother and this alters all her relationships. Pregnancy brings with it physical and emotional changes. Many women feel nauseous, tired, and there are physical changes in the breasts, hair and skin. Something very small, the size of a pound coin, can have an enormous physical and emotional impact, with body temperature increasing by up to 10%. The fetus produces more oestrogen than a woman makes in the whole of her lifetime and this affects the serotonin levels in the brain. This chemical is linked with feeling happy and, combined with hair growing thicker and faster and more blood in the lips, gives what is commonly thought of as the 'pregnancy glow'. However, some women do not experience the glow of pregnancy.

Motherhood and pregnancy are seen as being 'natural' and many first-time mothers do not expect to have problems. However, Wolkind & Zajicek (1981) reported that from a sample of 105 pregnant women in London, 43% reported indigestion, 68% lack of energy, 46% breathlessness, 68% leg cramps and 48% backache. Many women also experienced emotional changes; crying, nervousness and worrying were all common, especially during the middle of the pregnancy. Major worries reported were fear of a miscarriage, fears that something was wrong with the baby and money worries. Although the pregnancy may be very much wanted, mothers might also experience feelings of loss; loss of some relationships, loss related to stopping work and loss of a period in life without family responsibilities. Some women suffer depression during pregnancy and a number of studies have shown that a significant number of these women continue to suffer after the birth of the baby (Fergusson *et al.*, 1996). It is not surprising that depression in pregnancy is common given the extent of the physical and emotional changes and changes in social circumstances. However, depression is often not recognised and instead is put down to the discomforts of pregnancy. There is an assumption that if the pregnancy was planned or 'wanted' there will be only positive emotional affects.

Fathers who are supportive can greatly reduce the stress of pregnancy. Lamb's (1997) review of research on fathering shows that fathers often take on more responsibility for the care of older siblings. Fathers can help set up a pattern of interaction that improves the way the siblings react to the arrival of a new baby. However, fathers who deny paternity, who are not supportive or who are violent greatly increase the stress for the mother. Around 30% of domestic violence begins in pregnancy and can cause miscarriage, still births and maternal deaths (Department of Health, 1998a).

During pregnancy when the mother is under severe stress, the flow of adrenaline is increased. One action of adrenaline is to decrease the blood flow to the placenta and this affects the amount of oxygen the fetus receives. As we have already seen, the fetus will try to compensate for these changes in the uterine environment by diverting blood away from other organs to protect the brain. If stress continues for a large part of pregnancy there is increased risk of miscarriage and premature delivery (Botting, 1996). Babies born to mothers who have felt very stressed during their pregnancies are more irritable and therefore a pattern may have begun before birth that interferes with the relationship between mother and baby.

Fathers also report physical symptoms during their partner's pregnancy. Wolkind & Zajicek (1981) found that 50% of the fathers in their study reported pregnancy-like symptoms, such as nausea, vomiting and loss of appetite. Fathers also found pregnancy stressful, feeling helpless about and partly responsible for the possible dangers facing their partners and unborn child. Men also reported feeling afraid of parenthood, concerned that it would create a distance between themselves and their partner, or that their partner would transfer all affection to the child. Scott-Heyes (1983) found that fathers who were depressed and anxious during pregnancy felt they not only gave less affection but also received less. The way the father adjusted to the pregnancy affected the quality of the relationship between the parents. This in turn would increase either the stress or the sense of wellbeing felt by the mother, altering the flow of chemicals and nutrients across the placenta to affect the developing fetus.

Most parents form a relationship with the fetus long before birth. Studies examining feedback during ultrasound scanning (Reading et al., 1989) showed how the visual imaging of the new baby directly affected the way parents felt about the pregnancy and changed their behaviour in ways which might affect the development of the fetus. For those parents where the scan revealed a healthy fetus the parents felt they could now identify the fetus as their baby and it made the pregnancy more of a reality, especially for fathers. However, those parents where the scan or other tests suggested that there might be something wrong suffered high levels of stress. Even when subsequent tests disproved the possibility of disability, mothers continued to worry and be highly anxious until the delivery of the healthy baby (Green et al., 1990).

Birth

The fetus begins the process of birth many days before the mother is aware that labour has begun. Labour as a biological process occurs in the same way throughout the world. The experience of giving birth, however, differs with the traditions of each culture. In most cultures it is a great event, whereas others treat it as an illness or believe only women should be present at the birth. The practice in recent years in Britain has been to allow women to make choices about their birth experience. Some births happen in 'high tech' environments; others in the home, some in birth pools, and others in unplanned places as the baby will not wait to be born! Many research studies have noted how women have compared their pregnancy to being on a conveyor belt with little continuity of care by professionals and with little control over events (Phoenix et al., 1991). A review of research on care in pregnancy and childbirth (Enkin et al., 1995) showed that many technological procedures which were routinely employed were of no value to the woman or baby and in some cases were harmful. In contrast, the non-interventionist techniques of the new midwifery such as maternal mobility, choice of position in labour, emotional and psychological support in labour were beneficial.

Studies in Britain have shown that a sense of control is a major factor contributing to women's positive assessment of the birth experience and future wellbeing. Control though is a complex set of behaviours and perceptions about events. It is not simply about being 'in control'. Green *et al.* (1998) found that women wanted to have faith in the experts caring for them. They wanted to believe that the professionals knew best but they also wanted to have the choice of disagreeing with possible interventions. This balance between personal control and support was very important. The mother needed to have the support of the midwife when she wanted it and to be able to hand over control to her when needed. The midwife taking 'control' at appropriate times was seen as supportive.

The period just after birth is associated with a steep rise in psychiatric illness. About two in every 1000 mothers experience a psychotic breakdown with many more experiencing less severe symptoms. Despite this, the risk of suicide is low, as the presence of a dependent baby seems to be a protective factor. Maternal deaths related to pregnancy or birth are rare events but still account for around 125 deaths each year (Department of Health, 1998a). However, black women born outside Britain have a three times greater risk of maternal mortality, primarily due to difficulties in accessing services (Acheson, 1999). Some maternal deaths are due to mothers being inhibited about seeking help but many deaths are due to substandard medical care, with, for example, an increase in deaths from embolisms. The Department of Health (1998a) is committed to improving practice in this area by making health professionals more aware of risk factors.

Although parents will have been told that nothing is ever the same again they now begin to realise just how different life is with a baby. Many cultures regard the month after birth as a vulnerable period in a woman's life. The Chinese believe that if a mother does not take proper care of herself she will suffer long-term health consequences such as arthritis, asthma and anaemia. It is the responsibility of the whole family to take proper care of her and provide special food. This time is known as 'sitting the month'. Similarly, mothers from Pakistan and India would, within their own traditions, expect to recover for about six weeks before taking a ritual cleansing bath and then returning to normal household duties. The support and expertise of mothers-in-law ease the transition from wife to mother. Husbands traditionally would not be involved in direct care but would be expected to carry out rituals according to religion. A Moslem baby must have a call to prayer whispered into the ear shortly after birth while Hindu babies have honey and ghee placed on their tongues.

Whatever their actual background, mothers in this country rarely have this level of support. Health professionals normally encourage mothers to move around as soon as possible after the birth as it is known this encourages healing and reduces the risk of thrombosis. Mothers from other cultural traditions may feel very anxious and afraid by the lack of support and different ways of approaching both the birth and postnatal care.

In this chapter we have seen that:

- The fetus is active in development. Development is a participatory process that is affected by genetic, social, emotional and environmental influences.
- Low birthweight is a key indicator of vulnerability across the lifespan.
- The social construction of childhood and parenting starts before birth.
- The positive discourses around pregnancy may prevent parents accessing professional help if they have difficulties.
- Cultural and religious beliefs need to be respected and understood by professionals working in this area if inequalities in health are to be addressed.

The period from conception to birth is a time of rapid growth for the fetus. Development is a participatory process with the fetus taking an active part. It is a period where much is still to be discovered. It is also a period of change for the parents as they become accustomed to their new roles and status. Relationships change between the parents, siblings and the extended family. The pregnancy may make the mother's and father's own parents grandparents for the first time. This is an important transition for them too and one they may, or may not, anticipate with pleasure.

Despite the dangers, most babies are born healthy and very quickly let their parents know they have arrived. A new person is part of their lives, with his or her own personality apparent from the moment of birth. The discourses around mothering and fathering begin to be felt in a new way after birth as the parents try to meet the needs of a new baby and balance this with their own family's needs and society's expectations. The next chapter will take up the story from birth until three.

Chapter 3
Infancy

Julie Selwyn

Recently I had another baby and as I carried him around with me to shop or collect my other children from school, strangers or acquaintances would come up and ask, 'Is he a good baby?'. I was completely absorbed with his beauty and responsiveness and there was only one reply I could make: 'Of course'. However, the question left something unsaid and it made me feel uneasy. The weeks went by and the same question was asked but now with a statement that suggested that if he really was a good baby he should be sleeping through the night and in his own cot. Advice was freely given about how to achieve this from giving up breast-feeding, letting him scream or adding alcohol to bottle-feeds!

The birth of a baby is tremendously exciting but it can also be a confusing and difficult time for parents as they cope with lack of sleep, care of their infant and maybe care of siblings and older family members. The reality for many families is different from the descriptions of family life found in books and parenting magazines. To explore these issues, this chapter is divided into two sections. The first examines the context within which the infant develops, focusing on areas rarely mentioned in parenting books, namely parenting more than one child, the role of fathers, disability in childhood and the impact of poverty. The second section focuses on the developing child. At birth babies seem helpless, but even the newborn has some essential survival tools. The baby can breathe, eat and cry. Infants are born into a bewildering variety of environments, from war zones to palaces. Their brains must be ready to adjust to whatever environment they confront. The 1990s were described as the decade of brain research and we will see what this research tells us about the importance for healthy development of the infant's active involvement with the environment.

Developmental context

Getting ready for a baby to be born in white Anglo-American cultures involves a great deal of preparation. Magazines are read avidly and there are shopping trips to buy everything that will be needed. Health professionals state that babies actually need very little. However, mothers are pressured to buy what is perceived as best for baby and this may include a separate bedroom for the baby decked out with matching curtains, wallpaper, cot and fluffy toys. Providing material goods for the new baby has become associated with being a 'good mother' and as the goods are covered with Winnie the Pooh or other corporate icons, babies and mothers are caught early in marketing attempts to link brand loyalty and future spending. Typical of the material aimed at new mothers is literature from major stores that combines educative material with advertising, linking healthy outcomes with products.

It is easy to assume that the same processes go on throughout Britain and the world. This is far from true. We will see in Chapter 5 that other cultures are shocked by the early separation of baby and mother at night as babies sleep in a cot of their own in less than 10% of the world's societies (Werner, 1979). Anglo-American discourses around parenting stress the importance of encouraging early independence by helping babies find their own sources of comfort, to be 'dry' as quickly as possible and be awake when adults are around to stimulate. Bornstein & Lamb (1992) have suggested that forcing infants to fit into adult time frames (often determined by work schedules) may be unhelpful for babies and create pressure and stress, particularly in the relationship between the main carer and the baby. Wolf *et al.* (1996) suggest that these cultural practices teach children to rely on objects (teddies or dummies) for a source of comfort rather than to rely on people. Parenting practices reflect the cultural values associated with being a good parent. These cultural values also tell us what it means to be a 'good' baby. Each society creates its own belief systems and assumptions about what is the best care for infants and what is 'good' behaviour. Consequently, the questions I was asked about my own baby were possibly a kind of check to see if he was fitting the expected norms of how a baby should behave and also a way of assessing my parenting abilities

In comparison with the Mediterranean countries or Scandinavia, Britain is seen as a child-unfriendly country, with young children only just tolerated in public places. It is hardly surprising that babies largely remain within the home with outings limited to 'safe' places such as mother and baby groups. The baby clinic is ostensibly the place where mothers can meet health professionals to get help and advice as well as complete early developmental checks. New mothers are often amazed at the number of babies and mothers attending clinics and wonder where the babies are hidden the rest of the time! Yet, infants have important symbolic value. This is evident as politicians (usually men) vie to be photographed kissing a photogenic baby. The photograph says: 'Look, here is man who will look after our future, the country is safe in his hands.' There is a paradox here, in that although infants carry significant symbolic meanings for all adults, and parents will make considerable sacrifices to ensure the best for their child, society is ambivalent about the value of children. For many families, caring for infants goes on behind closed doors with parents expected to take full responsibility. The isolation of mothers and the pressure to make their baby match or exceed developmental norms increases stress on parents. When the stresses of parenting are combined with other stressful life events such as unemployment or domestic violence and the mother feels unsupported, there is a far greater risk of postnatal depression (Cooper & Murray, 1998).

Caring for an infant can bring great joy and pleasure, a sense of fulfilment and can be tremendous fun. At times it can also feel like a lonely responsibility. Many first-time mothers talk of the shock of realising that the baby in the cot is their responsibility to feed, clothe and help develop into a mature adult. Parents seek help and advice from family, friends, and health professionals and turn to parenting magazines. The number of magazines and childcare books has grown rapidly in the last 20 years and these aim to guide women in their role as mothers. Fathers are hardly mentioned and the images of parenting are almost exclusively female.

The advice mothers receive has changed dramatically. In 1934 Frankenburg was advising:

> 'Babies and children ... are all the better for a little wholesome neglect. From the beginning an infant should be trained to spend most of his time lying alone. He gets quite enough handling whilst being fed and dressed ... Reserve singing, talking and playing for his playtime (half an hour a day): let "being amused" be a treat – do not let him expect it always, for then he will get no pleasure from it.'
>
> (p171)

In 1999, the titles of the latest babycare books give a flavour of the shift in the social construction of parenthood: 'Raising a happy confident successful child – 52 lessons to help parents grow,' or 'Secrets of success'. The word 'success' is repeated in numerous other titles. Parents are expected to stimulate, entertain and ensure that their child develops into a well-balanced adult. Books offer opposing advice and mothers try to weigh up how far their own infant is meeting developmental norms or use the books and magazines for advice when they have concerns.

Some infants do not fit in with developmental norms, for a number of reasons including temperament, disability, illness or the effects of poverty. The inability to 'fit' may be temporary or be indicative of difficulties that will continue to have an impact on the developing child. It is often parents who first identify that their child is not developing at the same rate as other children. Parenting books and magazines do not reflect the reality of many people's lives. They present a stereotypical view of parenting and infancy that does not show the diversity of parenting and childhood experiences. It can also leave parents feeling more isolated and blamed and children not receiving the services they need. To examine this diversity we will begin by taking a brief look at the rise in poverty, the role of fathers, the way disability is perceived and, to begin with, parenting more than one child.

Siblings

Mothers having their second child are often ignored in hospital as it is assumed that 'they know it all'. Dunn's (Dunn & Kendrick, 1982; Dunn, 1993) research investigating young children's relationships shows that family difficulties can escalate with the birth of a second child. Mothers have on average only five hours sleep each night until the second baby is over three months old and this makes caring for the first child very difficult. The birth of a second child for the first born is an overwhelming experience which often is acted out through increased confrontations. Parenting books discuss this as though it does not matter as it occurs so frequently, but many parents seek help either informally from friends or formally from professionals, as they are concerned at the level of sibling rivalry and hostility. It is a matter to be taken seriously.

Sibling relationships are the longest relationship most of us will ever have and during the early years young children spend more time with their siblings than with any other child or adult including their parents. Dunn's studies showed that families began to settle down again around 10 months after the second birth. Parents who helped their first child understand that babies had *feelings and needs* were the families where the transition to having more than one child went smoothest. These were the families where the carer said to the first child 'Oh look, the baby is hungry, he is crying, what shall we do?' However, it is not clear from this research if it was the style of parenting or the temperament of both children that encouraged the carer to discuss the baby in this way. Nevertheless, children under two are especially sensitive to *how* people are talking and families where feelings and needs are recognised are more likely to promote pro-social behaviour in their children.

Disability?

You may be wondering why this section starts with a question mark. Disability as a concept has been debated by academics, by disabled people and by pressure groups. For many years the individual model of disability dominated. This model located the 'problem' of disability within people themselves and saw the 'problems' as caused by the physical or mental limitations which were assumed to arise from the disability. The model became increasingly unsatisfactory as it did not fit the experience of disabled people (Oliver, 1996a and b).

The development of the social model distinguished between impairments and disability. Disability is seen as being caused by society's failure to provide adequate services. It is the range of restrictions from prejudice to lack of public transport that imposes a disability on an individual. In comparison with the individual model that sees disability as a personal tragedy occurring at random, the social model stresses that it is the systematic discrimination against disabled people as a group which creates disability.

'Consequently there is increasing rejection of approaches based on the restoration of normality and insisting on approaches based upon the celebration of difference. From rejections of the "cure" through critiques of supposedly therapeutic interventions such as conductive education, cochlea implants and the like, and on to attempts to build a culture of disability based on pride, the idea of "normality" is increasingly coming under attack.'

(Oliver, 1996b, pp43–44)

The proponents of this model do not support the kinds of medical intervention that were described in Chapter 2 or intervention after birth such as cochlea implants for deaf children. Those supporting the social model of disability stress the diversity of humanity; children have different shapes, sizes and abilities. All children are 'normal'; it is society's attitudes that are disabling. Others see this clear distinction between impairment and disability as unhelpful. Corker & French (1999) comment on how disability has been stressed whilst the impact of the impairment has been marginalised and silenced. This, they argue, prevents a full understanding of disability and silences certain groups. To illustrate, there has been a great deal written about including disabled children within mainstream schools but less about how their lives are also affected by the pain of their impairment and the medical interventions they need to stay alive. Corker & French (1999) call for a reconceptualisation of disability theory which would look at the relationship between impairment and disability and address the ecology of individual lives. They argue that this would allow new knowledge and understandings of disability and the liberation and acceptance of 'silent voices'.

This discussion of models is not just of interest at a conceptual level. These models influence the kinds of research that has been undertaken and influence professional training, law and policy. The individual model can still be seen operating in the Children Act 1989 and in service responses. This model also seems to be deeply ingrained in popular magazines. During pregnancy, the possibility of having a child with an impairment is mentioned in magazines and self-help books advising mothers to avoid a range of substances and certain behaviours. Magazines rarely include discussion of living with a disabled child and when it is discussed it is described in terms of either a mother's or a child's heroic efforts to overcome or cope with disability. It is evident that the disability is being seen as a personal tragedy. Yet two out of every 100 babies are born with an impairment which will be disabling in this society (Gregory, 1991). Parents find it difficult to access information about their child's condition and babies with impairments are missing from media images of infancy. This is not to say there are no images but that disability is portrayed elsewhere as abnormal, often ugly and associated in children's books with evil (e.g. Captain Hook) or to be pitied (e.g. Heidi).

As we noted in Chapter 2, there is a great deal of medical expertise being put into reducing the number of babies born with an impairment. This is countered by the rising numbers of small babies kept alive by technology and a failure of community resources to keep up with needs. A number of different studies have suggested that one result of more low birthweight babies surviving has been both an increase in the rates of cerebral palsy and death delayed until infancy rather than at birth. Guillemin & Holstrum (1986) consider this may not necessarily be progress. They argue that families have little input into medical decisions about whether to intervene. Some families in their study watched their tiny babies undergoing intensive intervention, suffering pain and dying, with medical professionals who stereotyped mothers as uncaring if they wanted a peaceful death for their baby. Other studies and case law (see Fortin, 1998a) have shown that parents have demanded expensive 'high tech' intervention once they had seen their baby. Parents wanted to give their baby every chance to survive and this has involved appeals to the High Court for invasive medical intervention. This has left the NHS unsure about how to deal with the ethical issues as well as having implications for resource management.

Parents find diagnosis of impairment a time of crisis. Parents often expect to have increased sense of fulfilment and an increase in self-esteem after the birth of a child, but when children cannot live up to parental expectations there can be a sense of failure, personal blame and sadness. For fathers the most disturbing events happen at this time as they are often not informed about the diagnosis or informed after the mother (Lamb & Billings in Lamb, 1997). Many fathers respond by being concerned about the child's future, wondering about providing for them and whether they will be able to be independent as adults. Mothers are more likely to be concerned about the emotional impact on the family and ability of the child to have friends and be happy. The important developmental stages such as talking or walking can remind families of their sadness. The social, emotional and physical demands placed on parents increase stress in families and divorce rates are higher than in other families. Mothers, in particular, report high levels of stress caused by the demands of caring with little support and with limited finance (Lamb, 1997).

The social model of disability places disability within an equal opportunities framework and it is important to recognise that issues around gender and ethnicity interact with disability. For example, in a study (Chamba et al., 1999) comparing severely impaired children living in white families with those living in Asian families, it was found that Asian families were even more disadvantaged. They were less likely to be receiving services and less likely to have been awarded the higher rates of Disability Living Allowance. Although inability to use English was a barrier to gaining information and benefits, discrimination was also apparent in the low levels of services they were receiving.

It is as difficult to generalise about the effect of impairment and disability as it is about all children. Parenting a child with learning difficulties is very different than parenting a child with a limited life span. Much of the literature is of the personal tragedy kind. There is, however, a different type of literature which describes how living with a disability has brought positive changes in people's lives, giving a different set of values, stronger marriages and personal insight (Lamb & Billings in Lamb, 1997; Oliver, 1996a). Beresford's study (1994) concluded that most parents caring for a child with impairments actively seek ways of managing their day-to-day lives so that children are cared for within happy and loving relationships. Professionals working with families need to consider involving fathers in all discussions and decisions. Fathers can play a key role in supporting the mother and reducing feelings of stress.

Role of fathers

Government policy has concentrated on the role of fathers as bread-winners, highlighting their financial responsibilities. While this is certainly one of the roles many fathers play, it omits the importance of the multiple roles that fathers play in the family. Contrary to early research on fathering, it is now accepted that fathers and mothers influence their children in very similar ways. The similarities are more important than the differences (Lamb, 1997). Warmth, nurturance and closeness are associated with positive outcomes, whether the parent is male or female. The quality of relationships is more important than gender characteristics. An important role is support for the mother. In Chapter 2, we saw the importance of men in supporting the pregnancy, and support during childhood continues to enhance the quality of family relationships. Newer perspectives on fathering recognise the indirect patterns of influence. Fathers and children are part of complex families in which each person is affected by and affects others' behaviour (Lamb, 1997). Fathers also play different roles in different cultural contexts; for example, the role of moral educator is more important in some cultures than others.

Lamb's (1997) review of the available research on fathering shows that generally fathers spend much less time with their children than mothers and assume no responsibility for important decisions such as looking after sick children or organising childcare. Their involvement in decision making does not depend on whether the mother works inside or outside the home. Fathers' participation is increasing gradually but not as much as suggested by the 'new men' rhetoric. While research has now begun to concentrate on the role of fathers, fewer children spend their childhood in families where fathers are present. Many men have removed themselves or allowed themselves to be excluded from their children's lives. Lamb (1997), reviewing the evidence on the effect of father absence, concludes that father absence may be harmful for children. This is not because a sex-role model is absent, but because other aspects of a father's role, such as providing economic, social and emotional support, go unfilled in families.

The present government is attempting to reassert the importance of fathers. The Labour government wishes to change the culture that surrounds fathers which sees them as 'walking wallets' only important in providing economic stability, uninterested in their children or as potential abusers. The 'Fathers Direct' initiative is intended to offer information, advice and support to all fathers. An example of this is the inclusion for the first time of information for fathers in the packs given to mothers after birth. The government is also keen to educate the providers of health, education and social services to include fathers in their assessments and interventions. As we will see though in Chapter 11, although more fathers are taking paternity leave, current legislation does not ensure this is paid leave. Consequently, families who are under the most economic stress are also the ones where the father is least likely to be able to take paternity leave.

Poverty

The number of children living in households with below half the average income has risen rapidly in the last 20 years. In 1995–6 about one-third of all children (4.3 million children) were living in these low-income households compared to 1.3 million in 1968 (Gregg *et al.*, 1999). This is at a time when the standard of living for the majority of the population has increased. Although part of the rise can be explained by the growth in the numbers of lone parents, children are also more likely to be living in poverty in two-parent families where no one is employed and this includes families where a child has a disability. Pakistani and Bangladeshi families are over-represented in the poorest fifth of income distribution (Department of Social Security, 1999).

Death rates for infants and children are at a historically low level but continue to show that gender, class and geography affect the likelihood of mortality. There are regional differences in death rates with the north and north-west of England having the highest infant mortality rate. The same birthweight babies from working-class households have infant mortality rates 68% higher than babies born to fathers from professional occupations. Similarly, babies born to single mothers (who are more likely to be poor) are twice as likely to die before their first birthday as those born inside marriage. Babies of mothers born in the Indian sub-continent and the Caribbean are also twice as likely to die before the age of two (for a full discussion see Population Trends, 1998).

From the age of one until four, accidents are the leading causes of death with most happening in the home. Children from poorer homes are at greater risk of accidents from lack of proper facilities and overcrowding (Whitehead, 1992). Accidents can also leave children with long-term health problems. The most common type of accident is a fall (45%) with burning the most common cause of fatality (Department of Trade and Industry, 1992). Accidents have two major causes: environmental hazards such as kettle flexes and dangerous behaviour where the curious child does not understand the danger. Accident prevention is one of the key targets of the Health of the Nation programme and health visitors advise parents (usually mothers) on ways of reducing risk.

It has been argued that educating parents is not enough (Roberts *et al.*, 1995). A review of the research (Alwash & McCarthy, 1991) showed that improving safety was not simply a matter of allocating more health visitor time to discussing home safety as parents reported low income as an important barrier to improving safety. Alwash & McCarthy (1991) argue financial help should be made available to low-income families to buy safety equipment and account should be taken of the cultural, economic and environmental circumstances that constrain families. Roberts (1995) argues that health professionals should go further and be more willing to act as advocates for child safety, taking every opportunity to be more vocal about the causes such as inadequate housing, homelessness and poverty.

Growing up in poverty affects nutrition, all areas of development, access to medical care, the safety and predictability of physical environments, the level of family stress and excludes children from many of the activities open to other children. In later chapters, we will see how poverty diminishes the life chances of children by reducing their aspirations, increasing their likelihood of ill health and reducing educational opportunity. Infants need good nutrition for physical and cognitive development and this leads us into the next section which examines the developing child.

The developing child

It used to be thought that a child's brain was a miniature version of an adult's brain and that all the connections were in place at birth. We now know this is inaccurate. With advances in scanning technology, brain activity can now be identified and measured and this has brought rapid advancements in knowledge. Development starts *in utero*, but at birth a baby's brain is only partially wired; millions of details are to be filled in by experience. After birth each brain cell (neuron) sends a long thin fibre to connect it to other neurons. The connections that neurons make with each other are called synapses and each neuron can make anything from 10 to 10 000 synapses, depending on the function. The brain will eventually contain well over 1000 trillion synapses and none of these are random (Atkinson *et al.*, 1993). This network forms the neurological foundation upon which a child builds a lifetime of skills; a map which allows learning to take place (Carnegie Corporation, 1994). Up to the age of ten, a child's brain shows twice the level of activity of an adult's.

The wiring of the brain has been compared to the setting up of a telephone system; first lines are laid between cities then between towns and then between individual houses (Nash, 1997). The most important factors in this process of developing connections are stimulation and repeated experience. Neurons that are stimulated continue to establish new synapses whereas those that are seldom or never stimulated are pruned and die off. The evidence emerging on synaptic development suggests that appropriate stimulation of the child's brain is critically important during periods in which the formation of synapses is at its peak (Berk, 1994). At the age of two, a child has twice as many synapses as an adult. This has led to the phrase *'Use it or lose it'* to stress the importance of stimulation during the early years. If the brain does not receive the right kind of stimulus, connections are not made and the opportunity may have gone forever or be very difficult to make up at a later stage. A classic experiment by Hubel and Wiesel (Berk, 1994) illustrates. A newborn kitten had one eye sewn up at birth. Even though the stitches were removed some months later the kitten remained blind as the visual connections had not been made. This explained why, if a baby has untreated cataracts and is not operated upon soon enough, the eye never recovers sight, whereas an adult after a cataract operation recovers sight as the synapses have already formed. Although the window of opportunity for visual experience is very short other connections take many years to develop.

Babies are acute observers. If they have a secure base, are given lots of physical affection and communicated with, there are physiological changes to the brain. Diet, poverty and stressful environments affect the quality and quantity of the wiring between cells. How the baby is nurtured plays a key part in the maturing of the brain. It is not simply that the brain matures and then behaviour change follows. Environmental stimulation which changes behaviour can lead to changes in the brain which in turn can then go on to support more complex forms of behaviour.

The brain does not know whether it is going to learn English or Urdu so it sets up a fundamental framework which is then pruned depending on experiences after birth. Within the first four months of life, infants are what Kuhl (1991) has called 'universal linguists'. Babies can distinguish each of the 150 speech sounds that make up every human language in the world but very quickly lose this ability to show preference for their native language. There are many skills that young children have that adults do not possess which disappear with maturation (Barrettt, 1999). There is a developmental window during early childhood where the power to learn language is so great that many languages can be learnt at the same time, including sign and spoken languages. From puberty as the brain becomes less flexible, the task of learning a second language becomes more difficult. The brain has pruned away the cells that would have enabled the young child to master a foreign language easily.

Different parts of the brain mature at different rates and times. The neurological foundations of maths and logic seem to be established by four years. Research has shown that babies less than six months old understand that items can be added and subtracted (Wynn, 1992). New insights (Lamb, 1999) are being gained into the development of dyslexia, cerebral palsy, and learning disabilities. A scanning technique known as PET has confirmed that there are inherent gender differences. At birth girls tend to be more attentive to faces and sounds while boys are attentive to objects and what they can see. These differences occur so early that it is difficult to attribute them to anything other than the way the brain is organised. However, culture also affects behaviour and as the infant grows the combination of nature and nurture produces differences in behaviour such as boys' preference for competitive games.

There are, however, very specific ways in which each gender uses the brain. The brain is divided into two hemispheres. Boys tend to use one hemisphere at a time whereas girls have far more synapses between the hemispheres. In girls, the hemispheres work simultaneously to process information. This ability allows girls to overcome damage to the brain more easily than boys and makes boys less able to compensate for faulty wiring (Springer & Deutsch, 1993).

There is debate about the evidence for critical periods and the arguments are particularly fierce around the evidence for emotional stability. PET scans show there is a large increase in brain activity in the emotional area between six months and two years and it has been suggested that this is the critical period for emotional stability (Dawson, 1997). Research following the adjustment of children adopted into British families from Romanian orphanages shows that although these children make impressive catch ups in height, weight and cognitive deficiencies, they are continuing to have difficulties in social behaviours such as in play and in attachment behaviours (Rutter & ERA, 1998).

The relationship between the main carer and the child is very important. It is through this relationship that the infant learns they are loved, secure, and feels able to explore the environment. Consequently, there has been considerable research interest in postnatal depression as evidence has accumulated of the long-term effects on children's cognitive and emotional development. In situations where the mother is the main carer, having a mother who is suffering from postnatal depression provides the baby with a different, less predictable and unresponsive relationship. Although newborn babies are near sighted, they can see their carer's face perfectly from the position where they are fed. Babies look intently at faces and babies who look at a mother's face which is expressionless and unresponsive quickly become unresponsive themselves (Murray & Trevarthen, 1985).

Depressed mothers tend to believe they are poor mothers and feel inadequate and unable to aid their baby's development. Depressed mothers interact less with their babies, are more unpredictable, and show less emotion and feeling towards their infant (Thompson, 1994). Murray *et al.*'s (1996) longitudinal study of postnatally depressed mothers and their children found that a predictor of poor cognitive outcomes for the babies was having a mother who was not able to adjust communication sensitively. Not only did the infant have poor cognitive outcomes at 18 months but also this trajectory continued to the age of five and beyond. Male children had significantly poorer cognitive outcomes. Dawson *et al.* (1997) has noted how different parts of the brain are stimulated by different emotions. Brains of children with depressed mothers looked different when scanned, with the area for positive emotion showing less activity and the area for negative emotions more active. Dawson believes this permanently affects the synapses made and sets up a predisposition to respond to stress negatively as an adult and be less able to respond positively to good things in the environment.

Tronick & Gianino (1986) suggest that some effects of postnatal depression might be positive. Becoming attuned to the emotional state of their mother, children might develop a greater sensitivity and awareness to the emotional state of others. Paradice (1993) argues that although the effect of postnatal depression on the child's development must be taken seriously, it is incorrect to assume that the child will be irreversibly affected. The whole environment needs to be considered, not least the other relationships the infant has, with siblings, with the father and other adults which may compensate for poor infant/mother relationships. The latter view is certainly of importance when assessing a child's protective environment, but, as we have already seen, many mothers and children are isolated within the home on low incomes. Our current state of knowledge suggests that postnatal depression, if untreated, is likely to have adverse emotional, cognitive and behavioural child outcomes which are persistent (Cooper & Murray, 1998). Depression is often missed by primary care teams although treatment is available which is usually very effective. However, even when medication is prescribed, it can interfere with the ability to breast-feed. Alternative medication is available but by failing to consider the interaction of mother and baby they can both be deprived of the physical closeness and other benefits associated with breast-feeding.

Early feeding

Breast-feeding has been shown to offer infants increased resilience to a wide range of viruses, parasites and bacteria and offer a range of other benefits to the growing infant (Palmer, 1993). Human milk contains more than 100 individual fatty acids and two of these combine to form LC-PUFA necessary for the development of the baby's brain and retina. Although a bottle-fed baby can make the necessary LC-PUFAs from other fatty acids, these cannot be made as fast as they are needed, particularly by premature babies. These fats may also be responsible for the better performances of breast-fed children than formula-fed infants in tests which measure verbal ability, cognition, and school performance (Makrides et al., 1994; Rogan & Gladen, 1993). However, these benefits may be related to more than just the content of the breast milk. For example, the intimacy and physical closeness of breast-feeding may be important for infant development. During feeding, mothers stroke, kiss, soothe, and talk to their babies. Babies reciprocate and communicate with sounds, gestures and enjoy feeling the breast. In Britain it is also the case that mothers who choose to breast-feed are often from a higher socio-economic group than mothers who feed formula milk. Differences in performance may reflect better nutrition, stimulation or better access to high quality education in the families where income is high. Other studies have tried to adjust for these factors with mixed results (for a fuller discussion of these issues see Morley, 1998).

There are other advantages to breast milk, not least the undisputed ability to protect the infant from a variety of viruses, parasites and bacteria. The mother's body has an amazing ability to continuously monitor harmful organisms in her infant's environment and respond by pouring specific antibodies into her breast milk. There has been an increase in breast-feeding since the 1970s but in 1990, only 63% of mothers in England and Wales were breast-feeding (White et al., 1992). That percentage declines rapidly so that by four months of age, only 25% of babies are breast-fed. The decrease has been associated with mothers not being made aware of shifts in feeding patterns of babies due to gender differences and age (Wright, 1990), work patterns, the social acceptability of breast-feeding and other factors (Botting, 1996).

Mothers from Asia traditionally believe that they should wait until the milk comes in before putting the baby to the breast. Colostrum (the first milk) is considered too strong and sugar water is frequently given. This belief can be misunderstood and it is assumed that the mother does not want to breast-feed (Kaseras & Hopkins, 1987). It is common practice in British hospitals to put the baby to the breast as soon as possible as the wish is to encourage bonding and allow the baby to begin suckling. For many Asian mothers public breast-feeding, especially if there are men in the room, is not acceptable and again a chain of events may be set in motion through lack of understanding.

Promoting and helping mothers to breast-feed receives little govern-ment support. The supply of free formula milk to those on low incomes could be seen to actively discourage it. Bottle-fed children are more likely to have infections from inadequately sterilized bottles, to be fatter and have less resilience to common diseases. Companies spend millions advertising and new mothers are encouraged to bottle-feed by intro-ductory vouchers and products given whilst in hospital. Hospitals hard pressed for cash have agreed that companies producing formula milk can sponsor maternity wards. It is hardly surprising that many mothers feeling anxious about feeding their baby in public, or whether they can produce enough milk, take some comfort from these positive messages and can see exactly how much milk their baby consumes from a bottle. The Department of Health estimates universal breast-feeding would save £35 million per year in hospital admissions from gastro-enteritis (DoH, 1995). There is no doubt that breast milk is by far the best first food for babies; just how protective and nourishing it is, we have still to discover.

Research on brain development confirms that good prenatal care, warm and loving attachments between young children and adults and positive stimulation from birth do make a difference to children's development for a lifetime. It confirms the tremendous diversity of humans; each brain is as unique as a face. The brain can be helped to compensate by appro-priately timed and intensive intervention. Studies of the outcomes for children who have faced adversities show that humans can and do overcome tremendous hardship (Rutter *et al.*, 1990; Garbarino *et al.*, 1991). The plasticity of the brain also means that there are times when negative experiences or the absence of appropriate stimulation are more likely to have serious and sustained effects. Plasticity or the brain's capacity to remodel itself has led to a radical operation for infants with extreme epilepsy. Half the brain is removed but the amazing flexibility of the developing brain allows it to remodel itself and the children develop with only minor physical and mental impairments (Chugani, 1996). This plasticity reduces with age which explains why it is more difficult to reverse negative effects once puberty is reached.

During the last 20 years there has been a great deal of research that has emphasised the abilities of newborn babies and infants. It used to be thought that babies could see or hear very little and there are still assumptions made about babies' abilities. The influence of theorists who advocated a stage approach can still be seen in the assumption that children grow up gradually increasing in competence. This view is too simplistic in that it does not reflect the way development includes the loss of some competencies and gain of others, depending on the environment. The same child may be progressing in cognitive skills and regressing in social skills. Development is not unitary (Barrett, 1999).

Much of the literature still concentrates on one aspect of the ecological system without looking at the interconnections and interrelatedness of all the systems. The full impact of poverty is only just beginning to be understood. In the US, the technological advances that enable better understanding of brain development are having a big impact on the political debates around the necessity of providing high quality childcare. Others fear the emphasis on early intervention leads to older children being 'written off' as beyond help. Burman (1994), on a cautionary note, questions these developmental approaches and wonders what they tell us about current discourses around childhood. Burman comments how only evidence that supports competency is highlighted whereas other contradictory evidence is ignored. By stressing competence, i.e. what babies can do, the introduction of hot-housing educational programmes can occur. Having a high regard for competencies that can be measured disregards infants' other behaviour, which is not competent and perhaps devalues characteristics that are not competency based. Thinking back to earlier in this chapter, how does this discourse affect the view of disability? What are we unable to see and recognise because of the emphasis on competency? During the twentieth century childcare experts offered very different advice to parents on the most appropriate way to raise their children; one wonders what the twenty-first century will bring in our understanding of development.

Chapter 4
Early Development: Critical Perspectives

Mary Fawcett

The word 'development' implies change. From the moment of conception (see Chapter 2) and through the years up to ten, dramatic changes and growth take place. Development implies, of course, more than simply change – it is about progress towards a goal. In early childhood, patterns of interacting with other people and making friends are already evolving. At this time children are constructing ways of thinking – about themselves, their strengths and weaknesses (and hence their sense of self-worth), and the groups they belong to. In these years a vast amount of knowledge is absorbed and processed, and each individual constructs a personal understanding of the world. Proficiency is gained in vital skills of all kinds. For those who encounter young children at this stage and have duties towards them – teachers, social workers, play-workers, parents – it can be a challenging but often positive time.

> '...children show us they know how to walk along the path to understanding. Once children are helped to perceive themselves as authors or inventors, once they are helped to discover the pleasure of inquiry, their motivation and interest explode. The age of childhood, more than the ages that follow, is characterised by such expectations.'
>
> (Malaguzzi in Edwards *et al.*, 1998, p67)

This vivid image of children setting out on their 'path to understanding' with competence and potential suggests that adults have great responsibilities in creating situations which allow them to develop fully.

This chapter is not only concerned with what adults who work with children might be expected to know but also how our current understanding of child development has arisen. The matter is not straightforward and the very concept of child development has become a contentious issue (Burman, 1994; Stott & Bowman, 1996; Woodhead, 1996 and 1999; Dahlberg *et al.*, 1999). What once seemed an uncontroversial field of study is being subjected to critical scrutiny. Given the close relationship between child development knowledge and early years practice, such examinations of long taken-for-granted theories and commonly accepted notions can be unsettling. All the same, these important debates can be invigorating and indeed are necessary given the recognition of the transient nature of knowledge itself.

Characterising child development

Actually defining 'child development' is not entirely straightforward. Different terms and subdivisions are used. The UN Convention on the Rights of the Child (adopted in 1989) recognises the categories 'physical, mental, spiritual, moral and social' in relation to children's development (Article 27). These universally accepted categories are very broad and child development textbooks (e.g. Berk, 1998; Cole & Cole, 1993) typically subdivide them more narrowly. *Physical* development will include not only general bodily growth, but also large 'motor' skills, such as walking, running, climbing, and small 'sensori-motor' skills involving hand and eye co-ordination. *Mental* development (which is often labelled *cognitive* or *intellectual* development, or even 'thinking skills') incorporates many elements such as reasoning, learning, remembering, understanding, judging, and using concepts (Meadows, 1993). Language may be included within mental development or counted as a separate category, perhaps called 'communication' in order to incorporate forms other than speech. *Social* development has traditionally focused on the process of becoming a socially acceptable member of society, but clearly, learning how to get on with other people incorporates cognitive and emotional elements too. *Emotional* development is sometimes, but not always, treated as a separate category, but there is a growing body of literature emphasising the role of the emotions in cognitive and social development as well, and indeed in everyday living (Harris, 1989; Goleman, 1996; Olson & Bruner, 1996). Emotions may either assist or hinder learning (Oatley & Nundy, 1996), while social relationships lie at the heart of almost all development (Chapter 5). *Spiritual* and *moral* development tends to be much less emphasised in current texts, perhaps because until recently the culturally embedded nature of child development had not been recognised.

All this goes to show that the developmental categories are not separate water-tight compartments, since each interacts with the rest. The holistic concept of the 'whole child', i.e. the complete person with all these 'domains' or aspects to their person, gives recognition to the breadth of human development and the interconnections between the domains. Figure 4.1 demonstrates the concept, yet such a view of the developing child remains inadequate on its own. As argued in the Introduction to this book, an ecological perspective of development is essential – one which situates all development within a social-cultural context in both historical time and geographical space (Bronfenbrenner, 1979).

Looking critically at child development

The next part of this chapter attempts to bring together and synthesise various perspectives in the debate about the concept of child development.

One significant issue is the degree to which the early years are formative. The usual view is that they are vitally important, but the issue is

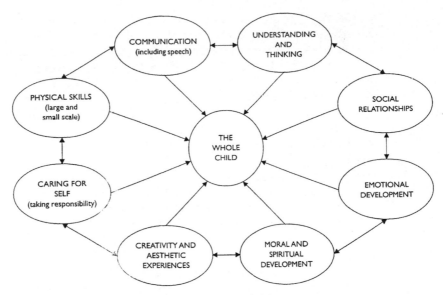

Fig. 4.1 A holistic view of the developing child.

complicated. There do seem to be certain critical periods for development: for example, the making of neural connections in the brain during the early months (see Chapter 3) and the acquisition of language in the first six years. Human beings, however, are generally resilient and can often 'catch up' on lost time. Moreover, development does not stop with the early years, and there is a growing body of literature taking a lifespan approach (see for example, Berk, 1998). Nevertheless, most psychologists would agree that the period before eight is foundational and that events can have cumulative, even multiplying, effects (Rutter, 1989; Rutter & Rutter, 1993). However, each individual is unique, and interactions between the child's genetic characteristics and diverse environmental elements (social, physical, cognitive and affective) ensure a complex and continuing process of maturation (Plomin, 1994).

Another question concerns the source of our personal knowledge of children's development. Much will come from our own up-bringing, in other words our own cultural experiences – sometimes called 'folk psychology'. People pick up information from the media and from books about childcare which is likely to be a filtered version of research studies and theoretical accounts. The consequences of the formal and informal assumptions we hold can be significant, profoundly influencing how we interpret research and how we act professionally. It is important therefore to set the original developmental theories and research into context and then to study how these relate to children and communities at the present time.

For more than 150 years the patterns and processes of human development have been the focus of investigation by academics and a source of fascination for the general public. In particular the search for a fundamental pattern of development, applicable to all people across the globe, has driven study and research. Charles Darwin and Sigmund Freud, and then later thinkers such as Erik Erikson and Jean Piaget, have contributed to a vast body of developmental literature, including theoretical frameworks, which has become the basis of most textbooks on the topic worldwide. But knowledge is not static and however influential these perspectives may have been, many of them are now under scrutiny.

Insights into child development have traditionally emerged from psychology and medical science. More recently anthropology, sociology and history have all added to the body of knowledge – even though these disciplines are still guilty of 'adultism' or at least condescension toward child-centred studies (Alanen in Qvortrup *et al.*, 1994).

According to Qvortrup *et al.*, there was no place for childhood in sociology until the 1980s, but since then various research studies have added to the body of thinking – the Vienna-based project Childhood as a Social Phenomenon: Implications for Future Social Policies (Qvortrup *et al.*, 1994), certain American work (Corsaro, 1997) and several British sociological investigations (Mayall, 1994a and b; Prout & James, 1997). We are now at the interesting stage of trying to bring together these different perspectives. It is an ideal time for reflection and debate and we hope that the following discussion may help students in evaluating research and practice texts as well as making their own observations.

The social construction of development

We have already seen how childhood is socially constructed (Chapter 1); so too is child development. One of the earlier standard bearers of the new critiques was Kessen who, in his seminal article 'The American Child and other Cultural Inventions' (1979, p815), asks the reader 'to give up debates about the fundamental [universal] nature of the child' and recognise that '... *child psychology* is itself a peculiar cultural invention that moves with the tidal sweeps of the larger culture in ways that we understand at best dimly and often ignore'.

Recent writers (Dahlberg *et al.*, 1999) believe that it is useful to 'problematise' developmental psychology in order to put it into perspective – 'recognising its specificity and limitations, making visible its particular assumptions and understandings...' (p15). Thus it is argued that all knowledge is socially constructed, developmental psychology not excepted. Besides, it is a personal process in that each of us constructs a private mental framework, an individual understanding of the world – social, physical, mental and spiritual.

The original intentions, as we have seen, were to find a universal, objective, scientific, and true-for-all-times account of human development. In forming a theory – a testable, systemised description – scientists and thinkers draw on the information of their own time, and their own cultural and educational background (see Appendix). All the major psychological theorists were men, whereas many educational thinkers in the early childhood field (such as Margaret McMillan, Susan Isaacs and Maria Montessori) were women.

By far the majority of published texts on child development are American (conceivably 95% of the world market) and consequently based on studies of children and adults of mainly white American cultural groups. Criticising this state of affairs Burman (1994) writes: 'The developmental psychology we know is tied to the culture which produced it ... In purveying what is advertised as a general, universalist model of development, developmental psychology is a vital ingredient in the "globalisation of childhood".' A growing number of anthropological studies and cross-cultural investigations, such as the Six Cultures Project (Whiting & Whiting, 1975), are revising the way development is considered. Gradually the sheer complexity of human development and the diversity of its contexts have impinged on the consciousness of psychologists, social workers and educationalists.

As we review the way in which our ideas about children are formed, the concept of 'children's needs' must be considered. This ubiquitous phrase in psychology, education and welfare seems harmless and obvious, but on analysis it turns out to be problematic. In particular it is almost always a cultural interpretation in a particular context. Woodhead's important chapter on this subject is recommended (1997).

Stage theories

In western countries the various stage theories (such as those of Erikson and Piaget), which chart a child's apparently systematic progression on his or her way to becoming a mature, rational and competent adult, have been a strong, often unquestioned, force. The example of Piaget's 'egocentric' infant is a telling one. Egocentricity in young children has become 'common knowledge' and implicitly accepted. The concept is, nevertheless, frequently used in an over-simplified and inaccurate manner, not actually reflecting Piaget's intention. Thus a restrictive (and mistakenly applied) concept has been used by adults to justify the denigrating view of small children as self-centred and unsocial. Yet over the last 20 years observational studies by Dunn (1988) and others (e.g. Trevarthen's video explorations, 1979) have proved that babies as young as eighteen months can in fact empathise with others.

> '...children from 18 months on[wards] understand how to hurt, comfort, or exacerbate another's pain, they understand the consequences of their hurtful actions for others and something of what is allowed or disapproved behaviour in their family world; they anticipate the responses of adults to their own and others' misdeeds; they differentiate between transgressions of various kinds.'
> (Dunn, 1988, p169)

The counter-assumption that adults are not egocentric is also patently untrue, and psychologists have shown the great similarities between the thinking of adults and children (Gardner *et al.*, 1996). Piaget's theory of progress towards mature abstract thinking and away from unscientific childhood notions of 'animism' (belief that objects have feelings) is certainly undermined by the fact that adults often retain simple nonscientific explanations for natural phenomena. New research is also demonstrating the remarkable competencies of babies – some of which they lose as they grow older (Barrett, 1999).

Criticism of stage theories does not mean that the principle has to be jettisoned. Human growth is obvious and physical changes in the first few years are dramatic. Emotional and cognitive growth is occurring too. A near universal example of growing maturity is evident around the age of six, when most children develop a clearer understanding of planning and forward-thinking and move beyond 'naive realism' (Olson & Bruner, 1996). Thus the choice by most countries of this age for starting formal school is no accident.

With greater understanding of the interplay between individual development and the environment it is evident that the ecology of development is more important and that the emphasis should be on 'ecological transitions' rather than stages (Barrett, 1998).

Norms of development

The history of the use of scales and charts of development helps to put these tools into perspective. Their purpose was to identify the chronological steps a child would follow in the sequence of 'normal development'. Though these studies were based on large samples it is worth noting that much of the (largely American) research on 'normal' development came from observations of children brought into special child-study centres set up in universities for just this purpose. Bradley evocatively referred to these studies as taking place *'in vitro* – on the social equivalent of a desert island' (1989, p155). He noted that the well-fed middle-class children under observation hardly represented the estimated 40% of the world's population of children living in poverty, on the streets, or in war-torn environments, nor the many other children trying to survive in struggling, violent, unhappy families – who may belong to any social class. The application of white western norms to children from other cultures, and the consequent disregard of variations in childrearing patterns, have been damaging and distorting (see Chapter 6). As we show in many chapters in this book, there is often a gap between rhetoric and reality.

The vogue for using developmental scales was probably at its height just after World War II. Figure 4.2 depicts the 'milestones' in a chart from one of several 'mothercraft manuals' based on simplified information from the Gesell Institute in the USA. Among middle-class British families especially, a culture of dependence on manuals, scales and normative progress was fostered by professionals trying to raise the quality of the nation's health (Hardyment, 1995, Chapter 4) and their own professional credibility (Cunningham, 1995). Some parents felt bound by the charted steps, to the extent that competitive pressures and anxiety about results blinded them to the strengths and capacities of the actual individual child.

One reason for the creation of scales of development was to identify children who were failing to reach 'normal' developmental milestones. In the first half of the twentieth century the emphasis was on segregating

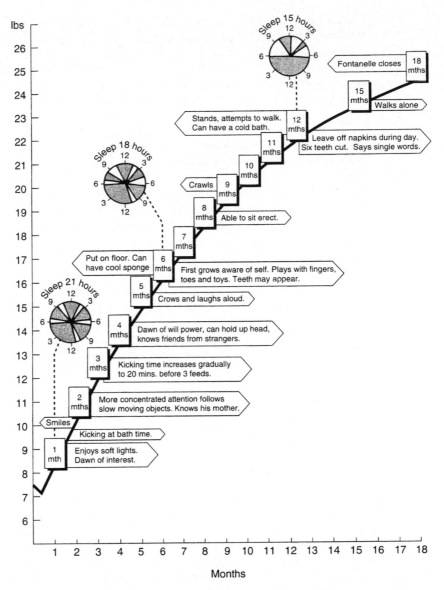

Fig. 4.2 Mabel Liddiard's 'milestones' of development, 1924.

and training (rather than educating) those perceived as problems for society. The language used at the time reflected the prevailing attitudes towards children whom we might currently describe as having learning difficulties. 'It now seems inconceivable that less than fifty years ago, the terms feeble-minded, imbecile and idiot were the accepted terminology of the day' (Fawcus, 1997). Such children were separated off into special institutions and some were deemed ineducable. Expectations then were low and even now the abilities of children with impairments may be seriously underestimated.

Different professions have tended to specialise in different aspects of children's development – medical science in physical development, teachers in cognitive and academic progress, social workers in social adjustment. Evidence of this kind of compartmentalisation (see Appendix) is seen in the importance Bowlby's theories have had for social workers and the stress on Piaget's theories in teacher training up to the 1980s. Jackson (1987) demonstrated how deficits in social work training led to insufficient recognition of children's cognitive and educational needs – an issue that remains relevant today especially for children looked after by the state. A new text for social workers (Daniel *et al.*, 1999) addresses this problem and takes a broad view of development.

The extent to which some scales (and theories) have evolved from the discipline of biology needs to be recognised. One practical text (Sheridan, 1973) uses four categories as a framework – Posture and Large Movements, Vision and Fine Movements, Hearing and Speech, Social Behaviour and Play – and labels them explicitly 'the four outstanding biological achievements'. Readers will note the absence of categories called 'cognitive' and 'emotional' development. Until very recently Sheridan's Stycar scales continued to be the recommended guide for social workers even though the focus was narrow and the source data from which they were designed came from the 1950s.

In discussing the use of norms and screening instruments, the critical elements to keep in mind are: first, which elements are claimed to be measured and which are missing (it is unlikely that one instrument can cover everything); second, what sources were originally used and whether these are culturally appropriate for the children being surveyed; and third, whether they are reliable and valid for the task.

Gender development

This short section is included to alert students to an area which is still under-researched and about which much remains uncertain. Our most familiar developmental theories are entirely the constructions of men, and were devised at a time when women had a very different profile in society. (Chapter 1, looking at historical perspectives, gives an indication of the oppressed position of females, young and old, in Britain's past patriarchal society.) This led to an over-emphasis on the mother–child dyad, and contributed to the tendency of society to vilify mothers for their children's inadequacies.

Over the last few decades much more information about various biological processes has become available through technical advances, for example, knowledge about brain development and the impact of hormones in the womb. Clearly such knowledge contributes to the big debate about the relative importance of biology and social patterns in gender behaviour. Many studies have found that girls mature more quickly, for example in the use of language. But the evidence is not conclusive. The social environment also has a part to play, and in Greece for instance, mothers value and interact with their sons more than their daughters, leading to more language use (Bjorklund & Bjork-lund, 1992, p424).

The culture in which children grow up obviously conditions their ideas of self, the gender-related activities they are allowed to take part in, and what they eventually achieve in education and careers. A large-scale research study of seven-year-olds in inner London schools demonstrated surprising differences in academic achievements. Most successful were black girls of predominantly African-Caribbean background. Next came white girls, then white boys, and, lowest of all, black boys from African-Caribbean families (Tizard *et al.*, 1988). This result shows the importance of looking in detail at both gender and specific cultures. It may also point to underlying tensions (e.g. racism) that affect groups differentially. We know that boys are more vulnerable to stresses of many kinds, including physical and psychological ones (Rutter & Rutter, 1993), and their responses are more overt and extreme. However, it may be that girls' response to psychological stress is different – being expressed through depression and self-harm.

Topics in early development

Work and play

The image of childhood as an innocent, carefree, separate period of life is typically held by affluent western societies. It is an image linked to 'romantic' views of early childhood and is based on play, not work. Woodhead (1999) in his recent project on child labour surveyed eight well-known child development textbooks and found one sole reference to 'work' (actually an account of the effect of part-time work on adolescents' school performance in the USA). In contrast there were 126 references to 'play'. When one considers that UNICEF (1997) estimates that at least 190 million children (aged 10–14) are obliged to earn a living and that many younger children contribute to family businesses and household work, the role of work in children's lives and its effect on their development can hardly be ignored. Supported by research and anecdotal illustration, Woodhead writes that 'Wanting to contribute is as much a feature of early childhood as wanting to learn or wanting to play' (1999). Cross-cultural research into participation and 'apprenticeship' in early upbringing that uses a Vygotskian framework is particularly helpful (Rogoff, 1990).

Play

Play is not easily defined. It is a cultural concept and means different things to different people. Phrases such as the suspicious 'What are you playing at?' or the stressed 'Oh go away and play!' or the western value judgement – 'Play is a child's work' – illustrate some of the perspectives. The value of play in childhood is recognised (though to varying degrees) in most western societies, but its relevance to poor, working children is more ambiguous, as Woodhead (1999) shows in his studies of children in Kenya and Bangladesh. Play may be thought of as a way of learning, or something that all small children do and will grow out of sooner or later. The example of Maria Montessori is pertinent: she based her method on the child's sensory exploratory drive but saw *imaginative* play as a childish weakness not to be encouraged.

Piaget and Lev Vygotsky were both fascinated by the powerful drive to play in young children and its possible purposes. Their theories view play as a means both of learning and of practising different competencies. Piagetian theory conceives play as active, hands-on, engagement and a way of experiencing symbolic representation. The striking ability of human beings to represent thought and action in varied modes – from spoken and written language to drawing, painting or modelling – appears very early. Play may be a vital practice arena.

Vygotsky identifies play as the means by which children gain mastery of their behaviour as a learning mechanism. It is not simply about affective (i.e. emotional) adjustment. For Vygotsky play offers a method of practising skills (both interpersonal and physical) and of co-ordinating various aspects of experience. His view of the unique quality of play in relation to the 'zone of proximal development' is interesting. The zone of proximal development (ZPD) indicates the developmental stage which the child is about ready to enter and is relevant because a sensitive adult may be able to give just the right amount of help – scaffolding – to enable the child to move forward. Vygotsky describes play as being a mental support system that enables children to use objects symbolically, so that an object signifies something other than what it is: hence a brick can be a sandwich. Play creates a zone of proximal development, therefore, which allows a child to operate at a higher level: 'In play it is as though he were a head taller than himself' (Vygotsky quoted in Miller, 1993, p102).

From these two perspectives one might view play as a form of preparation for life – almost a kind of work in itself – which is available to most children in affluent societies. On the other hand, children in agrarian or other working societies have to spend much more of their time preparing for life through actual labour.

The benefits of play, for children and adults alike, go beyond skill development. Garvey's (1977) definition of its characteristics is still valid. It is freely chosen and self-motivated, has shifting goals and is of a pleasureable, active, often non-literal (imaginative) nature. It is frequently social in character, involving other people; and the participative, cohesive, and sometimes creative ethos it engenders may be very beneficial to all involved. The rewards of play are strong, not only for humans but recognisably for other creatures too. Relaxation of tension and active engagement of the deeper parts of the brain are also evident. For Pellegrini, years of observational research led him to conclude that children's play times (breaks from classroom tasks) are highly beneficial and any reduction, on the grounds that time in school might be used more efficiently, would be counterproductive. This is especially true for younger children (under six), for whom sedentary, directed school work could be regarded as particularly 'unnatural'. All children gain social and demo-cratic experience from the relaxed interaction which play affords. The benefits of variety of movement and change of location, too, are much more significant than the discharge of energy – 'letting off steam' (Pel-legrini & Bjorklund, 1996).

Play is a form of behaviour adopted by all mammals, but it is especially characteristic of human beings and manifested throughout their lives. The Dutch cultural historian Huizinga described our species as '*homo ludens*', the playing animal. Play, however, is probably at its most significant and valuable during the early years. The period from birth to six is sometimes called the 'play years'.

Play may be used by adults for diagnostic or therapeutic purposes. But the role of adults in children's play, beyond making it possible by pro-viding the time, space and perhaps resources, is a challenging one because of the very nature of play. It is essentially a self-chosen, self-motivated activity which adults should join in on these terms. Since it is open-ended and free-flowing, and because children often change direc-tions as they play, adults must be alert, open and responsive in order to take part (Bruce, 1991). Thus arises the issue of power and control over the play activity, for it is all too easy for adults to dominate.

Understanding and supporting early development – some key areas

Human beings have adapted for survival through an evolutionary pro-cess. Three of the topics discussed next – attachment, mindreading, and language – are all examples of human characteristics which seem likely to help ensure survival and psychological wellbeing (Baron-Cohen, 1995).

(i) Attachment

Although this vital concept is considered in detail in Chapter 6, it is mentioned here in order to comment on some associated problems. There is no question that all humans have need of a 'secure base', that is, close, reliable relationships, especially in the earliest months and years. This attachment relationship is a biological basis of development. It is of course associated with social adjustment, growth of self-esteem and confidence, the ability to deal with stress and anxiety, and the development of later relationships. Furthermore it is a potential catalyst for cognitive development.

Attachment theory, as it is called, should none the less not be employed uncritically. Difficulties stem in part from misconceptions of Bowlby's actual theory, but in addition many child development texts over-emphasised the role of the mother as the primary attachment figure. Rutter's (1981) critique highlights the importance of the quality of relationships and the fact that a person of either gender can take on the role of 'mothering'. From the work of Bowlby another assumption has caused problems, '...that the "traditional" nuclear family provides a superior child-rearing environment' (Daniel *et al.*, 1999). A particular danger of this assumption is the devaluing of other cultural family structures; forms of group childcare are common internationally and indeed are much more supportive for an individual parent. The narrow focus on the nuclear family also risks denying the importance and potential of the local networks surrounding the child and family (Boushel, 1994). Both within the family and in wider group networks, attachment relationships are fundamental. It follows that professionals should consider how they can be compensated for when children are separated from key people in their lives.

(ii) Mindreading

Some refer to this phenomenon as 'theory of mind' but Rutter & Rutter (1993) more helpfully call it 'everyday mindreading'. The topic is currently the focus of much psychological investigation (Astington, 1994) and is now coming to the attention of the general public. It could be defined as the ability to make sense of how other people think, what their motives are, and what they really mean (the subtext may be different from what they say). At the same time it is to do with awareness of one's own thinking processes (metacognition).

The earliest indication of this remarkable human attribute appears around six months when babies reveal that they know other people can also focus on the object that personally interests them – thus the baby will point to a toy, look at an adult, and then back at the toy. This early intersubjectivity, or sharing of thoughts, is of major importance. Later, the ability can be observed in imaginative play and in the imitation of roles.

Three-year-old children demonstrate some notions about feelings, but have yet to understand about secrets, tricks and lies. For example, Emily, aged three, opened the door to greet her grandfather with the words, 'We're having a surprise party for your birthday! And it's a secret!' (Astington, 1994, p98). It is only around four that clearer understanding of the difference between appearance and reality becomes established. Children can then understand that it is possible to trick someone into believing something which is false.

The child's capacity for mindreading, another 'prewired' competence, develops universally at similar ages (Astington, 1994, p123). But certain experiences can enhance or hinder the ability. Dunn (1996) has identified several ways in which this may come about through relationships with adults and with children; for example, mindreading skills may be related to the quality of early attachments. Adults inevitably contribute in many ways, both consciously and unconsciously, positively and negatively, because children 'tune in' to the relationships and interactions between the adults in their lives. There is growing evidence, for instance, that marital discord and conflict can impact seriously on children's development (Hester & Radford, 1996).

Most studies of theory of mind have been based on samples from middle-class, well-educated families, but Cutting & Dunn (1999) have begun to explore the relationship of family background – education, occupation, family structure, number of languages spoken – to children's development of this ability. They found compelling evidence that family context was significant and suggest several reasons why this may be so; for example, the family's interactions and discourse about feelings.

However, not everyone gains the ability to read other people's minds. 'Mindblindness' is the key problem for people with autism or its milder form known as Asperger syndrome (Baron-Cohen, 1995). Without the capacity to mindread a person is unable to comprehend the reasons for other people's actions; events may be taken at face value and mistaken reasons ascribed to the behaviour of others. This is not a lack of empathy, since feelings are recognised, but rather an inability to 'read minds'. We need to know more about the development of mindreading and to examine the consequences for professional practice. Those with autistic tendencies, who therefore fail to read people's minds accurately, are especially vulnerable. This puts extra responsibility on those who work with them such as parents, social workers and teachers. Expectations, assessments and communication should take into account the particular levels of mindreading of these individuals, because what seems quite obvious may actually need to be spelled out.

(iii) Language

Everyone recognises that language is crucial for all kinds of life experiences – achieving goals in everyday circumstances (such as asking for food), expressing pain or pleasure, making friends, learning in school (language and literacy are inextricably entwined) and in human contacts of every form. It is a further essential adaptation for survival and positive wellbeing which has evolved over time. No society in the world exists without this form of symbolic expression – language (Pinker, 1994). Language in its many forms, including sign language, is of course only one facet of communication. *Non-verbal* communication may actually carry more information than the words we use. In adopting the phrase 'shared total communication framework', which includes words, tones of voice, actions, postures, gestures, and facial expressions, Gonzalez Mena (1993) notes that this is an essential element of cultural heritage.

The acquisition of language starts even before birth as the fetus hears and absorbs sounds in the womb (Chapter 2). In the first few months after birth all humans can both hear, and have the potential to reproduce, the sounds of any language in the world, no matter how subtle and complex. By nine months, though, this competence is lost for good (Barrett, 1999). We do not know precisely how the remarkable facility of using human speech, which virtually everyone has mastered by the age of five, is acquired. Yet there is no doubt that humans are, as it were, programmed for language. Chomsky's 1950s theory of the innate Language Acquisition Device (LAD) was developed in response to behaviourist theories. More recently Pinker (1994) has extended Chomsky's insights, using the phrase 'language instinct'. Bruner has contributed the notion of a Language Acquisition Support System (LASS), which strengthens the idea that we can only achieve language in a social setting (Bruner & Haste, 1987). The role of adults and older children in providing the 'scaffolding' support is most effective when it starts from the child's own interests, and through careful listening enables children to solve the problems they have set for themselves. Children who have benefited from attentive, supportive experiences and also shared story books with adults, before attending school, were found to have a marked academic advantage at the age of seven (Wells, 1985).

Language fulfils many roles for humans, and it may be central in cognitive development, as Vygotsky claimed. He considered that by talking to themselves, perhaps narrating what they are doing, children were helped to solve problems. For Piaget this was another aspect of egocentricity, with self-commenting speech indicating that a child was unable to take another person's perspective. He thought that egocentric speech would just fade away as the child grew older. Vygotsky, on the other hand, suggested it becomes internalised and that we continue to monitor ourselves silently. Berk's studies support this view (1998).

Scales and models of development have until now overlooked multi-lingualism, and even bilingualism, yet a majority of children across the world use more than one language as part of everyday life. In Britain, bilingualism has for too long been regarded as some kind of problem rather than an asset. The potential benefits of bilingualism include a greater awareness of the symbolic nature of language (e.g. that names of objects are in fact arbitrary), greater sensitivity to non-verbal expression, and increased creativity and divergent thinking (Hazareesingh *et al.*, 1989). Besides being a vital part of our individuality and self-concept, language may also be an indicator of progress and even of future development. Language delay at around the age of three has been found to be an indicator of future behavioural difficulties (Richman & Stevenson, 1982).

(iv) Cognitive development

This topic will be considered here very briefly. As readers will have recognised, it is an essential element in all the areas discussed above. Meadows' (1993) text on children's thinking covers the role of cognitive development in many aspects of their lives, and also discusses three theoretical models – Piaget's, 'information-processing models' using computer analogies, and Vygotsky's explanation.

'Piagetian theory,' she writes, 'was a tremendous intellectual achieve-ment … [and] has shaped the field in quite remarkable ways' (p198). Despite this, it has been much misunderstood, has its own inadequacies, and has created problems which have already been mentioned (for an extended critical account see Donaldson, 1978). 'Information-processing models' offer another perspective on children's development, but they tend to concentrate on how the child's mind works and ignore the eco-logical setting. The third model, Vygotsky's, differs from the other two in being founded on the social, cultural and historical elements in the child's development (Meadows, 1993, pp235–51).

To Vygotsky the child is not like the 'lonely scientist' of Piagetian theory trying to make sense of the world alone, but is seen instead as an integral member of a cultural group from birth onwards. His concept envisages sensitive adults, aware of the child's progess and readiness for the next stage (i.e. the zone of proximal development), engaging constructively with the child. Vygotsky claimed that cognitive development involved the internalisation of ideas and skills which are learned through social interaction.

This last theoretical view – of the scaffolding role of adults – currently seems the most positive and useful approach. Rogoff has developed Vygotsky's rather abstract ideas and has provided more detail, describing cogntive development as an 'apprenticeship in thinking' (1990).

(v) Emotional wellbeing and competence

This section might equally have been titled 'mental health', an issue which has not been given proper weight, even though it affects many children. *The Big Picture*, a report from the Mental Health Foundation, has calculated that at any one time 20% of children and adolescents are suffering from a range of psychological problems (Kay, 1999). Many of them will experience depression, a problem not much associated with young children in the past, but increasingly recognised as an important matter (Kovacs, 1997). Two particular factors have hindered understanding of the problem of depression. One is the failure to see the child's perspective, together with an unwillingness to accept that young children might ever be depressed, in spite of concerns about withdrawn, anxious or disruptive behaviours. A second factor is that worrying behaviour patterns have very often been attributed to the kind of parenting (usually mothering) the child has received. It is more helpful, however, to look widely at possible causes of childhood depression. The cause may be internal to the child (e.g. learning impairment), within the family (neglectful or abusive behaviour), or external (homelessness, discrimination) or indeed it may be all three interacting together (the mesosystem). It may be a persistent or transient depression; it may affect the child's whole life or only limited areas (Daniel *et al.*, 1999, p106). Children at risk of developing mental health problems must clearly be identified as soon as possible, and action taken at an early stage.

Smiley & Dweck (1994) in the USA have examined the possible processes by which children develop self-esteem and confidence in the classroom context. They suggest that it used to be commonly thought that children as young as four and five were unlikely to be affected by failure. Their research found the opposite: that even by this age children's self-perceptions and self-confidence were already becoming fixed and highly susceptible to negative as well as positive experiences. At this age, children's response to successful achievement of prescribed tasks, or failure to achieve them, goes beyond simple satisfaction or disappointment; it is internalised and starts to shape a wider self view. Children who have grown confident and see themselves as generally competent are self-motivated, able to concentrate longer, and will persist when the going gets hard. On the other hand children with low confidence and limited goals were observed to be easily discouraged, and anxious in the face of challenge. Once children had characterised themselves as poor performers, they tended to adopt a helpless style of behaviour, disliked attempting novel tasks, expected failure and defined themselves as 'not nice or good'. These potentially negative consequences of curricula too much dominated by performance targets ought to be taken seriously by practitioners, local authorities and government alike in planning programmes for young children.

Conclusion

This chapter has been grappling with current issues about child development, where the ideas have come from, their strengths and limitations. The important concept of the social construction of knowledge about child development has been discussed, as well as the overdependence on American sources. We now recognise the limitations of earlier beliefs that every child develops according to similar norms and could be studied in isolation. Children do not develop in a vacuum – each person is born into an ecological context, familial, cultural, geographical and historical. The final part of this chapter has tried to highlight some important insights about developmental processes which may help professionals understand their practice better.

Chapter 5
Childrearing across Cultures

Margaret Boushel

The Efe in northeast Zaïre are a tribe of semi-nomadic, forest-living hunters and gatherers, small in stature. In the early 1980s, when Tronick and his colleagues studied their way of life, the Efe moved camp every four to six weeks, in flexible groups of from six to fifty people. Most of the work of cooking, cleaning etc. was undertaken as a group. Efe mothers did not hold their infants after birth because of the belief that some harm would come to them if they did so. Instead, the newborn was passed amongst women and suckled by them before being held by the mother several hours later. Women other than their mothers nursed most infants and crying was responded to quickly – within ten seconds in 85% of situations. Each infant was carried by between five and twenty-four different people – contact time with individuals other than mothers ranged from 39% at three weeks to 60% at eighteen weeks; with three-week old infants transferred between members of the tribe about 3.5 times per hour, and eighteen week-olds 8.3 times (Tronick *et al.*, 1987).

How very different this seems to childrearing practices in Britain and the Western world! In this chapter we will consider some cross-cultural variations in childrearing – how they can be understood, their causes and their impact. This is not just an exercise for the inquisitive or the anthropologist. Work with or on behalf of young children constantly involves reflection about the influences of childrearing patterns and often involves assessments about what is 'good enough' parenting. Therefore we need to understand what underpins the childrearing approaches of our own and other cultures, their limitations, advantages and capacities for change. If we learn from parents and share our understandings with them, then parents and professionals can be better placed to identify the cultural practices they wish to foster or to change.

Childrearing has been described as 'an investment of material and psychological resources in infants aimed at accomplishing three universal goals: child survival and eventual reproduction, economic self-sufficiency, and enculturation' (LeVine, 1980 in Tronick *et al.*, 1987, p97). Of course the quality of childrearing will vary within groups and cultures as well as between them, and, for the individual child, within-group variation will often be the more important issue. Its main determinants are the childrearer's own personality and psychological wellbeing, the adequacy of the supports available and the child's characteristics (Belsky, 1984; see also Chapters 7 and 11). In this chapter we will concentrate on the broader picture, the context created by the childrearing 'culture'. 'Culture' is a difficult term to define. It covers the range of beliefs, customs and way of life of a particular group, from religion to dress codes, musical traditions to behaviour in personal relationships (Boushel, 1994).

There is immense cultural variation in the way the universal child-rearing goals are approached. Well-designed cross-cultural studies do more than describe this variation. They encourage us to re-examine cultural assumptions, to distinguish between biological and environmental influences, and they illustrate how processes of adaptation take place. Very importantly, they help distinguish the impact of socio-economic development from that of culture (Kağitçibaşi, 1996).

To understand how culture shapes the everyday activities of child-rearing we must explore the child's world and consider the impact of the wider ecological influences on it. Super & Harkness (1986) suggest that the child's micro-environment, which they refer to as her 'developmental niche', is best understood by considering three interconnected components – the physical and social context in which childrearing takes place; culturally determined childrearing customs; and the psychological characteristics of the childrearers. It is these three components, they argue, that mediate the child's developmental experience, and 'from which the child abstracts the social, affective, and cognitive rules of the culture' (Super & Harkness, 1986, p552). This model of the 'developmental niche', with the child as an active participant, is used to guide the discussion below.

The interconnectedness of the three elements can be seen by considering the 'developmental niche' of the Efe child. The childrearing behaviours are adapted to the physical and social setting – the Efe babies are genetically small and the early suckling by non-mothers helps keep up their fluid levels; the tribe needs to be mobile to ensure its survival – carrying the infants and transferring them from one adult to another facilitates this whilst keeping the infants active and warm in low forest temperatures. Shared approaches to tasks like childrearing are imperative for survival and reflected in cultural customs that emphasise co-operation and strong group attachment. The researchers found that the infants were not overly stressed by their pattern of care and that the attention given to the child's acquisition of co-operative social skills led to precocious social development and helped the children avoid conflict.

However, childrearing contexts change over time, sometimes very rapidly, and what is suitable in one context may not be so in another. For example, think of the impact that war, environmental disasters or planned deforestation would have on the Efe community. Other social changes such as the introduction of compulsory education, changes in technology or religious beliefs may also affect childrearing patterns. On a global scale, one of the most profound and rapid changes has been widespread migration from rural to urban areas (and sometimes across continents) in search of employment (Kağitçibaşi, 1996). These changes, especially if enforced, can give rise to tensions between childrearing aims and the way in which they are or can be pursued. Sometimes, the aims themselves change.

What happens when childrearing practices are transferred from one culture to another? Does cultural variation matter? Is there such a thing as 'good enough' childrearing, and if so, how is it best evaluated at a cultural level? These are important questions for all who work with young children and their families, especially in a multi-cultural society such as Britain. Some of the 'needs' we identify for young children are similar no matter what the child's culture, whereas others are culturally specific. Western child development theorists have been accused of sometimes confusing the two (Woodhead in James & Prout, 1997; Woodhead *et al.*, 1998). For example, to survive, all children need food, shelter and protection from physical dangers, and most have the ability to alert those around them to these basic needs. All young children are predisposed to pay attention to the human face, to seek 'proximity, comfort and nutrition' from caregivers (Woodhead *et al.*, 1998, p69). From about seven months most protest if separated from an attachment figure and these behaviours are evident across all cultures (Kagan *et al.*, 1978).

However, sometimes childhood experiences considered essential in one cultural context are ignored or actively discouraged in another. This does not mean that 'anything goes' – that all childrearing practices are equally helpful to children. As we shall see below, differing practices are likely to have different outcomes. Some effects depend on their social meaning – the effects of multiple mothering, for example, seem to be closely related to the context in which it takes place and on the overall stability and quality of the caregiving environment (Rutter, 1981; Berk, 1998). It's a question of cultural 'fit'. Schaffer (1977) makes an analogy with two species of monkeys to explain this idea of 'fit' – the bonnets are gregarious and share infant care, the pigtails live in close family groups:

'A bonnet-reared child is unlikely to become an effective pigtail parent; any particular cultural tradition rests on continuity between child-rearing, personality development, and social setting. Yet that is very different from equating any one such tradition with mental health and all other traditions with ill-health.'
(Schaffer, 1977, pp109–110 in Woodhead, 1997, p73)

Other effects may be the same across cultures, e.g. opportunities for verbal interaction seem to be related to increased cognitive abilities wherever they occur. Compensatory behaviours may minimise detrimental outcomes, e.g. in some cultures babies are strapped to cradle boards to keep them out of danger or to keep them still. Despite the physical restrictions it imposes the practice appears to have no ill effects when high levels of physical activity are encouraged when the infant is off the board. In cross-cultural analysis questions about the rationale for and the outcomes and transferability of practices need to be constantly considered.

For the cross-cultural comparison of 'developmental niches' sufficient information needs to be available to allow specific practices to be understood within their wider context. This is difficult to achieve, as there is as yet limited inter-disciplinary research on which to draw. The main examples in the following sections have been chosen from two countries, Britain and Turkey. This, it is hoped, will provide a useful contrast between an urban, westernised, multi-cultural state, familiar to many readers, and Turkey, the country of origin of one of Britain's largest minority ethnic communities and which provides an example of a semi-rural, traditional culture experiencing rapid industrialisation. Turkey was a participant in an extensive cross-cultural survey of parenting attitudes (Value of Children Study (VOC), see Kağitçibaşi, 1996) which included Indonesia, the Philippines, Singapore, Taiwan, Thailand and the USA, and some comparisons may be made with those countries also. Kağitçibaşi, a developmental psychologist, has built on this and other cross-cultural work to analyse, intervene in and evaluate Turkish child-rearing practices. The approaches selected for discussion here include some that challenge accepted UK practices, but there are many more, explored in depth in Kağitçibaşi's book *Family and Human Development Across Cultures: A View from the Other Side* (1996). For an analysis of a wider range of cultures readers are referred to the work of Whiting & Whiting (1975) and Whiting & Edwards (1988) and the *Handbook of Cross-cultural Psychology* (Berry *et al.*, 1997).

Physical and social setting

A child's survival and growth is in many ways determined by the time, place and class into which she is born. These physical and social settings also determine the wider social and developmental opportunities available to her. Three aspects of the childrearing setting – the number of people it contains, its gender dynamics and the social responsibilities of young children – are explored here to illustrate some cultural variations and their consequences. We will consider first the physical and social settings common to many British children.

Whatever her ethnic background, the young British child is most likely to be raised in a two-generational household living in a self-contained home in an urban environment. Seventy-five per cent live with both parents but a growing proportion, about one in five, lives with a single parent, usually their mother (Clarke, 1996, p75–9). A much smaller number live in stepfamilies (p78). The statistics mask class and ethnic variation. For example, in 1993, 15% of white, 27% of African, 44% of African-Caribbean but only 10% of Asian families lived in lone parent households (Graham, 1993, p49) and these families were more likely to be on low incomes. Pakistani and Bangladeshi children were more likely to live in large families (Office for National Statistics (ONS), 1998) and they and other young south Asian children were more likely than other groups to live with their extended family (Owen, 1993). Nevertheless, family size is decreasing for all groups. The immediate physical and social setting for most young British children is, therefore, a relatively isolated one.

The family's wider networks will temper isolation. Working-class children in particular are more likely to live near their grandparents and relatives. However, smaller family size means that cousins, aunts and uncles will also decrease in number. Compensatory experiences help reduce the impact of isolation. Television brings access to the outside world and plays a major part in the life of most British children. Other opportunities, such as those presented by toys, books and social activities, are often circumscribed by financial circumstances. Poverty increases isolation. Many poor mothers and their children are 'communication and transport-deprived' (Pearson *et al.*, 1992 in Graham, 1993, p97) and disabled children can be particularly isolated. Middle-class families tend to be more mobile and have less contact with relatives, but they are better able to afford outings, preschool activities, etc. and thus to provide compensatory experiences for their children.

Childrearing in British society remains a highly gendered occupation across all classes and ethnic groups. Most mothers feel they should have the primary responsibility for looking after their children and 'anticipate(d) that having children would be the most fulfilling aspect of their lives'(Graham, 1993, p73). The gendered division of labour around childrearing is sharpest in households with younger children. A survey of 900 British mothers with six-month-old babies found that '96% were with their baby most of the day', spending three-quarters of the day in the house (Graham, 1993, p97). British mothers (or substitute carers) spend a much higher proportion of their time alone providing continuous care and contact for their infants than do most mothers in the non-Western world. Three-generational British Moslem households, with the grandmother undertaking 'both the doting and the disciplining' whilst mothers do 'the domestic work', are an increasingly rare exception (Afshar, 1989 in Graham, 1993, p75).

Although there are indications of change, cultural expectations of fathers in Britain remain linked primarily to the role of breadwinner and of social support for the mother, with limited expectations of their direct participation in childrearing. So when working-class mothers of dependent children take on part-time jobs they chose them to fit in with childcare responsibilities and with their partner's working hours, very often working evening, week-end or early morning 'shifts' (ONS, 1998, pp52-3). Middle-class dual-earner families are most likely to employ a nanny (40%) or arrange out-of-home paid care (Gregson & Lowe, 1994). The employment patterns of British full-time workers, who work the longest hours in Europe, are not fashioned to take account of childrearing responsibilities and arrangements.

In Britain, protective legislation forbids the paid employment of children until they are 13 years old. Where family size is small the care of younger siblings is also unlikely to be a major responsibility for young children. The children of disabled parents are exceptional in that many shoulder major caring responsibilities from an early age (Aldridge & Becker, 1995). Studies suggest that Western children have far more 'free' time than children in many other cultures do. In 1975, Whiting & Whiting reported that 41% of Nyansango (Kenya) children's time was devoted to work, compared with only 2% of US children in Orchard Town, New England. As part of recent attempts to re-evaluate childhood, however, Qvortrup challenges current notions of what constitutes children's 'work' and suggests that time spent in school and studying is included, as its function is to prepare children to contribute to society and the economy (see James *et al.*, 1998). From this perspective, British children are expected to take on academic 'work' responsibilities at an increasingly early age.

Turkey

Turkey has experienced enormous economic and social change over the past few decades, as it moves from a rural subsistence to an urban-based economy. Infant mortality at 49 per 1000 live births remains very high and life expectancy is low (INFOPEDIA World Almanac Map, Futura Vision, 1995). Mass migration from rural to urban areas in Turkey and northern Europe has lead to a rapid increase in the number of women, including mothers of young children, employed in non-agricultural jobs outside the home (Kağitçibaşi, 1996; Tekeli in Ozbay, 1990).

Turkey's population is mainly Moslem, with a social structure that has much in common with its non-Moslem Mediterranean neighbours. The traditional family is extended and patriarchal, but changing economic conditions have meant that by 1990, 72% of households were nuclear and only 21% extended (Women's Indicators and Statistics (WIS), 1999). The average size family household is larger than in the UK, with 4.8 members, whilst the average for extended households is 6.9 (WIS, 1999). Turkish marriage rates are high and divorce rates the lowest in Mediterranean Moslem countries (Tekeli in Ozbay, 1990, p148). However, because many Turkish men migrate to find work, a large number of women are effectively parenting alone.

Childrearing is seen as a mother's responsibility, but with closely linked networks of female relatives expected to provide help and social support. The traditional role of fathers in urban as well as rural settings is to be the family breadwinner, to shop and to undertake the 'outside' work needed to maintain the household. These strongly sex-segregated socialisation patterns have implications for the ways in which children's social settings have adapted to economic change. Where fathers migrated, mothers' 'activities in the ordinary course of the day are not very different from what they would be if their husbands were present' (Kiray in Ozbay, 1990, p80). When mothers in urban areas are employed in factory work Bolak (1997) found that the presence of older girl children or female relatives made it less likely that either parent expected fathers' traditional household work pattern to change. Since the 1980s the childcare responsibilities of mothers have, if anything, increased to include children's education and discipline, traditionally male roles. Despite their equality under the law since the 1920s, a study of eight countries in 1982 found the degree of role-sharing and the influence of women in family decision-making was lower in Turkey than in any of the other countries. It is only when education is combined with employment that women approach equal status (Kağitçibaşi in Ozbay, 1990).

Especially amongst the less well educated, boy children are favoured and expectations of boys and girls differ markedly. In rural areas, Kiray noted 'women's extraordinary spoiling of male children compared to their treatment of girls', so that 'the status of a boy of 10 or 11 years of age was higher than that of his mother and he could impose his wishes upon her' (in Ozbay, 1990, p81). This, she and others (Tekeli, 1995) associate with an economic structure and patriarchal culture which provides few opportunities for women to live independent of their families. However, these attitudes change as migration and a dwindling rural economy undermine traditional patriarchy.

In low-income urban and rural areas children are likely to have very few toys or books (Kağitçibaşi, 1989). Only 7% attend formal preschool – most of which is privately owned and fee-paying. Compulsory education lasts for six years and attendance is high, at 95%. Female literacy used to be seen as 'functionless', but for the past three decades has been seen as increasingly important as women become more economically independent (Kiray, 1990, p79).

In low income areas children take on responsibilities from a very early age, with girls in particular helping with childcare and domestic chores. Kağitçibaşi points out that 'in socio-economic contexts where children's material contribution to the family is substantial, a utilitarian value is attributed to children and their work is seen as important', but as lifestyles change 'especially with urbanization and increased parental education, child work loses importance' (Kağitçibaşi, 1996, p27). In Turkey she found that children's 'material help' lost its importance with parent's education (with 56% of parents with no education considering it important compared to only 20% of university-educated parents (p27)).

What do we know of the implications for young children of these different physical and social settings? Much remains to be understood, but some interesting cross-cultural findings are beginning to emerge. It seems, for example, that children who between the ages of about three and ten have the opportunity to look after infants and toddlers gain a great deal from this experience. Little children tend to invite and respond positively to nurturing behaviours from those around them, giving satisfaction to the older child and encouraging them to develop competencies and nurturing qualities that transfer to other situations (Whiting & Edwards, 1988). Once puberty begins, children's interests and energies are taken up elsewhere, whilst peer relationships tend to encourage competition and domination rather than nurturing behaviours. In Britain, such opportunities are available to an increasingly small number of young children within their families and the organisation of preschool care and education further limits the numbers of mixed-age group settings available.

Many cultures demand more work and responsibility of young girls than they do of boys of a similar age. In four communities in a major six-country comparison boys were 'found farther from home than girls' the same age and also spent 'more time than girls do in undirected activity (that is free play and idle time)'(Whiting & Edwards, 1988, p57). One of the consequences, according to Whiting & Edwards, is that boys then have greater opportunities to learn about the environment, whilst '(T)here is no doubt that, across cultures, girls get more practice in nurturance and pro-social dominance, boys in egoistic dominance and challenge' (p278). It is not known whether this is because of active choices by children or 'their assignments to settings by adults' (p278). Whichever, there are other consequences. Kağitçibaşi comments that in patriarchal cultures where there is little adult role-sharing between men and women, not only is the transition from boyhood to manhood likely to be abrupt (and often accompanied by painful rituals), but men tend to be more aggressive and women to have lower status and be subjected to more violence. Whilst gendered expectations are less extreme in Britain than in Turkey, it would seem that attempts to facilitate the increased participation of men and boys in childrearing would benefit both countries.

Customs of childcare

The second component outlined by Super & Harkness is the customs of childrearing – those taken-for-granted behaviours, routines and rituals, 'community-wide solutions to recurrent issues in childrearing', 'so thoroughly integrated into the larger culture' that they seem the 'reasonable' or 'natural' response (Super & Harkness, 1986, p555).

As we saw from the Efe example, these customs are in evidence from the earliest moments of a child's life. To consider their influence we will examine practices that encourage or discourage physical proximity and those that relate to skill learning.

Custom exerts a considerable influence on patterns of behaviour related to the physical proximity of young children. Solitary sleeping is common amongst white, majority ethnic children in Europe and North America but uncommon in Turkey and elsewhere. In Britain, a study comparing 'white British' and Gujerati families found that white British babies usually slept in a cot from birth and moved out of their parents' room at eight months, whilst their Gujerati counterparts occupied their parents' bed until they were over three years old (Hackett & Hackett, 1994). The toddler of Gujerati origin, like his Turkish peer, was less likely to have a fixed bedtime and more than twice as likely to share a bedroom or bed. Perhaps as a result, he showed much less interest than the white British child did in bedtime rituals and comfort objects. Two generations of Punjabis in Britain had similar attitudes to the Gujeratis in relation to sleeping patterns (Dosanjh & Ghuman, 1997; 1998). Western childrearers are more likely to use a pushchair or car seat than to carry young children, further limiting opportunities for physical proximity. Carrying young children also encourages their limbs to move to the rhythm of the care-taker and is thought to account for their superior reflexive and gross motor development (Super & Harkness, 1986). In the cultures in which it is common, it is a task which often passes to a slightly older sibling once a new baby is born, providing the older child with opportunities for social skill development.

In impoverished agrarian cultures high infant mortality and hazardous environments mean that the survival of individual children is by no means guaranteed. To maximise survival rates, such cultures are usually associated with 'conformity-oriented child socialization' along with high fertility rates (Kağitçibaşi, 1996, pp29–30). In 1966 in a Turkish village Helling noted the prevalence of a parental teaching style based on demonstration, imitation, and motor learning rather than verbal explanation and reasoning. He found no appreciable change on his return twenty years later (Kağitçibaşi, 1996, p36). Kağitçibaşi noticed that many 'less-educated, traditional Turkish mothers, talk about the child growing-up (buyur), rather than being brought up (yetistirilir)' (p37).

These patterns of learning by demonstration and imitation are effective but have limitations. Bandura (1989, 1997) has shown that young children actively develop their own behavioural standards and sense of competence by trying to understand and model what they see around them. However, the more interactive and consciously stimulating style of childrearing found amongst British and middle-class Turkish mothers is more conducive to cognitive development. 'It appears that learning specific procedural skills (*how* to do something) does not easily transfer to new tasks, but when conceptualization is involved, transfer is seen' (Hatano, 1982 in Kağitçibaşi, 1996, p40). Even when the skills acquired are quite complex, such as the arithmetical skills required by young street-traders, a Nigerian study found that non-working students taught to use more abstract principles outperformed their trader peers (p40).

The psychology of caretakers

Childrearing customs are not all carried out unthinkingly. On the contrary, all cultures have an idea of what a well-adjusted child or adult in their society is like, and these parental belief systems shape parents' behaviour, influence the developmental outcomes for their children, and are remarkably diverse (Super & Harkness, 1986).

Once again, a very important dimension of variation is 'along rural-urban and socio-economic status (SES) differences' (Kağitçibaşi, 1996, p27). In rural (and some urban working class) societies where survival demands a high level of physical labour by all, children are more likely to be valued for their material contribution, whilst in more affluent and technologically rich societies children are more likely to be valued for their psychological contribution (p27). Thus, in Western societies childrearing objectives might include, in addition to healthy physical development, a happy, confident assertive child, polite to adults, doing well at school, not getting into trouble, independent as an adult, but supportive of parents, etc. In Turkey, on the other hand 'uslu' – defined as being 'good mannered, obedient, quiet, not naughty, not boisterous – is a highly valued characteristic, especially of girls' (p41). The VOC study found that when asked about the most desired characteristics of children, 60% of Turkish respondents identified 'obeying parents', and only 18% 'independent and self-reliant'. Thai respondents had similar priorities, and those in Indonesia and the Philippines placed even more stress on obedience. In Korea and Singapore, on the other hand, countries that were industrialising at a very fast rate at the time of the study, qualities of independence and self-reliance were rated even more highly than by US parents.

Childrearing approaches to control and discipline are closely related to the values and goals of socialisation. 'In general, higher levels of control are common wherever childrearing does not stress the development of individualistic independence in the child' (Kağitçibaşi, 1996, p21). Thus, in traditional working-class and rural Turkish families, it is assumed that adult conversations take precedence over children's demands. In a study of 6000 Turkish mothers, Kağitçibaşi found that 73% 'would not tolerate' a child interrupting adult conversation and in the low income areas of Istanbul, 40% seldom or never gave a child full attention outside mealtime (1996, p45). She also observed the prevalence of physical punishment and the limited use of verbal reasoning (Kağitçibaşi, 1989). This limits opportunities for children to develop an internalised sense of control (1989, p141) and helps account for the large differences in vocabulary size between middle-class and working-class Turkish fifth grade children. But, as we have seen, these outcomes would not necessarily be viewed in a negative light by those involved.

These higher levels of control do not reflect a lack of affection for the child. Rather, Kağitçibaşi found that 'dependency and conformity expectations from children in more traditional societies with extended or joint families (are) characterized by closely knit bonds' (1996, p60), but the emphasis is on social interdependence, and social as opposed to cognitive intelligence. This difference in emphasis is noticeable also in south Asian cultures. For example, British Gujeratis were less tolerant of peer aggression than their white counterparts (Hackett & Hackett, 1994). Kağitçibaşi criticises Western psychology and psychiatry for its 'promotion of individualism' and agrees with Campbell's statement that it 'not only describe(s) man as selfishly motivated, but implicitly or explicitly teach(es) that he ought to be so' (Campbell, 1975 in Kağitçibaşi, 1996, p57).

In dominant cultural settings in Britain and the USA, where physical survival is less of a challenge and the macro-environment is individualistic, competitive and achievement-oriented, parental attention, especially in middle-class families, tends to focus on children's cognitive and socio-emotional needs. Mothers behave competitively with 'good' mothers ensuring that their children are ready to take on the social and academic norms of school – to manage dressing, know colours and numbers, act sociably, etc. The style of discipline and interaction is more likely to be authoritative and inductive, i.e. child-centred and reasoning-oriented, rather than punishment-centred. This reasoning-oriented approach not only helps develop internalised controls but because it relies greatly on verbal interaction, it lays the ground for further cognitive development (Baumrind, 1967; Bradley & Caldwell, 1982).

Immigrants, especially those moving from rural to urban areas, and poorer families may experience problems if cognitive rather than social competence is valued in the new setting. Nunes (1993) notes how Mexican parents believe that if children are quiet and obedient they will succeed well in US schools. Okagaki & Sternberg (1993) found the same beliefs amongst US immigrant parents from Cambodia, Mexico, the Philippines and Vietnam, who believed that these qualities were more important than cognitive characteristics such as problem-solving skills, verbal ability and creative ability. In fact, however, 'parents' beliefs about the importance of conformity correlated negatively with children's school performance' (Kağitçibaşi, 1996, p44).

Issues in multi-cultural contexts

For many cultural groups, childrearing takes place in settings where a more dominant group has some different traditions and goals. This may occur where members of a group migrate, where there has been colonisation of indigenous peoples or where groups have maintained distinctive cultures over a long period. Here, we will consider some issues arising for groups that have migrated to Britain, in search of work or as refugees. Cross-cultural research suggests that the mental health outcomes for immigrants are most positive where 'some degree of cultural integrity is maintained, while at the same time the individual seeks to participate as an integral part of the larger social network of a multicultural society' (Berry & Sam, 1997, p297), and that this tends also to be the preferred position of most immigrants. Thus, in Britain, many minority ethnic parents see the development of a strong sense of personal and cultural 'identity' as an important developmental goal and task, often accompanied by a wish for their children to learn their language of origin (Graham, 1993; Dosanjh & Ghuman, 1997; 1998).

However, successful integration depends on several factors. Welcoming policies and practices within the dominant group, as well as the presence of supportive networks within the minority group, make integration easier to achieve. Pre-immigration experiences may have a major impact. For example, adults who migrated from the Caribbean between 1955 and 1960 in response to job recruitment campaigns brought with them 6500 children, but a further 90 000 had to be left behind, to be cared for by the extended family. For some of these children, the separations and later reunifications caused severe adjustment problems (Arnold, 1997). On the other hand, although the dominant culture in Britain makes integration for south Asian families difficult, a different immigration pattern has allowed them to maintain strong extended family and social support networks which have had a positive buffering effect in helping psychological adjustment (Berry & Sam, 1997).

Most minority ethnic children are members of families who migrated here within the past two or three generations, often from rural areas in their countries of origin. As a result, many have experienced both socio-economic and cultural changes. Much remains to be known about their experiences and attitudes, but a number of small-scale studies illustrate some themes. Like the Turkish migrants described earlier, minority ethnic groups within Britain have generally adapted their cultures whilst seeking to retain valued traditional practices. Second generation south Asian Punjabi families, for example, have retained familial interdependence and a dislike of physical punishment as important childrearing values, but tend to give their children more freedom and stimulation. There has also been a significant increase in men's involvement in childrearing (Dosanjh & Ghuman, 1997). African-Caribbean families have retained a more matrifocal family structure. A traditional openness to intergroup relationships also continues, so that nearly a third of young African-Caribbean men and a quarter of women have white partners (Owen, 1993).

Is there a universal standard of 'good enough' childrearing?

This brief exploration of childrearing across cultures indicates how much practices differ – in the contexts in which they take place, in the behaviours they take for granted, and in their developmental goals. It has been seen also that this variation makes a difference – to children's experiences, to their opportunities and to their development. Perhaps most importantly, the evidence suggests that childrearing practices are inextricably connected to the wider socio-economic context, in what they seek to and can achieve, and in their need to adapt to changing circumstances. 'Best fit' is a moving, changing criterion.

An inter-disciplinary group of experts from 20 countries has begun to meet to identify indicators of the wellbeing of children on a global scale, seeking indicators that go beyond mere survival. A consensus is emerging from their work that indicators of a 'good enough' context for rearing children need to include measures of adequate opportunities for social connectedness, for the development of 'civil' life skills (co-operation, respect for others), 'personal' life skills (self-esteem and the capacity to learn and work), safety and physical development, and respect for children's own subculture (Andrews & Ben-Arieh, 1999).

Cross-cultural analysis demonstrates that not all contexts and cultures provide optimum opportunities for development in each of these areas. The way young children learn in rural and working-class urban Turkey, for example, may not provide them with the personal life skills necessary to survive and thrive when faced with an advanced industrial and technological environment. Indeed, it is because she believes that these children are disadvantaged compared to their wealthier peers that Kağitçibaşi (1996) undertook a long-term project with the aim of improving their cognitive development. She then compared the longer term outcomes of a range of professional interventions designed to improve young children's cognitive development. She found that working with mothers was most effective because it encouraged a long-term family readjustment of cultural norms. The example illustrates two important issues that are pertinent to an understanding of the child-rearing practices of both dominant and minority cultures – value judgements cannot be avoided and professionals play a significant cultural role in constructing the idea of what childrearing should be.

British and Western majority group childrearing practices, if carried out well, provide a good 'fit' for this society, but are achievement-oriented, individualistic and provide relatively few opportunities for the development of nurturant behaviour. It can be argued that this reduces young children's opportunities for social connectedness and for the development of civil life skills. Is this what we want to encourage? What might young children want for themselves? Cultural childrearing practices and the assumptions on which they are based are a matter 'for personal choice and political discussion' as Woodhead suggests (1997, p68). A commitment to the rights and interests of young children demands that these debates are regularly undertaken and informed by up-to-date knowledge, by children's views and by a commitment both to value and critically evaluate the cultural practices we and others may take for granted.

Chapter 6
Relationships

John H.W. Barrett

People are social animals. More than half a century of research has now confirmed that effective relationships are central to the development of ability, communication, emotion, personality, identity and self, culture and even the quality of consciousness itself. However, it is a two-way process, and all these characteristics in their turn influence relationships, and of course each other. So earlier relationships influence later relationships in continuing spiralling transactions. In this brief summary of recent research findings only a few aspects can be touched on, focusing on those with the most immediate implications for caregiving, intervention and prevention. In particular, most of the hugely important contributions of cognitive, communicational and emotional processes will have to be left for another discussion.

When do relationships start?

Before birth! Mothers who visualise and think about their unborn child long before the birth, and regard him or her as already a responsive individual human being to be treated with consideration tend to develop stronger relationships with their infant. Likewise, fathers who share the pregnancy by listening to the fetal heartbeat, feeling the body movements, and discussing and planning how to live with the child to be are more likely to become more involved with the infant both practically and emotionally. But processes which influence relationships go back before pregnancy. Couples who before conception, perhaps long before, prepare and plan their caregiving environment and style have been shown to be more likely to adapt more effectively to the lifestyle changes which go with childrearing, and to become part of a healthier family relationship network.

However, influences on parent–child relationships go back even further. The relationship experiences parents have enjoyed or suffered throughout their lives, and particularly during their own childhoods, can also make powerful contributions. Childhood is the first phase of a life-long apprenticeship in life skills, which include childrearing, relationship and emotion management skills. Other processes being equal, parents who themselves have been ineffectively or inconsistently reared, or who have been neglected or abused as children, are more likely to develop problematic relationships with their children.

The processes underlying these 'granny' or transgenerational influences have attracted much research. Many of the most powerful processes are cognitive. People's own experiences of being parented contribute to their construction of the 'internal working models', or scripts, with which they guide their behaviour towards their children. However, it is important not to conclude that people with unhappy or deprived childhoods will necessarily become poor parents. What matters is not what actually happened to them, but how they *perceive* it, how they come to understand or forgive it, and how they modify it in the light of later experiences and ideas. Where later circumstances are favourable, the effects of severe maltreatment during their own upbringing can 'wash out'. Unfortunately, where families are trapped in cycles of poverty, disadvantage and poor educational opportunities, a family tradition of unhealthy relationships can be passed on over many generations, and in these circumstances 'washout' is rare. The likelihood of 'washout' is highly experience-contingent, and depends among other things on the particular life pathways followed by individual children.

Enculturation

Another very powerful influence on the development of our 'internal working models' is the culture which we belong to and identify with. Because we often have little opportunity for comparing *our* childcare habits with those of others, or do make comparisons but decide our approach is better or more normal, we are often largely unaware of many of the implications of the highly varied family traditions we hand on. We tend to be even less aware of the implications of wider cultural traditions and values. For example, while Anglo-American children are allowed and often encouraged to become self-centred, individualistic and competitive, Thai children learn from their culture to develop smooth and harmonious relationships by putting others first, and being cooperative, patient, generous and gentle.

Absorbing skills, attitudes, emotions and behaviour from our culture, often without realising that it is happening, is the most powerful of the educational processes, and developmental and cognitive researchers have dubbed it 'enculturation'. The importance of enculturation in general is discussed in Chapter 5. Here we focus on just one aspect of it, the way skills and the internal cognitive processes which contribute to intelligence, for example, are acquired, often without realising it's happening, from the culture. The development of language, music and occupational skills have been shown to be highly influenced by enculturation processes, especially the efficiency of the thinking and practical tools available. A particularly well researched example is the way the characteristics of the language, number system, counting aids and attitudes to learning we inherit from our culture affect the ease and effectiveness with which we learn maths (it is more difficult in English-speaking cultures than in many Pacific rim languages and cultures). But the importance of enculturation is also well supported in many other areas of development, including learning, thinking, feelings and relationships. Increasing differences in relationship styles have been found from Britain through Northern Europe through the Mediterranean countries and through the Pacific rim. For example, although many Europeans would regard shy or withdrawn children as socially immature, most Chinese would see them as socially mature and advanced in understanding.

Enculturation processes are part of what Bronfenbrenner has called the 'macrosystem'(see the Introduction). Many researchers have been surprised to find that macrosystem or exosystem influences can often have more powerful effects on what happens in the microsystem of the family than behaviours and attitudes initiated within the family. Many parents, despite striving to provide what they consider to be an 'ideal' upbringing environment, and paying great attention to quality of relationships, have ended up sadly wondering why their children have turned out so differently from their hopes. There are very many reasons for this, as parents are one of many influences on development, but powerful macrosystem and exosystem influences often play a major role (Bronfenbrenner, 1997).

Bullies and charmers

A classic example of exosystem influences is provided by a multivariate study of relationships in a French nursery school, which longitudinally followed young infants from before their second birthday for several years. They were systematically observed, and on the basis of their relationship behaviours, mostly non-verbal, they were classified into a number of categories, including 'withdrawers', 'isolates', 'bullies' and 'charmers'. Both the 'bullies' and the 'charmers' had a strong though very different influence on the other children. The 'bullies' hardly need describing: they were takers, for example snatching toys other children were playing with, and they were domineering and aggressive. The 'charmers' were givers: they gave objects (including objects which did not 'belong' to them!) and more importantly they gave time, attention, services, smiles and affection. Most of the 'bullies' came from families where the parents were stressed and pre-occupied, particularly with their jobs, gave their children relatively little time and tended to manage them in an 'authoritarian' style through quick instructions. On the other hand, most of the 'charmers' came from families which gave significantly more time, attention and warmth, were responsive to their children's individuality (thus providing 'goodness of fit', which will be discussed later), and influenced them in a more 'democratic' style through rather more lengthy two-way discussion.

Longitudinal biochemical measurements indicated the 'bullies' were under stress, and as both stress and the lack of close warm relationships impair the immune systems, it is no surprise that the 'bullies' suffered far more colds and other infections than the 'charmers'. During the course of the study a few parents of 'bullies' moved into less stressful jobs, and were able to spend more time in a more relaxed and 'democratic' way with their children. These 'bullies' tended to become less aggressive, and some developed into 'charmers'. Many researchers have also emphasised that although time often helps, what is more important is the quality of the parent–child interactions. And many studies have pointed to the major influence of 'exosystem' variables such as occupational stress, and especially management style, on many aspects of the development of employees' children, including their developing relationships. Some studies have even found that bully and victim both wanted a positive relationship but had only experienced opportunities to learn strategies for conflict (Boulton & Smith, 1994).

What part do genes play?

So far our discussion of bullying by very young children suggests that bullies are made rather than born. What about older bullies, and are there genetic influences as well? A recent large-scale study of 1500 twins carried out in both Sweden and Britain provides some answers. The findings, which show no difference between boys and girls, suggest that some bullies may have a genetic predisposition towards aggressive behaviour, but as is the case with most genetic predispositions, genes make an indirect contribution and are neither necessary nor sufficient for bullying to develop. The researchers emphasise that they have no evidence for specific genes for bullying, and that the rearing environment can facilitate, inhibit or reverse the predisposition. The practical implication is that rearing influences which discourage the development of bullying will be effective whether it might originate from social learning alone or from interactions between social learning and a genetic predisposition, although in the latter case a little more effort might be required. Further research will be necessary to discover whether these findings apply outside the similar cultures of Sweden and Britain.

Shyness is another of the many aspects of relationships which fit this pattern. Working with Caucasian children in the US, researchers have found physiological differences between some shy infants and some sociable infants. From the early weeks, some of the shy children tend to have higher cortisol levels, higher heart rates, and to show greater increases in heart rate, blood pressure and pupil dilation in response to unfamiliar events. Researchers point out that shyness and sociability usually result from interactions between many influences, and that as genes may sometimes make a modest contribution, rearing practices then become especially important. If parents shield children who withdraw from unfamiliar people or events from minor stresses, it becomes more difficult for the child to develop the effective strategies for coping with stress and the unfamiliar which we all need. Conversely, if parents help their children to develop strategies for coping with new experiences, an initial tendency to withdraw can be reversed. Here again, we see the benefits of 'goodness of fit' or continuously matching parenting to the changing characteristics of the developing child (Kagan, 1998).

Bio-ecology and perceived relationships

Bullying and shyness provide examples of the way the often separate and conflicting nature or nurture approaches to development seen in the past have now converged into a unified biopsychosocial approach. For example, Bronfenbrenner (1994, 1997) has extended his original ecological model into what he now calls a bio-ecological model. This incorporates the most influential current model of behaviour genetics, that arising out of the research of Plomin and his collaborators.

A fundamental feature of Bronfenbrenner's original model is that what matters for behaviour and development is the environment as it is perceived rather than as it may exist in 'objective' physical reality. It is the environment as attended to, perceived, interpreted, assimilated and remembered which influences the development of people's ideas, attitudes, feelings, stress, and behaviour, including relationship behaviours. Plomin incorporates Bronfenbrenner's model explicitly using the term 'experience' rather than 'environment' to convey the way we actively filter and cognitively construct our environments. Both adults and children actively choose what they attend to and which parts of the environment to make use of. Ecologists call this niche-picking. What is more, from infancy onwards people create their own environments, or niche-build. As Plomin (1994) puts it, 'Socially as well as cognitively children select, modify and even create their experiences'. This means that how relationships are perceived is crucial.

Non-shared environmental influences*

In the past it has usually been assumed that living in the same household means children share the same environment, including the same relationship environment. But more precise methods have shown that shared environmental influences are small compared with what have come to be called non-shared environmental influences (Plomin, 1995).

Shared influences include relationship opportunities, disciplinary practices and stressors which could potentially influence all family members in similar ways, though opportunities, even in the relatively rare cases where they are similar across children, are not necessarily used, and different children may respond differently to similar relationship practices. Non-shared influences are of two kinds. First, environments 'objectively' non-shared because children spend time in different parts of the house or garden, or with different friends on different streets in the neighbourhood, or going out to different places with different caregivers, or because of differential parental treatment (Hetherington *et al.*, 1993).

---

* Parts of this section are adapted from Barrett, J.H.W. (1998) New knowledge and research in child development. *Child and Family Social Work*, **3** 267–76.

For example, Dunn (1993; 1996) found preschool children talked with their sibs about topics they had never been observed to talk about in the presence of their parents, and with peers outside the home about topics they never mentioned in the family.

The second kind of non-shared influence is provided by environments which are 'objectively' shared but perceived differently. A variety of research methods have been developed to measure these differences in perceptions. For example, the **Sibling Inventory of Differential Experience** (Plomin, 1994) asks siblings to rate their experiences relative to their siblings rather than in an absolute sense.

Such methods, based on ecological approaches which directly measure children's perceptions, are showing how very differently children in the same family perceive and react to what have previously often been assumed to be aspects of a shared environment. These methods have been corroborated by systematic observation and analysis of videotapes. And they have also been used to explore children's relationships with peers, friends and teachers, while similar methods are employed to explore parents' perceptions of their relationships with their children. As Plomin (1994) writes: 'The evidence from behavioural genetic research seems clear that environmental influences play a major role in the development of individual differences in behavioural dimensions and disorders. However, this environmental influence is largely of the nonshared variety.'

The nature of relationships

The major roles of the non-shared environment, individual perceptions and cultural differences pose serious problems for generalising about relationships. Although we live in a society characterised by an increasing variety of ethnic, cultural and value backgrounds, most of the research has been carried out with only a few cultural groups, the majority relatively undisadvantaged English-speaking Caucasians.

Dunn (1993) cautions against overgeneralising and oversimplifying. She emphasises that children's relationships are multifaceted, multi-dimensional and change with development; that all partners in relationships contribute to their quality; and that the quality of a mother–child relationship does not predict in any direct way the quality of the child's relationships with others. She points out that many findings may be relevant to children growing up in comfortable, relatively stress-free families, but not to children growing up in more stressful circumstances. And so she pleads for findings to be tested in a much wider variety of situations and family structures.

Sibs, peers and only children

The details of research on children's relationships have been excellently presented and evaluated by Dunn (1993; 1996; Dunn et al., 1998). Now that research in developmental psychology is moving it beyond the stage theories of the past into a lifespan approach, most of the underlying general principles and processes we discuss throughout this chapter of course apply across all ages and all types of relationship. Here there is only space to bring out a few further points.

The differences between children in the behaviours and relationships actually seen on the surface arise from the interactions between the past experiences, present context, and perceptual and cognitive processing of the particular children in the relationship, and so simple generalisations can be highly misleading. The need to avoid oversimplifying is reflected in many of the assessment instruments now in routine use. For example, the **Child Behaviour Check List** involves hundreds of variables as well as 'triangulation', that is, comparing the independent assessments of at least three assessors, including the child herself, and presents the results as profiles over a variety of underlying dimensions.

Relationships with other children can start early. For example, even by three months infants display more vocalising, reaching and squirming in response to another infant than to their own mirror image. By the primary school years, children have opportunities to develop associations, and these often amplify characteristics they have already picked up in the family. For example, although children who have already developed pro-social and considerate behaviour tend to behave in a caring way towards others, they also tend to prefer to associate with other like-minded peers, and this sometimes means that children who have acquired more aggressive strategies are more likely to be left only with other aggressive children as friends. Their relationship then tends to become a context for mutually amplifying antisocial behaviour.

Where initially 'pro-social' children find themselves, either in school or in the street, in the company of more aggressive or 'antisocial' children, they are sometimes vulnerable to acquiring some of the 'antisocial' characteristics. However, where the child hails from a 'pro-social', 'democratic' and 'responsive' household, more often than not these deviations will tend to be superficial, limited to certain contexts and relatively short-term. Caregivers influence the relationship environment experienced by their children not only by how they organise the household, where they take their children and where they allow their children to take themselves, but also by how much they discuss with their children their dealings with contacts outside the home, and through such 'counselling' help them to understand and cope with all sorts and conditions of people. For example, serious stress and lasting problems are often suffered by victims of bullying who do not feel able to discuss their worries with parents or teachers (Boulton & Smith, 1994). And although there is a traditional view that as children develop they turn for intimate support and advice from parents to peers, many studies, including the very large-scale longitudinal cohort studies in Britain (Hill, 1993), find this only applies to a minority. For a majority of children peer relationships do not replace family relationships and support: they extend and enrich them. Lifespan studies find the same applies throughout life.

Because poor peer relationships are frequently symptoms of current psychiatric and psychosocial problems as well as predictive of yet-to-develop future problems (Rutter & Rutter, 1992; Rutter and the ERA team, 1998; McCarthy & Taylor, 1999), much effort has been put into their assessment and classification. One important source of evidence comes from children's self-reports of whom they would choose to play with, work with, invite to their party, be helped by if they felt unwell, and so on. Systematic forms of this are known as 'sociometry' and frequently identify four categories of peer acceptance or 'likability': 'popular', 'rejected', 'controversial' and 'neglected' children, into which half to two-thirds of young children in Britain and the US fit. The rest are average in peer acceptance (Newcomb et al., 1993).

'Controversial' children are those who attract many positive and many negative choices, and 'neglected' children attract few or no choices, either positive or negative. 'Rejected' children, those who are actively disliked, fall into several sub-groups, including the 'rejected-withdrawn', who are often vulnerable to bullying, and the 'rejected-aggressive', who are poor on mindreading and empathy tasks, show cognitive distortions and biases such as perceiving and reacting to hostility where none is intended, and display high levels of aggression and impulsivity.

The recent longitudinal study of 4–10 year olds by Fordham & Stevenson-Hinde (1999) suggests that just one good peer relationship can buffer children who are shy with unfamiliar people against the loneliness, low self-worth and anxiety to which some studies have found shy children to be vulnerable. The degree of reduction in vulnerability such buffering provides remains controversial, and more research is needed. As usual, cultural differences are important, and in many cultures cautious and inhibited children of primary school age are regarded as advanced in social competence and leadership, and reflecting this their peers rate them as above average on popularity and peer acceptance.

Many 'rejected' children, after trying hard to gain acceptance, conclude, together with their parents and teachers, that they will never be liked, and that their social incompetence is a part of their make-up which cannot be changed. However, we have already seen that even where there may be a genetic predisposition, programmes which offer shy children training in social skills have produced large and lasting improvements in social competence, peer acceptance and relationships (Lochman et al., 1993). Such programmes can be particularly helpful to children whose peer acceptance is compromised by problems like obesity or severe learning difficulties.

Are only children vulnerable? In some countries, including Britain and the US, it is commonly believed that only children will be 'spoilt', selfish and deficient in relationship skills. However, they turn out to be at least as well-adjusted as children with sibs, to develop higher self-esteem, and to perform better educationally. This fits in with what we would expect from analyses of family size: there are opportunities for closer parent–child relationships which both the parents and the child often claim to prefer, and these are often accompanied by more pressure for achievement (Falbo, 1992).

Body language and non-verbal communication

Starting a conversation (especially with someone who is unfamiliar), keeping a conversation going, and bringing a conversation to an end are all examples of the many skills which are normally used to foster and maintain relationships. Much research has been devoted to the development of these skills from birth onwards. Indeed, most parents are amazed when they first begin to realise the complexities of the relationships which are constructed in the first week of life. From the start, non-verbal communication (NVC) skills play a very large part, and recent research has shown that they continue to play a very important part after the development of verbal communication skills and throughout life. For example, in acting like traffic lights, and regulating turn-taking in conversation.

Use of new tests of NVC signals, ranging from eye-movements to posture and tone of voice, has shown that people with low skills in receiving or transmitting NVC, or both, tend to be loners, to have difficulty in forming relationships, and to suffer from far more than their share of problems such as anxiety, depression and low confidence and self-esteem. Remedial training during childhood or adulthood in NVC skills can make a large contribution to helping people to get on with others, and to reducing these psychiatric problems (Nowicki & Duke, 1992).

Where do emotions come in?

The important role played by emotions in the making and breaking of relationships has long been recognised. However, recent research has shown that underlying the surface of feelings and emotional behaviours, the processes include many which have traditionally been labelled 'cognitive'. Indeed, Strongman (1996), in his recent survey of over 150 ways of looking at emotion, ranging from the psychoanalytic and the physiological through to the cognitive and the social, concluded that those which currently provided the most comprehensive and useful explanations were those which afforded a central place to cognitive processes. Particularly useful for thinking about relationships is Oatley's (1994) model.

For Oatley, relationships develop from 'mutual plans'. When two people become interested in spending more time with each other, they share thoughts and feelings about what to do when they are together, and generate plans for the future which incorporate a role for both of them. Typical of this process is when two people are contemplating marriage or partnership, when the development of their 'mutual plans' often includes discussion of lifestyle, hobbies, holidays, values, demarcation of responsibilities, and the location and features of the housing they aspire to share. Frequently these shared plans will include plans for children: how many to have, how to bring them up, what sort of education to aim for, what careers and lifestyles they might eventually follow. Whole families, nuclear or extended, and close-knit groups of friends can share 'mutual plans'. (For many years, social psychologists have regarded shared objectives as central to the creation and survival of social groups.)

Once a baby is born, 'mutual plans' start developing between caregiver and baby. Short-term examples are provided by research on the way a baby quickly develops scripts (plans) for cooperating (or otherwise!) with feeding, nappy-changing, bathing and other caring routines. Often a baby learns different scripts or plans for the same routine with different carers. When the infant is still very young, the caregiver usually contributes much of the plan, but as the child develops she contributes more and more, particularly where the caregiver adopts a 'democratic' parenting style. Gradually, too, these child–caregiver 'mutual plans' come to include longer-term and more complex expectations.

When an adult or a child perceives herself to be part of a stable 'mutual plan' she tends to feel secure and happy. When the stability of the 'mutual plan' is threatened, or just perceived to be threatened, worry and anxiety are generated. And when there is threat of loss, or actual loss, of one of the partners in a 'mutual plan', the consequences for the survivor can be severe. The classic example is bereavement. Feelings of uncertainty, sadness, depression, helplessness and emptiness are characteristic. Hormonal and other physiological changes are reflected in sleep, appetite and digestive problems. The immune systems are depressed with consequent vulnerability to infectious and other illnesses. And because the lost partner is part of the current and future daily routines as well as of longer-term plans, and partly because so many of what were once regarded as characteristics within individuals are now regarded by researchers as emergent properties of relationships between individuals, there is often a severe loss of identity and sense of self.

The implications for therapy of 'disrupted mutual plans' are clear and direct: help the child who has suffered the loss of a relationship to develop new 'mutual plans' with one or a few new people. And as research continues, the evidence is building up that the physiological, psychological and social consequences of the disruption of 'mutual plans', or of failure to develop them in the first place, are similar across the lifespan from birth onwards.

Do we need (the concept of) attachment?

So far we have managed to discuss relationships without using the word 'attachment'. Does this mean 'attachments' are unimportant? Far from it. However, the term has many different everyday meanings, and the term as used technically in the research and childcare literature also carries with it some problems. And over the years even the technical concept has provoked much controversy (see Rutter, 1995; Cowan, 1997). 'Attachment' has typically been used to refer to reciprocal close, affectionate relationships which provide security and fear reduction, and which are impaired by insensitive parenting. Earlier in its evolution the term 'attachment' was used to emphasise the child–mother relationship, which was seen as different in kind from all other relationships. It was seen as qualitatively different from children's relationships with fathers, grandparents, sibs, other caregivers and friends, as well as from relationships, including marriage, partnership and friendship relationships which might develop later in life.

So in what ways was the child–mother relationship seen to be different? First, it was a relationship unique to the biological mother. She was the only person who could provide the 'secure base' from which the young child could venture forth with little anxiety and much confidence to explore the environment, and to whom she would regularly return for reassurance and emotional support. Second, it was universal, and applied across all cultures. Third, it would not develop so well if there was early mother–child separation. Fourth, the child would only form a real attachment to one caregiver. The more extreme attachment views, sometimes known technically as 'bonding', held that separating mother and infant during the first day or two, as in 'rooming out' in the maternity hospital, could lead to permanent damage not only to the mother–infant relationship, but also to the infant's ability to relate to others throughout life. There was thought to be a very narrow 'window' or 'critical period' for the development of relationships, and the consequences of missing it or messing it up were both severe and irrevocable. This threatening and pessimistic view was worrying to many mothers and families. What if the infant required early hospitalisation and there was a delay before the mother could start caring at home? What if the mother was ill and substitute caregiving had to be provided? What are the implications for the child, the father and other caring relatives if the mother dies early in the child's life? What about adoption and fostering?

Fortunately, this extreme view has steadily weakened as the evidence has built up. Caregivers other than the mother can provide the 'secure base'. In some contexts relationships with the mother are particularly important, while in other contexts other people can provide relationships which can be just as healthy for development. And in some contexts, relationships with the mother can be very damaging. If it provides consistency, benevolence and security, multiple caregiving often works well.

Earlier, in the section on 'When do relationships start?', we discussed the way relationships are guided by the 'internal working models' or scripts people construct from both direct experience and culture. Bowlby made very influential contributions to theories of attachment and emphasised how from experiences during the first two years or so the child constructs an inner representation or working model of the caregiver–infant relationship which guides later relationships. By the end of Bowlby's career, the initiation and maintenance of attachment, through the continuous lifelong modification of the 'working model' in the light of experience, was regarded as important not just for young children, but for people of all ages (Parkes et al., 1991). Although when Bowlby first discussed it, the 'internal working model' was a hypothesis, it now fits comfortably into the models generated by current research into cognitive psychology in general, where constructed and continuously reconstructed representations of experience underpin our strategies for coping with the present (Collins & Read, 1994).

Collaborating with Bowlby, Ainsworth developed the **Strange Situation test**, which attempts to measure patterns of attachment in 1–2 year olds by observing the child's behaviour towards the parent before and after a couple of brief separations during which the child is left with a stranger. On the basis of these observations, it classifies children as showing 'secure attachment' (actively approaching parent when she returns), 'avoidant attachment' (slow to approach returning parent), 'resistant attachment' (angry and resistive behaviour when parent returns) or 'disorganised/disoriented attachment' (confused and contradictory behaviour towards parent, for example approaching with blank or depressed facial expression).

However, there are problems about drawing conclusions because the standard methodology lacks important controls. For example, it is usual to employ only one stranger in the test. If a series of strangers is employed, even in children classified as 'secure' the earlier, less strange 'strangers' tend to evoke much the same response as the parent. A single measure cannot reflect the complexities of caregiver–child relationships even within one culture. (For older children, up to five years, a newer test, the 'Attachment Q-Sort', has proved a little more efficient. The Q-Sort method involves sorting cards bearing pictures or words into piles representing different responses or categories.) In the context of wider cultural differences the test can lead to misinterpretation of the quality and implications of children's relationships. In some cultures, an absence of closeness, touching and hugging does not indicate an absence of healthy relationships with warm and sensitive responsiveness to children's needs. And, although 'secure attachment' is reported for over half the infants in most cultures, 'avoidant attachment' is reported to be seven times as common in German as in Japanese children, and 'resistant attachment' five times as common in Japanese as in German children.

Given these problems about the validity of the classification, we need to be cautious in interpreting the conclusions of studies which have used them. However, many researchers have found that compared with the other categories of attachment, 'securely attached' children have more friends, have better physical health and develop a clearer and more positive sense of self. And these benefits typically lead them into 'pathways' which not only maintain these qualities through the lifespan, but also transmit them over the generations. In this way attachment styles, both advantageous and disadvantageous, are often passed on by both the culture of the family and the wider cultures in which the family is embedded. As we have already seen, however, given appropriate opportunities, effort and resources, especially educational resources and an understanding of the way relationships develop, a disadvantageous 'pathway' can be broken.

The idea that attachment style, and 'the internal working models' underlying them, become a characteristic of the child is also problematic.

Many infants develop different attachment relationships with each carer with whom they become familiar: as always the nature of the relationship emerges from the interaction with the other person. When the developing person continues to live in a similar social environment, earlier attachment classifications sometimes predict later relationship problems, and this has led to the notion of 'attachment disorders', which to some extent reflect the lack of opportunity for 'washout' or reconstruction. But the 'internal working models' can change when different pathways are followed, particularly under the influence of educational or relationship experiences. The development of warm and secure relationships seems to be more likely when both partners respond sensitively and accurately to each others' shifts in attention and mood, and consider each other's feelings by developing ever more effective strategies for empathy.

So healthy attachment can be flexible and adaptable, multiple rather than to one person, lifelong rather than once for all, context and culture dependent rather than universal, and cannot be validly measured in individuals. The importance of relationships cannot be over-emphasised. But does the concept of 'attachment' now add very much to our understanding of them? It carries with it much unhelpful 'baggage' which predates much of the research on the underlying psychological processes. In keeping with the expectations of the lifespan approach, the processes of what was once thought to be unique to young children have been shown to apply and be important from birth to death: rich relationships can develop with people first encountered late in life and can lead to the development of new relationship styles and 'working models'. So do we still need a special term for children? Or should we become less attached to 'attachment'?

The construction of relationships

How can relationships be fostered if an infant has to spend months in an intensive care baby unit? If the infant goes home after several weeks or months during which care has been provided solely or largely by hospital staff, building relationships with the mother and the rest of the family can be slow and difficult, and the stress involved can sometimes be demotivating, especially if the parents have picked up from the more extreme ideas on attachment the assumption that it is already too late. The result, although by no means irrevocable if time and effort are later put into it, can be a start on a 'pathway' of relatively weak relationship development. However, when the mother is encouraged to visit the unit frequently, to stay overnight, and to take part in as many aspects of the care of the infant as possible, then the relationship can develop before the homecoming, and does not have to be constructed from scratch when the baby arrives home. When other family members are encouraged to visit and share in the caring as well, the results are even better, and the developing relationships, both short- and long-term, do not differ from those seen in children who have not been detained in hospital.

This is an example of the way relationships need to be constructed.

They don't just happen. Parents can and do start constructing relationships even before the conception of the infant, and longer term transgenerational and cultural influences also contribute to the construction.
Later, if parents discuss with their two-year-old firstborn child the feelings and needs of their newborn sib, they are helping the firstborn to
construct an affectionate relationship with him or her. Later still, by the
early primary school years if not before, effective 'democratic' parents are
gradually handing over a greater share of the decisions about everyday
activities and relationships to the child.

Maccoby (1984) dubbed this transfer 'co-regulation', and stressed the
need for parents to monitor and support at a distance, to use the times
when they are together in face-to-face contact effectively, and to continue
to help their children to construct safe and effective strategies.

The construction of these internal cognitive strategies for coping with
the world is vital to development. The bio-ecological model sees individual development as in part actively self-constructed by the individual
through the choice and use made of the genetic and environmental
resources available to him or her (see Bronfenbrenner, 1994; Plomin, 1994;
Barrett, 1998). The cognitive strategies include strategies for attending,
learning, problem solving, communicating, making rational decisions,
and higher level strategies (known as metastrategies or metacognition) for
choosing which lower level strategies to use. Internal strategies of this
kind contribute a major part of what at a surface level has in the past been
observed and measured as 'intelligence'. They are constructed through
experience and opportunities for learning in a particular family or culture.
Also based on such internal strategies are reading and writing skills, the
skills of listening to, performing and composing music, craft and sports
skills.

A very important aspect of skill development is trying out strategies,
and, if they are not effective or simply not available, 'strategy switching',
trying out alternatives, and so gradually constructing a combination
which works. Some trying out will be in the real world, much will be
through 'thought experiments' or mental rehearsal, and much by testing
out against the experience of others through conversation with them.
Learning on the job by doing, watching people already more skilled, and
discussing ways of going about the task with them, is the most efficient
way of developing skills. In one word, apprenticeship.

Relationship skills, too, are constructed through apprenticeship: social
skills of getting on with others; skills of conflict reduction, of using
humour, of cooperating, of making others feel good by boosting their self-
esteem; skills of sussing out what other people are thinking and feeling,
what would help or please them, how we can best serve them and help
them to 'feel good'. These add up to what Rogers called 'unconditional
positive regard' and they are the foundation of constructive relationships,
not only with children but also with others throughout life. It has also
been shown that households and families vary hugely in the opportunities they provide for children to learn NVC and other relationship skills.
Coaching in the construction of relationship skills forms a major part of

the impressively successful **Collaborative Process for Working with Parents who have Children with Conduct Disorders** (Webster-Stratton & Herbert, 1994).

Many relationships founder because people assume that they are incompatible with each other and cannot change. However, compatibility has mutually to be worked for, and people do change. There are, of course, constraints on change, such as fear and insecurity, lack of knowledge or experience or other resources, expectation of failure or learned helplessness, and these can trap us in what we feel is familiar and habitual. As William James perceptively put it, 'Habit is the enormous flywheel of society'. Adaptive habits are highly efficient coping strategies, and we could not survive without them. However, when habits are maladaptive, they threaten survival.

The cultural habit of leaving relationships to fend for themselves does threaten survival. As we have seen, however, an antidote is suggested by much of the research: providing apprenticeship in relationships. How would this operate? By encouraging awareness that relationships are dependent on skills, and that skills have to be constructed through effort, practice and physical and mental rehearsal. By developing mutual plans and mutually trying out ways of collaborating to put the plans into effect. The longer we go on putting thoughtful mutual effort into constructing our relationships, the stronger, the more adaptive and the more satisfying they become.

What are the implications for the development and construction of relationships of the research we have sampled? Some of the many answers are implicit in the discussions throughout this chapter. Let us summarise some of them in the form of questions. Less stress on family life? Less age segregation? More opportunities for young people to develop their relationship skills by working cooperatively together with people of all ages on constructive community and leisure projects, rather than playing competitively or passing time and spending money in passive commercial entertainment centres? More focus on the collective values of Mediterranean and Pacific rim cultures, and less focus on individualism and the relationship neglect and self-centred pursuit of careers and personal leisure it often encourages? But perhaps one of the most profound implications was voiced by Bronfenbrenner (1974) in 'The origins of alienation' where he pleads for more time and no-cost opportunities for people of all ages to walk or sit and talk together. Let's have more gossip!

Chapter 7

Young Children's Rights and Needs

Margaret Boushel

> 'giving children rights has the effect of drawing attention to the fact that children cannot expect to have equal rights to adults...'
>
> (King, 1997, p170)

In this chapter, we focus particularly on young children's rights within child–parent relationships. To help do so, we first explore briefly the concept of children's rights and their interpretation within UK law. This is followed by a more detailed discussion of three areas – physical punishment, child protection and family breakdown – before finishing with a short discussion of the link between rights and responsibilities in the lives of young children. In part, this parent–child focus is an acknowledgement of the central importance of the family microsystem to the wellbeing of young children. A restricted focus also makes it easier to explore how attitudes and responses to the concept of young children's rights are shaped and to guide our own attempts to develop personal and professional views in this complicated area.

Children's rights are a complex and contentious area (see Fortin, 1998b for an excellent discussion of children's rights and the law). Some theorists argue that children, and especially young children, cannot be legal 'rights-holders' at all, since they have not got the capacity to make free informed choices in exercising them. Others suggest that it is more appropriate to view children's rights as the right to have their interests protected (MacCormick in Fortin, p15) – which begs the question of how, and by whom, their interests are identified. In the field of child welfare the traditional emphasis has been on children's 'needs' rather than their rights. Martin Woodhead, a leading theoretician in this area, counsels caution in the use of the term 'needs'. He points out that 'needs', like 'interests', 'are not a quality of the child; they are a matter of cultural interpretation which will certainly be context-specific and may well vary amongst various stakeholders who believe they have the wisdom to shape children's futures. In these circumstances, a "rights" perspective provides a powerful antidote to "needs"' (Woodhead, 1997, p80).

John Eekelaar (1996) deals with this tension by an approach which he calls 'dynamic self-determinism'. He suggests that objective measures are used to help broadly define a 'reasonably secure' environment, but within that the child should have the right to determine choices, through a 'dynamic' process, i.e. one that reviews the situation 'as the child grows up'. He adds that '(t)he very fact that the outcome has been, at least partly, determined by the child is taken to demonstrate that the outcome is in the child's best interests'(p48). This approach seems a particularly helpful one in considering the needs and rights of young children.

When relationships between parents and children are positive and respectful, the law may be of little significance, but it nevertheless provides an essential framework in determining children's rights. It identifies what rights there are, how, and by whom, they are to be implemented and decides what degree of participation will be allowed to young children in these processes. As we shall see throughout this chapter, confusion and contradiction are some of the hallmarks of the law in this area. We begin with a brief outline of the international and national 'rights' framework.

The UN Convention on the Rights of the Child is the most comprehensive and universal attempt to codify children's rights. It has proved a 'startling success' (Fortin, 1998b, p43) and of enormous influence worldwide even though it goes 'far beyond the scope of what is recognizable as law' (King, 1997, p171). Many of the rights identified are 'claims based on ideals regarding how children should be treated' (Fortin, 1998b, p14) rather than legally enforceable rights. It was completed in 1989, after ten years work, and lists 40 rights applicable to 'every human being under the age of eighteen'. All nations of the world, with the exception of the USA and Somalia (which disagree with its curtailment of parental rights), have signed the Convention. The UK ratified it in 1991. Although it is not legally binding, in becoming a signatory governments make a commitment to implement its terms and are obliged to provide regular progress reports to a special Commission.

The Convention is concerned mainly with the basic rights to survival and protection, which are central to the wellbeing of all children. The rights included are more extensive than this, however. They can be grouped into four areas – survival rights, membership rights, protection rights and empowerment rights (Fortin, 1998b, p38). They include pathbreaking rights to autonomy and participation – the right of all children to be consulted on matters that affect them, to give their opinion and to have it taken into account, with due regard to their age and understanding (Articles 12, 13, 14; Franklin, 1995).

The rights identified in the Convention are not unequivocal. They are circumscribed firstly by Article 3(1) which sets out the overriding principle that 'the best interests of the child shall be a primary consideration'. They are also circumscribed by considerations of children's competence and an explicit identification of the special rights of parents and those *in loco parentis*. In introducing these qualifications the Convention is in many ways quite different from a convention on the rights of adults and illustrates the paradox that children need protection as well as rights, as King points out in the quote at the beginning of this chapter.

The European Convention on Human Rights (ECHR) (1950), which the UK recognised in 1996, takes a different approach. It has as its main focus the protection of fundamental human liberties (such as the right to bodily integrity). It enshrines family privacy in Article 8 and includes no specific attempt to protect children's rights or identify appropriate boundaries for child–parent relationships. It has been strongly criticised for its 'adult-oriented nature' and emphasis on parents' rights (Fortin, 1998b, p367). However, unlike the UN Convention, it is legally enforceable through the European courts and it includes an individual right of petition, by which children, as well as adults, can challenge infringements of their basic human rights. Although currently a very lengthy process, it has proved one of the most successful ways for children to challenge British legislation. Once the Human Rights Act 1998 comes into force in 2000 the ECHR will form an integral part of domestic legislation.

In 1995 the Council of Europe adopted the European Convention on the Exercise of Children's Rights (ECECR). Although the UK has neither signed nor ratified it as yet, it will come into force once ratified by one more member state. There are concerns that it offers fewer rights to children than current UK legislation and 'is seriously restrictive of the provisions of the UN Convention' (Sawyer, 1999, p162). In particular, the position of young children and other children 'held not to be of "sufficient understanding" is extremely weak' (p163) and it contains no rights for children to initiate legal proceedings.

At a national level, the allocation of rights and responsibilities in the relationship between parents, children and the state varies greatly between states (Fox Harding, 1991) – and even, as we shall see, between England and Scotland. However, throughout the UK, domestic legislation tends to emphasise parental autonomy in childrearing, despite the fact that children, especially young children, are often most dependent on the very adults who may be breaching their rights.

The law of England and Wales reflects the European Convention, rather than the UN approach to children's rights within the family. It is just ten years since UK legislation made its first explicit reference to an overarching concept of 'parental responsibility' (Children Act (England and Wales) 1989, Sections 2 and 3). However, these responsibilities are not specified and, much influenced by the European Convention, the Act also includes a 'no order' clause, making state intervention a last resort. In practice, once 'significant harm' is avoided, parents are given the authority to raise their children in whatever way they wish and young children have no right to have their views considered and no redress, regardless of the impact these decisions may have on their general well-being. It is only in situations where the state becomes involved in children's upbringing that they have the right to be consulted and a vast range of regulations governing their treatment takes effect.

The more recent Children (Scotland) Act 1995 takes an approach that is closer to the UN Convention. It identifies explicitly the responsibilities and rights of parents – to 'safeguard and promote the child's health, development and welfare'; to provide 'direction' and 'guidance'; and 'to maintain personal relations and direct contact' if not living with the child (Sections 1 and 2) and gives children the right to sue if these responsibilities are not met (Section 1). It also obliges parents to consult children about 'any major decision' related to parental responsibilities, 'taking account of the child's age and maturity' (Section 6 (1)). However, a child has to be 12 years old and over before it 'shall be presumed to be of sufficient maturity to form a view' (Section 6 (1)).

In the first of our examples – physical punishment – these themes and their implications for young children's relationships with their parents will be explored.

Physical punishment

'the hitting of children remains, for the moment, a prime example of the privacy model of family life and family law.'

(Barton, 1999, p63)

The current debate about smacking provides a graphic example of the conflicts in this society between parents' and children's rights and their legal and moral base. Do young children have the same moral rights to bodily integrity as adults, and if so, what measures are most likely to encourage their acknowledgement? By the time this book is published, smacking children may be prohibited in the UK. The criticisms of the European Court of Human Rights and the UN Committee on the Convention on the Rights of the Child may have pressurised the UK government to make illegal 'inhuman and degrading' physical punishment of children in the home and elsewhere. If this happens, it will be in contravention of the wishes and beliefs of the majority of British parents.

A nation-wide survey of 700 parents commissioned by the BBC Radio 4 *Today* programme (August 1999) found that more than 70% supported the physical punishment of children. We know that parents act on these beliefs. In a study of 500 parents undertaken in the early 1990s, Marjorie Smith and her colleagues found that over 90% of the children had been smacked at some time (Smith in Department of Health, 1995b). When Nobes & Smith (1997) interviewed both parents in 99 of these families, a quarter of mothers and fathers reported that they used some form of physical punishment at least weekly.

The younger the child, the easier it seems to legitimate their physical punishment – as many as three-quarters of babies were smacked before their first birthday. Fifty-two per cent of one-year-olds, 48% of four-year-olds and 35% of seven-year-olds were punished at least weekly in this way. Where one parent smacked, the other was likely to also. These punishments were sometimes harsh. The researchers estimated that 57% of seven-year-olds had been subjected to 'severe' punishments 'that were intended to, had the potential to, or actually did cause physical and/or psychological injury or harm to the child' (p275). Nobes & Smith's findings, when compared with earlier research (Newson & Newson, 1989), suggest that there has been only a small reduction in the amount of physical punishment meted out by parents over the past thirty years, although the use of implements has diminished. This is in stark contrast to much of Europe, where the physical punishment of children has been illegal in Sweden for twenty years and is now illegal in at least eight countries.

Parents in the UK are acting within their legal rights in physically punishing their children. In England and Wales their legal authority is outlined in Section 1 of the Children and Young Persons Act 1933. This makes it a criminal offence to cause a child unnecessary suffering or injury but adds in Sec.1 (7) that 'Nothing in this section shall be construed as affecting the right of any parent, ... or other person having the lawful control or charge of a child or young person to administer punishment to him'. This legislation, which harks back to a judgement made 140 years ago (*R v. Hopley* (1Russ.Cr.751) 1860), was not amended by the Children (England and Wales) Act 1989, which says nothing of the expected behaviour of parents in disciplining their children once it does not cause 'significant harm' (Sec. 47). In fact, following the successful appeal of a childminder to the English courts (*Sutton London Borough Council v Davis* (1994) 1 FLR 737), the Children Act's Regulations have been altered to allow young children to be physically punished by childminders where parents give their permission. The Scottish Law Commission considered a ban on harsh physical punishment, but its determination to continue to allow 'an ordinary smack by a loving parent' meant that a suitable form of words could not be found and references to corporal punishment were omitted from the Children (Scotland) Act 1995.

In addition to persistent campaigning by the pressure group EPOCH (End Physical Punishment of Children), pressure for legal change has come from Europe and from the Commission monitoring the progress of the UN Convention. In a recent case, a child who at the age of eight had been severely beaten with a garden cane over a period of a week saw his stepfather acquitted of assault by an English jury. In summing up the case the judge commented 'It is a perfectly good defence that the alleged assault was merely the correcting of a child by its (sic) parent provided that the correction be moderate in the manner, the instrument and the quantity of it ... It is for the prosecution to prove it was not' (Newell, 1989, p130). With the help of his birth father the boy appealed to the European Court and won his appeal (*A v United Kingdom Application no. 25599/94* (Eu Comm Report 18-9-97). The Court unanimously decided that the punishment was 'degrading' under Article 3 of the European Convention and moreover, that the UK government had a responsibility to ensure that its domestic laws protected children from such punishments. It awarded costs and damages of £10 000 against the UK government.

Our reluctance in the UK to give children the same rights to bodily integrity as have been granted to all other citizens (since the 'right' of a man to beat his wife was abolished in 1861) reflects, at least in part, the power of custom and culture to shape attitudes. Hitting children is culturally condoned across all social classes in the UK. The Prime Minister has admitted to it, the Archbishop of Canterbury George Carey has supported it if 'done with love' and in his response to the 'garden cane' case, Paul Boateng, the then Under Secretary of State for Health, 'respected the right' of 'parents who exert discipline by smacking their children when they misbehave' (Leach, 1999, p2). Perhaps the most frequent comment from parents is that 'it never did me any harm'. However, if we are to consider the child's best interests we need to move beyond cultural beliefs and examine the evidence on the impact on children of such treatment.

Only a very small percentage of physical punishments could be viewed as constituting child abuse. However, excessive use of physical punishment is often associated with abusive parenting and the extent of 'severe punishment' identified in the Nobes & Smith study (1997) is worrying. The degree of control parents feel in using physical punishment is relevant in assessing both the risk it presents and its effectiveness as a boundary-setting measure. According to Leach's (1999, p.1) review '(M)ost parents tell researchers that they hit because they are angry and "lose it" or because they need to do something and cannot think what else to do'. This suggests it is unlikely to contribute to effective boundary setting in the longer term. Indeed a US study found that one-year-olds who were frequently smacked 'had a 58% higher rate of non-compliance with mother's requests than did children whose parents rarely or never spanked them' (Power & Chapieski, 1986, reported in Straus et al., 1997, p762).

Several studies have found a relationship between physical punishment and children's aggression. Links have now also been found with low self-esteem, depression and diminished cognitive development. However, it is very difficult to separate the longer-term impact of physical punishment from its broader social context and from other individual factors such as parental warmth. This issue has received little attention as yet in the UK, but recent US studies have tried to explore whether there is a direct causal relationship between physical punishment and a range of psychosocial problems.

One of these studies took a sample of 910 children aged 6–9 years old, measured their scores on an index of Anti-Social Behaviour (ASB) and noted the amount of physical punishment they had received in the previous week. The study also used measures of maternal warmth and cognitive stimulation. Two years later the process was repeated. It was found that the more often a child was smacked in the week prior to the study the greater the increase in the ASB score two years later (Straus et al., 1997). The relationship between smacking and ASB was stronger for boys than for girls and 'somewhat' stronger for 'European American children compared with minority children' (Straus et al., 1997, p765–6). Other studies have also found differences between children depending on gender, ethnicity and household form, with reports of aggressive behavioural outcomes most likely for white boys in single-parent households (Gunnoe & Mariner, 1997). The suggested explanation is that smacking is likely to be less harmful when it is not accompanied by lack of affection and where children accept it as a culturally 'legitimate expression of parental authority' (p768). Another study examined the relationship between harsh discipline, low warmth and cognitive development in a large sample of 1–3 year old low-birthweight babies (Smith & Brooks-

Gunn, 1997). It found that harsh discipline and low warmth made no statistical difference to the boys' IQ scores, but the scores of girls subjected to harsh discipline were eight points lower than their peers and twelve points lower when it was combined with low maternal warmth.

The balance of the evidence so far indicates, therefore, that the impact of physical punishment on children's social and cognitive development is more often negative than positive. Children also have strong views about it. Children aged between five and seven, when asked about smacking, were very clear that it hurt physically and emotionally and often left them feeling angry and resentful towards their parents: 'you feel sort of as though you want to run away because they're sort of like being mean to you and it hurts a lot' (Willow & Hyder, 1999).

The question then is how best to bring about a change in parental views and practices. Is change best sought through legislation? Given the recent decisions of the European Court, this question may be hypothetical, but it is instructive to consider how use of the law may affect parental practice.

Two examples seem relevant. The first relates to the banning of corporal punishment in UK schools. In 1979 Gerry Lee, an Executive Member of the NUS/UWT union, echoed many teachers' views with his remark that 'Corporal punishment is one of the tools necessary for the job. It's (abolition is) like a Ford worker having his spanner taken away' (STOPP, 1979, p3). Twenty years later and following three lengthy and well-publicised appeals to the European Court (*Tyrer* v. *United Kingdom* (1978) 2 EHRR 1; *Campbell and Cosans* v. *United Kingdom* (1982) 4 EHRR 293; *Costello-Roberts* v. *UK* (1994) ELR 1), the UK finally abolished corporal punishment in all state and private schools – the last country in Europe to do so. What is interesting about this process is that although it took nearly 20 years to achieve it seems to have been relatively successful. Despite recent attempts by 40 Christian schools to have the ban revoked, Lee's comment strikes one as far removed from the perceptions of most of today's teachers.

The second example is that of the comparison between Sweden and Denmark. In both countries, the physical punishment of children was culturally condoned. At different times (Sweden in 1979 and Denmark in 1986), both countries made it illegal. In Sweden, this move was accompanied by a large-scale public advertising campaign, using household items like milk cartons as well as a nationally disseminated leaflet, to take the message to the heart of family life. The campaign sought not just to remind parents of the new legislation but to provide them with ideas for alternative ways of setting boundaries and to reassure them that the aim of the law was to change hearts and minds rather than police minor contraventions. The effect was positive as later attitude surveys have shown (see Newell, 1989). In Denmark, fewer attempts were made to effect cultural change and less has been effected. These examples suggest that legal interventions in this area, even when at odds with public opinion, can help to shape cultural views and are likely to be particularly successful when well supported by advice on alternatives.

Child protection

What happens when 'smacking' turns into abuse or when young children are severely neglected, emotionally deprived or sexually abused? Are their rights to protection adequately safeguarded? To explore these questions we will look first at what is known about the extent and impact of abuse on children and then consider whether UK legal and professional interventions are sufficient and sensitive enough to protect young children. The Children (Scotland) Act 1995 and the Children (England and Wales) Act 1989 both give local authorities a legal responsibility to investigate situations where they receive information that a child (in Scotland) 'is likely' 'to suffer unnecessarily' or 'be impaired seriously in his health or development, due to a lack of parental care' (Section 52 (c)) or (in England and Wales) 'has suffered or is likely to suffer significant harm' and the obligation to take action to prevent further harm. As a result of these investigations, in 1998 local authority Child Protection Registers in England identified nearly 32 000 children as at risk of 'significant harm' (Department of Health, 1998b).

Children under ten make up 70% of those registered. Altogether, about four or five children under five in every 1000 in the UK population are at sufficient risk to be included on the Register (Browne & Herbert, 1997, p112). The abuse suffered by younger children is most likely to be physical abuse or neglect – 'NSPCC figures show that over 80% of the physical abuse most likely to cause death or handicap (i.e. head injury) occurs to children aged less than five with an over-representation of boys' (p112). However, parent-report studies suggest that much abusive behaviour never reaches the public arena. Some types of abuse go unrecognised and may be overlooked – for example, sexual abuse was not included in UK central government child protection guidelines until 1986. Studies of children living in families where there is domestic violence have found that they are abused in between a fifth and two-thirds of such situations (Hester & Radford, 1996) but that their abuse often remains hidden. Most of these children are very young – in Brandon & Lewis' (1996) study 55% were under five years old and a further 29% aged six to twelve. The impact was traumatic, with preschool aged children displaying the most distress.

Neglect is now the biggest recorded category of abuse. Often accompanied by emotional abuse, it can lead not only to failure to thrive but also to long-term organic, cognitive and emotional damage (Minty & Patterson, 1994; Stevenson, 1998). In a 20-year follow-up of children identified as suffering from non-organic failure to thrive, Iwaniec (1999) found that those who remained at home without services had very poor outcomes, with severe emotional and behavioural problems in adolescence and early adulthood. The research suggests that emotional abuse – which is often linked with neglect and other abuses – may be a more significant risk than is currently acknowledged (Gibbons et al., 1995). In a ten year follow-up study of children registered on the Child Protection Register because of physical abuse before the age of five and a matched group of their peers, Gibbons found that long-term harm was most likely in cases of 'parental punitiveness, highly critical attitudes and recent physical punishment' (p64).

Despite such evidence, and a general consensus that children have both moral and legal rights to be protected from severe abuse, in the UK there are deeply-held concerns about state 'interference' in family life (see Chapter 1). As a result, the process of state intervention is highly regulated and, in practice, nine-tenths of registered children remain at home.

Can we be satisfied, then, that the rights of young children who are abused are adequately upheld? To answer this, we will consider the impact and outcomes of English and Welsh legal processes. Legal processes in Scotland are very different and cannot be discussed in the space available. Readers are referred to King (1997, Chapter 3) for a review. The English and Welsh law, by adopting 'significant harm' as the threshold for intervention, has been accused of encouraging 'an obsession with simplistic notions of severity of behaviour' (Fortin, 1998b, p391). One of the results is a 'front-loaded' system. Professional interventions tend to concentrate on the identification of the abuse and the abuser. Once satisfied that the child is protected from further abuse in the short term, professional help is rarely available to deal with its impact on the child or family (Department of Health, 1995b). This, and a focus on mothers, often leaves non-abusing parents feeling undermined, provides insufficient help with parenting skills and allows men's violence to remain unaddressed (Boushel & Lebacq, 1992; Farmer & Owen, 1995; Brandon & Lewis, 1996).

The capacity of young children to participate in formal legal processes, however child-centred, is inevitably limited, so interventions which aim to prevent abuse, or reduce its impact, are those most likely to ensure that their rights are upheld. The evidence suggests that whilst potential abusers cannot be accurately identified (Browne & Saqi, 1988), there are factors which increase risk. For example, risk is increased by poverty, when coupled with other social disadvantages such as large family size, young age at first parenthood, isolation, overcrowding, violence and the absence of a supportive primary relationship for the main carer (Belsky & Vondra, 1989; Boushel, 1994; Quinton & Rutter, 1988). Recent research, including the findings of studies on child protection processes, has led to an attempt to 'refocus' professional practice towards preventive initiatives which aim to diminish family stress and improve long-term capacity to parent effectively (see Chapter 11).

Evidence about the efficacy of specific types of intervention is still limited, but is improving. Gough's (1993) review of research has shown that long-term visitation by a variety of professionals or paraprofessionals can be effective in preventing physical abuse and neglect in families where there is poverty, or parents are single or teenagers. Cross-cultural studies show that where gender roles and childrearing responsibilities are shared, it is more likely that women will be respected and levels of male physical and sexual violence will be low (Kağitçibaşi, 1996). Parenting skills programmes, especially those including cognitive-behavioural techniques, can be helpful. We also know that increased verbal skills in conflict resolution and other anger-management techniques reduce the likelihood of physical violence (Browne & Herbert, 1997).

What happens when preventive strategies are insufficient to protect a young child? Does the law enable those concerned with their welfare to protect them? What part do young children play in these processes? The interests of most young children would best be served by remaining in familiar surroundings with a well-supported, non-abusing parent. In theory, this is now partially recognised by the power available to local authorities in England and Wales (with the consent of the other partner) and in Scotland to apply to the court to remove an alleged abuser from the family home. However, in England and Wales when an exclusion order is applied for under the Family Law Act 1996 the court considers the 'balance of harm' to adult and child rather than giving paramountcy to the child's best interests. When the local authority initiates care proceedings to ensure that a child is looked after adequately and in a safe place, recent case law suggests that 'the courts are becoming increasingly concerned with protecting adults from false accusations of abuse rather than fulfilling children's rights to state protection' (Fortin, 1998b, pp379–80). Indeed, the more serious the abuse, the higher the standard of proof demanded by the court (p385).

Until 1990, the English law of evidence as it related to children under six has been described as 'something of a child molester's charter' (Flin & Spencer, 1995, p173). It remains confused, confusing and inadequate. Young children's rights to give evidence and have their views taken into account vary between Scotland and England and between civil and criminal proceedings. They do not have the right to appear in civil proceedings, where major decisions concerned with their own future – such as where and with whom they should live – are made. In care proceedings, for example, their interests are represented by a court-appointed social worker called a guardian ad litem and, very rarely and with court permission, an 'official solicitor' represents their views.

Since the Criminal Justice Act 1991 children are presumed to be competent witnesses in criminal proceedings and if called upon have no choice but to attend court, give evidence and be cross-examined. Few cases ever reach a criminal prosecution, but where they do, children as young as six have been required to give evidence against their parents in trials that take place, on average, as much as ten months after the investigation (Fortin, 1998b). The Pigot Committee (Home Office, 1989) described these court experiences as 'harmful, oppressive and often traumatic' and frequently a 'secondary victimisation' (p430). As a result, some changes were made. At the discretion of the judge children may give evidence by live video link and (in England and Wales only) earlier videoed evidence may also be presented (Home Office, 1992). Many of the Committee's other recommendations – such as providing support for children, giving them choice about the method they wished to use in giving evidence, expediting hearings and 'ensuring that cross-examinations are conducted without causing the child distress' (Fortin, p431) – were never implemented. It is hardly surprising that under the present system only a 'tiny number' of the abusers of younger children suffer legal sanctions (Fortin, p428). These rules of evidence bear little relation to children's competence – government-commissioned psychological research indicates that they can be reliable and competent witnesses even by the age of three or four, if properly interviewed and when some 'pronounced age differences' in ability to recall and report events are taken into account (Flin & Spencer, 1995, p179).

When children are asked for their views about how best to deal with abuse within the family, younger children in particular express two wishes – that the abuse is stopped and that their family does not split up. Children often feel responsible for family breakdown – and may indeed have been encouraged to believe so by the abuser. Sharland *et al.* (1995) found that older children who disclosed sexual abuse also felt frightened and betrayed if no action was taken against the abuser. Lack of a clear, supportive child-friendly legal framework contributes to these unjust pressures (Cloke & Davies, 1995).

Other countries have tackled these difficult issues in a different way. In France a specially appointed *Juge des Enfants* co-ordinates the investigation (Cooper *et al.*, 1995); in the Netherlands a 'confidential doctor's service' aims to decriminalise child abuse where the abuser is prepared to co-operate with child welfare specialists (van Montfoort, 1993); in Ireland, Italy and New Zealand the law permits cross-examination of children to be carried out by the judge only (Flin & Spencer, 1995); in Scotland, the Children's Hearings system goes some way towards providing more child-friendly procedures (King, 1997). If children's rights were to be taken seriously, then comparative research on the merits of each system from a child's perspective would need to be undertaken. However, the resistance so far shown by the English legal profession to less fundamental changes leaves little confidence that there is much interest in redressing current adult-centred procedures.

Family breakdown

In this third example we consider how the rights of children to participate in decisions affecting them, to have their views 'given due weight' (Article 12) and to 'seek, receive and impart information' (Article 13) might apply to young children in the circumstances surrounding family breakdown.

Family break-up is no longer an uncommon event in the life of children. In 1994/95 data indicate that about 7.5% of children under five experienced divorce. The figure rose to 18.7% of children under ten, a 3% increase on the 1988/89 figure (Rodgers & Pryor, 1998). These figures underestimate the numbers of young children affected by parental separation, as they do not include the separations of cohabiting parents. Neither do they reflect the changes that take place when new adult partnerships and new family units are formed.

Interviews with children indicate that the separation itself is a time of crisis, with effects that last for many years. Most children wish their parents would stay together. In the short term at least, children are likely 'to experience unhappiness, low self-esteem, problems with behaviour and friendships, and loss of contact with a significant part of their extended family' (Rodgers & Pryor, 1998, p4). Young children are more likely to be confused by events and to blame themselves. Because of the importance of location in their understanding of events, young children, in particular, may believe that the parent who leaves has ceased to be their parent (McGurk & Glachan, 1987). Other studies also indicate that younger children are more likely to consider as family only those who live with them (O'Brien et al., 1996).

To avoid traumatic feelings of abandonment it is particularly important, therefore, that children are provided with repeated, understandable, age-related explanations of events and given concrete reassurance of the continued involvement of their absent parent. In an early study of children's views of divorce, Walczak & Burns (1984) found that lack of information about what was happening was the most difficult aspect of the process for children. This and other studies have shown that children adapt most successfully across a range of educational and psycho-social outcomes and are more likely to continue to enjoy positive relationships with both parents when they are given clear consistent explanations from the outset. This is not to say that it is in a child's best interests to be given detailed information about parental conflicts or expected to participate by taking sides. Indeed, it is more likely that '(i)f conflict during marriage is contained within the adult sphere, children may be protected from its ill effects' (Richards, 1993 p313). This may be a somewhat optimistic view, since studies of domestic violence and of children's worries (Butler & Williamson, 1994) suggest that children are far more aware of family conflicts than adults expect or intend. Nevertheless, children's rights and best interests are best protected in most situations by acknowledging and encouraging the positive aspects of their own relationships with the protagonists.

A recent review of the research on the longer-term outcomes of divorce and separation makes it clear that '(t)here is no simple or direct relationship between parental separation and children's adjustment, and poor outcomes are far from inevitable' but that '(a)s a rule of thumb, many adverse outcomes are roughly twice as prevalent among children of divorced families compared with children of intact families' (Rodgers & Pryor, 1998, p5). UK studies suggest that parental separation when children are young significantly increases the child's vulnerability (Rodgers & Pryor, 1998). However, much remains to be understood in this field, and it is not yet fully clear to what extent the reported longer-term negative consequences for some children (such as greatly reduced levels of socio-economic achievement, poorer educational performance, increased psycho-social problems and earlier marriages) are related to the financial insecurity and parental conflict which often surrounds divorce, or to the more specific emotional impact of the separation (Richards, 1993; Rodgers & Pryor, 1998). What is clear is that it is important to consider parental separation not 'as a single event, but rather seeing it as part of a process occurring over an extended period' (Rodgers & Pryor, 1998, p13), a process that has considerable significance in a young child's life.

On separation, two decisions of tremendous importance to a child – whom she will live with and what contact she will have with her other parent – will need to be made. According to Rodgers & Pryor, recent evidence 'does not appear to support the suggestion that children living with a same-sex parent do better than those who do not' (1988, p39). However, both US and UK research shows that when families break up, 'many fathers disappear. Whether pushed or falling, they move away to begin new lives elsewhere'(Richards, 1993, p313). In the USA, Seltzer (1991) found that three to five years after separation only one-third of children saw their fathers each week and 18% once a year or not at all. A UK study suggests that fathers are far more likely to lose contact with their daughters than their sons (Cockett & Tripp, 1994). Without this contact, children may also lose half their kinship network.

In most cases it will be in their interests for children to have ongoing contact with their non-resident parent in a manner that takes account of their understanding and timescales. For young children frequency and consistency is most important, whilst older children value contact arrangements that are flexible enough to suit their changing lifestyles (Rodgers & Pryor, 1998). Young children's potential to participate in decision-making is often underestimated and insufficiently encouraged. In establishing contact arrangements there are many areas – such as the preferred timing, methods and venues, access to extended family – where principles of dynamic self-determination can be put into practice and the rights of even a young child to have their views heard and respected can be upheld. In cases of domestic violence, however, Hester & Radford (1996) point out that children's rights need active protection long after custody arrangements have been agreed as even very young children may feel forced to give in to the demands of the abusive parent in order to protect themselves and other family members.

Remarkably little attempt has been made to promote children's rights in situations of family breakdown, by, for example, helping parents understand the implications of their actions for children and how they might best deal with these events, providing opportunities for children to participate in decision-making or even to have their views acknowledged, or by the provision of counselling and support services for the children involved. Some changes are beginning to take place. In the USA, court-affiliated parent-education programmes for divorcing parents now exist in the majority of states and in some states they are mandatory. In Connecticut, they 'focus on getting parents to view their situation from their children's perspective' (Corsaro, 1997, p269–70) by including videos of parental conflict and interviews with children. Ninety per cent of those attending 'approved of the requirement' (p270). However, much more information is needed about whether the programmes have positive outcomes for young children.

At present, the legal framework in this area in the UK is in disarray. The

Children (Scotland) Act 1995 lists the maintenance of contact after separation as a parental responsibility but does not specify how this is to be achieved or deal with the rights of young children in the process. The Family Law Act 1996 proposals to change English and Welsh divorce legislation to include access to mediation did not include opportunities for children to participate directly and have recently been abandoned. In any event, the benefit to children of mediation and other measures linked to court proceedings in divorce and separation cases is disputed because they exclude separations where parents are not legally married (Douglas *et al.*, 1996) and their timing, often after the separation already has taken place, is unlikely to meet children's needs to have their care arrangements agreed within child-centred timescales (Richards, 1993).

Legal remedies are important in a minority of cases, but if we are to support young children's rights to have access to the information they need to make sense of major changes in the most important relationships in their lives and to have their wishes and views taken into account when new parenting arrangements are being planned, then we need to think more creatively. We need initiatives which help all adults (not just those already in conflictual relationships) understand how the processes of separation may be approached in ways that are most likely to prevent harmful outcomes for children; the role that extended families can play; how parental contact can best be maintained. We need advice and counselling provision for parents and for children to deal with difficulties that may arise before, during and after family breakdown. We need to provide ideas and opportunities which will enhance contact arrangements. Perhaps most importantly, we need to ensure that children are given opportunities to develop an understanding of family life and relationships which will help them cope with the parental separations that will affect so many of them. In this context, a recent government instruction to primary schools to teach children that the preferred model of family life is a legally approved, two-parent one is particularly unhelpful. It may deprive young children of information that enables them to situate their own circumstances (whatever they may be) within a wider context. It may encourage many to believe that their family life is inadequate and stifle the very discussions that may help young children cope more confidently with the potential impermanency of any particular family form.

Young children's rights – and responsibilities

In this chapter we have explored young children's rights within their families from two angles – the way these rights are regulated by the state and the way they are practised in parent–child relationships. The state's reluctance to interfere in family life discriminates against children because it fails to acknowledge the huge imbalance of power in the relationship between young children and their parents. It has no clear intervention strategy to help parents manage their power in ways that respect children and promote their best interests; and when it does intervene, its civil and criminal legal procedures are adult-centred, take inadequate account of young children's capacities and needs and rarely provide legal redress even when they are severely abused. Where attempts have been made to increase children's rights to have their wishes and feelings taken into account, they have been targeted at older children. So far, there is little evidence of any real attempt to encourage the 'dynamic self-determinism' that would allow young children 'to participate in the process of defining their "needs", treatment and destiny' (Woodhead, 1997, p81).

The private nature of the home makes it difficult to find out how children's rights are reflected in parent–child relationships. In a comparison of health visitors' and mothers' reactions to young children's health Mayall (1994a) found that mothers saw their children as active participants in their relationships to a far greater degree than did the health visitors. The form these interactions take and what they can tell us of children's participation in decision-making around the activities of daily life needs more research. The examples used here suggest that their participation is quite severely curtailed and its limitations generally unchallenged.

We need to remember, also, that the concept of 'rights', unless balanced by a commitment to the common good, can serve merely to reinforce the individualism of Western cultures. In drawing up the African Charter on the Rights and Welfare of the Child (1990) the Organisation for African Unity emphasised the mutual 'responsibilities' and 'duties' between child and family. In Western societies, as far as young children are concerned, we seem to avoid identifying either. Does this reflect a protectiveness that denies young children their capacity to act independently of us and an unwillingness to acknowledge the inter-relatedness of responsibilities and rights? Perhaps a feudal relationship rather than one based on emerging citizenship is less challenging to us as lords and ladies of the family manor!

Chapter 8
Early Childhood Care and Education Services in Britain

Mary Fawcett

Is it harmful for children to be in day care, away from their parents, in their preschool years? A simple answer is just not possible. As this chapter will show, there are many aspects to this awkward question, not least of which is the concept of quality.

Here the word 'services' will be used to cover day care and education provision before statutory schooling. The services that are now available to children and their families are the result of an evolutionary process which includes political decisions (or the lack of them), economic forces, employment patterns and family structures, as well as educational and social theories. This chapter will consider first their historical development over the last 80 years or so, secondly the present-day situation in terms of what is available (and the reasons why), thirdly the various partnerships that now exist (between parents and services, and among the services themselves) and finally the daily experience of children in education and day care services. One might describe this as an ecological structure (Bronfenbrenner, 1979).

The historical context – the chronosystem

From the earliest times every generation of human beings has had to find a way of looking after its young children while parents were occupied in hunting, growing food, earning a living, or engaging in myriad activities outside the home. In addition to this basic need to care for the younger children there gradually arose the idea of 'educating' them. Different approaches to early education up to World War I – many of which have remained influential – have already been mentioned in Chapter 1. By 1920, thanks to pioneers like Froebel, Montessori and McMillan, the belief in nursery education was beginning to take hold in Britain and some other Western countries. But while nursery schools, preparatory schools and day nurseries did become more common in Britain between the two World Wars, they still catered for relatively small numbers. For most families the traditional practice of women looking after each other's children, i.e. childminding, would have been the norm.

The trigger for a significant expansion of services for Britain's preschool population was the outbreak of World War II. Mothers had to fill jobs vacated by service men and their children needed day care. Day nurseries (offering all-day places) were seen as the solution rather than nursery schools, and by 1944 provided 70 000 places (Ferri *et al.*, 1981) – not a large number relative to the population.

After the war, there was no driving force to maintain these – largely custodial – day nurseries. Jobs were needed for men returning from active service and women were sent back to the kitchen. All the same, the flickering flame of vision that a proper nursery school experience was of significant value for children was kept alive – notably by the Nursery School Association (now the British Association for Early Childhood Education) which had been founded in 1923. The extent of preschool provision may still have been limited, and unavailable to many families, but the quality of what did exist was generally high. Indeed throughout the 1950s, 1960s and even into the 1970s, English nursery schools and infant schools were renowned across the world and the focus for many international visitors.

But the seed of a new movement, a mainly British phenomenon, was sown in 1961 with Belle Tutaev's letter to a national newspaper proposing *parent-run* preschool groups. The concept suited the moment. In the early 1960s women generally did not expect to join the work force before their children were of school age. This development happened to coincide with fresh thinking about the possibly critical importance of children's early years. The result was an amazingly rapid spread of playgroups in church and village halls (as well as in private homes) representing an extra-ordinary dedication of energy by huge numbers of women of all classes, whether as playgroup leaders and parent-helpers or as committee members and fund-raisers. If the original intention had been to create an approximation to a nursery school – that is, to give children good play experiences in the belief that this would enhance their later academic school work and their social development – playgroups soon discovered other remarkable benefits, not simply for the children but for the women (and a very small number of men) too, as they organised and ran the groups, particularly fostering their self-confidence and imparting useful skills.

Innovative energies of women were channelled not only into the playgroup movement but also into childminding. Furthermore the specific role of childminders became a subject of interest for the minders themselves and, as with playgroups, a self-improvement and support movement evolved. This eventually became the National Child Minding Association. In part this was a response to public unease about the care of children by childminders. Research on childminding in industrial cities by Jackson & Jackson (1979) graphically documented the poor quality of daily care at that time, particularly for black children. Twenty years on, unregistered childminders can still be found, but there is now much more training and awareness in this important area which remains the most common of all childcare services outside the home.

Through the 1980s and 1990s, as the rest of Europe expanded and improved its services for young children, many educators became increasingly concerned about the serious inadequacies of British provision. Not only were services patchy in their geographical availability, they were extremely uneven in quality (Audit Commission, 1996; Moss & Penn, 1996; Pugh, 1996). The shaming contrast with our partners in Europe (only Portugal had less public provision), together with increasing research support for the long-term benefits of appropriate early experiences, at last began to force the Conservative government into action. Starting in 1995 that action took the form of the Nursery Education Voucher Scheme, which allowed half-time 'nursery' schooling for four-year-olds in term times. This bureaucratic, ill-thought out and untried scheme had a dramatic effect on the balance of provision, leading to significant closures of playgroups and private nurseries – a trend which continued after the election of a Labour government in 1997.

In the closing decades of the twentieth century developments in other parts of the world show similarities to changes in Britain over the last hundred years. As populations move to cities, away from traditional and family support networks, and as women's roles change, these causal factors bring pressure to bear on governments and other agencies to set up programmes for children (Cochran, 1993, p628 ff). It is only as countries become politically stable, however, and once they have established statutory schooling (typically around the age of six), that the youngest children become the focus of attention. Even then it will depend on national budgeting priorities. Cochran's comparison of services in Europe and the rest of the world (1995) shows that in countries outside Europe and the USA the emphasis of care is normally on parents' rather than children's needs, and on private rather than public funding, with services largely unregulated and very limited in extent.

Early childhood services now – the macrosystem and exosystem

The picture of services in Britain at the beginning of the twenty-first century, with its great variety, is difficult to grasp. The majority of under-twos are cared for in home settings with relatives or childminders, most three-year-olds still attend preschools (playgroups), while four-year-olds are largely in state nursery schools, nursery classes and reception classes. On the other hand, there also exist nannies, independent private schools, day nurseries (local authority and private), family centres, and combined centres (the new Centres of Excellence). In 1995 a survey showed a 500% increase in private nurseries over the preceding ten years (Penn, 1995). An accurate picture of the take-up of day care and education services before school has long been difficult to obtain. While national statistics are now at last being published these still do not break down the information by age, nor make clear the multiple use of services.

We still therefore have a fragmented and, indeed, confusing scene which poses serious problems for governments trying to create a more universal service. Each of the three groups of 'stakeholders' involved –

Type of service	Number of providers	Number of places			Places per 100 children 0–4 years	As percentage of 3–4 year olds
		Full-time	Part-time	Total		
Childminders[1] (Registered)	94 700			370 700[3]	11.93	
Day nurseries[1] Local authority[4] Registered private nurseries	500			18 670	0.60	
Playgroups[1]	15 700			383 600	Children 3–4 years 30.15	54.27
Nursery schools[2] Nursery classes Total – Nursery schools and classes	533 6 015	8 247 30 662	40 389 289 060	48 636 319 722 368 358	28.95	
Infant classes[2]		321 122	30 998	352 120		27.68[5] 55.48 (as % of 4-year olds)
Independent schools (under fives)		29 406	24 353	54 353		4.27

References:
[1] Children's day care facilities at 31 March 1998 England (DoH, March 1999).
[2] Pupils under five years in LEAs, England, January 1997 (DfEE, Statistical Bulletin, 1/99).
Notes:
[3] Childminders places are recorded 0–7 years. These figures assume most are under five.
[4] Family centres and workplace nurseries may be included.
[5] LEAs collect information in different ways. Treat these percentages with caution; the great majority of children are 4–5 years.
A general point:
Statistics about the use of preschool services are notoriously difficult to compile; indeed no one knows the precise figures since many children attend several of these services at any one time.
(Figures compiled by Early Childhood Unit, National Children's Bureau.)

Fig. 8.1 Under fives and preschool services in England, 1998.

parents, children and staff – have their own practical needs and agendas. They are also regarded by politicians in particular ways.

Parents

Most of the European Union countries believe that the health, welfare and education of the next generation must be a shared concern for society at large and should be universal in scope. In Britain, though, preschool children have traditionally been seen as the private responsibility of parents to provide for as they think fit, the state becoming involved only when a parent was deemed to be incompetent, or to be putting the child's development at risk. Today this concept of primarily compensatory state intervention continues in the project for disadvantaged families, known as Sure Start (DfEE, 1999). This interdepartmental programme, implemented from April 1999, has the stated aims of raising standards in school, improving the employment prospects of young people, and reducing crime and school-age pregnancy. It operates in selected areas of social disadvantage to deliver support 'at every level' to families expecting a baby and to other families with children under four.

Parents, usually mothers, seek services to provide childcare while they are occupied in employment or education, or perhaps to reduce stress and loneliness. Services may be particularly necessary for single parents, though the social class of the parent and cost of childcare can create very diverse situations. Beyond their own needs parents may also turn to preschool services for the sake of the child's social and educational progress. The UN Convention on the Rights of the Child (1989) has recognised that parents should, of right, have help with childrearing (Article 18.2) and to enable them to work (Article 18.3). Indeed, if women are to have the civil right of equal access to the job or education market, childcare is a prerequisite. General acceptance of this need for childcare does not mean that it is fully available in practice. Thus, the present system of half-time attendance for four-year-olds (and increasingly for three-year-olds), and only during the three school terms, fails to match the timetable of many working parents. In addition, parents usually have very little choice of childcare within their immediate neighbourhood, and typically they do little 'shopping around' according to Nic Ghoilla Phádraig (in Qvortrup *et al.*, 1994). As a result they may, without meaning to, simply collude with poor practice, not least because they have no models of excellence by which to evaluate local services. Though working parents tend to prefer the more individual service of childminders for children under two (Meltzer, 1994), they likewise use home-based services for their older children when schools are closed. Another form of care, after-school clubs, is only just beginning to spread.

The government has now adopted a 'national child care strategy' (starting with a national baseline survey) which will be realised through the agency of the Early Years Development and Childcare Partnerships. At the time of writing it is too early to comment on the strategy other than to point to concerns about the quality of the staffing (see below under 'Staff') and about continuity for children.

Children

As already mentioned, Britain has a great variety of provision for young children. Within these there co-exist many kinds of practice, as well as staff with varying amounts of expertise and training, and informed by diverse philosophies or none at all. They include nursery schools with a clear ethos of the competent child who learns through self-directed activity; preparatory schools emphasising academic preparation; and preschools struggling to compromise between their belief in play and the external demands of the government. It is in recognition of the very uneven nature of United Kingdom practice that the government has chosen to intervene through inspection based on the *Desirable Outcomes* (DfEE, 1996) and its replacement, *Early Learning Goals* (DfEE, 1999b).

In formulating its childcare strategy the particular agenda of government seems evident. There appear to be two main elements. One is the attempt to draw as many adults as possible into the workforce through the 'New Deal', so requiring the 'preschool child' and the 'after-school child' to be 'cared for' in order to free up their working parents. The other is closely linked to the policy for older school-age children, i.e. the National Curriculum. Both emphasise adult work opportunities and the need to train children for a competitive work environment, rather than children's rights and all-round development. While it would be wrong to deny children equal access to a broad curriculum, it is neccessary to consider the nature of the approach which is developing in this country. The *Early Learning Goals* approach is over-prescriptive in relation to language and literacy, apparently disregarding research findings in psychology, sociology and education which demonstrate the very early drive for competence in communication in *all* its forms. The emphasis too is on preparation for the next stage, in this case the National Curriculum in statutory school, rather than giving sufficient status to the preschool years as a valid and vital part of life in its own terms.

This rather limited image of children is perhaps not uncommon in England – children are somehow 'unfinished' – empty vessels into which facts must be poured, clay to be moulded to fit prevailing social norms. In a thoughtful contribution to the debate ten years ago, one study drew on Indian, Chinese and African concepts of children and childhood.

> 'This concept of the child as an 'unfinished' adult shifts the focus away from the child's own intentions, attachments, and strivings – which might in fact open up many learning horizons for the adult, on to an end-product notion of adulthood which is unwisely equated with 'achieved knowledge'. It might be said that this represents a specifically Western, 'rationalist' approach to both childhood and learning which, by separating the mind from the heart, effectively denies the essential unity of the child.'
>
> (Hazareesingh *et al.*, 1989, p18)

In Britain the current dominance of academic goals for very young children worries early years educators on several counts (Nutbrown, 1997). While children in virtually every other country start formal schooling around the age of six, Britain, by an accident of history, chose five – which in practice often means four. Coupled with this is the danger that anxious staff, trying to meet national goals, will resort to a sedentary, talk-based, teacher-directed style ('direct instruction') rather than an active programme that encourages a young child's autonomy and sense of mastery. The American High/Scope project and its longitudinal research study have explored the benefits and risks which may be attributable to the patterns of behaviour and learning established even before children start school (Ball, 1994). In their most recent report Schweinhart & Weikart noted the consistent long-term effectiveness of both High/Scope and the traditional nursery school curricula and argued against using direct instruction at the preschool stage (Schweinhart & Weikart, 1997). Though their much-quoted research is based on a particular (and not very large) cohort in the 1960s, this study is a significant indication that early educational experiences should encourage children to be active and, moreover, to take responsibility for their actions.

Young children in Britain often have to cope with different out-of-home arrangements in the years before school – another consequence of an unplanned set of services which fail to put the child first. Typically children may experience several childminders, attend more than one pre-school group, and then have a year at a nursery school. Even in a single week some children attend a morning nursery class, two playgroups on different afternoons, and a childminder's house to cover the gap before their parents come home from work – moved around 'like so many small parcels' (according to one nursery head). Parents would not wish to see their secondary-age child attending seven different schools in the two years between the ages of eleven and thirteen, so why is the equivalent acceptable in the two years from three to five?

It would be interesting to know what children (the youngest, but most affected stakeholders) think about this and other matters, though in practice their views are rarely sought. Many children believe nursery school is obligatory (Evans & Fuller, 1998). The ESRC Children 5–16 project is beginning to provide valuable insights into children's experiences at a later stage, but we need to know more about the youngest children's ideas and preferences.

Our present situation is rather confused. The government, through the New Deal, is putting pressure on women to work rather than be full-time parents, while society generally has conflicting views about childcare. On the one hand parents are ready to shuttle children between different services, as described above, while on the other there is concern that out-of-home care of any sort might be damaging to their future development, a view often underpinned by a notion that the proper place for mothers is in the home. The review of research by McGurk and his colleagues (1993) demonstrates the complexity of the debate about whether childcare services are harmful or not. Among the factors bearing on this question are the age of the child when starting day care, the hours involved, the frequency of changes and multiple use of services, the types of care, the quality of the environment and curriculum, the training and experience of the staff, and the child's own family circumstances. Research has not been sufficiently detailed or based on large enough samples to give conclusive evidence. The latest review of American studies on the consequences of a large cohort of young children receiving day care (part of the National Longitudinal Survey of Youth) does not significantly alter the prevailing view that it is not harmful, even though it recorded certain small negative consequences from very early and long hours in day care. Unfortunately the investigation omitted any measure of the quality of the services used which, as the author notes, may have a much larger impact (Harvey, 1999).

Sweden's major longitudinal research study (Andersson, 1989 and 1992) appeared to show that the long-term educational and social benefits of day care were actually greatest for children introduced to it before their first birthday. In this case the preschool institutions were of very high quality, besides which all the supporting services (for example health) were also exceptionally good. Swedish policy now, however, is not to allow children to attend any day care unaccompanied by a parent until their second year, in the belief that the first year should be a time to build up strong relationships between infant and parents. Paid parental leave makes this a reality.

Thinking about children not just as adjuncts to their family, but as a distinct social group with their own perspectives, has a long way to go in this country. Taking international evidence, Frønes (in Qvortrup *et al.*, 1994) examined the institutionalisation of childhood and how children are inevitably situated in day care, schooling, and after-school leisure time activities. All these organisations incorporate forms of social control; most are age-specific; and they take place in special locations which separate children off from other parts of society.

One increasingly influential model of a community approach to providing for young children is found in the Italian city of Reggio Emilia. Here the preschools exemplify a community-based state institution which is democratic at all levels, which incorporates parents, and which makes possible a system of relationships and a forum for discussion (Malaguzzi, in Edwards, *et al.*, 1998). As the key theorist of this approach emphasises, the fundamental point is that it embodies a concept of children which is explicit:

> 'Our image of children no longer considers them as isolated and egocentric, does not see them only engaged in action with objects, does not emphasize only cognitive aspects, does not belittle feelings or what is not logical and does not consider with ambiguity the role of the affective domain. Instead our image of the child is rich in potential, strong, powerful, competent and, most of all, connected to adults and other children.'
>
> (Malaguzzi, 1993, p11)

Staff

When talking about preschool staff the phrases which might come to mind, especially in a British context, are 'women's work', 'low pay' and 'low status'. There are several reasons for such widespread negative and devaluing perceptions. The first is economic. With pay levels very poor, career prospects extremely limited, and the overwhelming female gender bias, the job is simply not seen as a serious professional option for most men (Penn, 1998). Such is not the case in every country; for example in the Scandinavian countries more men are gradually being recruited (Jensen, 1996).

Another reason for poor status – and this creates a self-perpetuating problem – is the low level of qualifications required, a situation which as yet shows little sign of improvement. Many practitioners have not been trained for the work. A very large national study (Blenkin & Yue, 1994) reports that fewer than one-fifth of all practitioners working with children under eight were graduates and a tenth had no qualifications at all. Another study (Calder & Fawcett, 1998) pointed out that whereas 23% of the general working population were now graduates, a mere 5% of staff working with under-fives had degrees. This is clear proof that most of those entrusted with our youngest children are quite poorly educated. Most of our European partners demand higher levels of training than Britain, by far the majority requiring at least three years of tertiary (degree-level) education for anyone employed in this sector. In an attempt to improve the culture of the early years profession in Europe as a whole, the European Commission Child Care Network (1996) has set a target of 60% of the preschool workforce to have degree-level education by the year 2006. This is still far from being the aspiration in Britain where nothing more than the National Vocational Qualification Level III (the equivalent of A level) is expected (see Calder, 1996, for a detailed discussion).

It is indicative that the low regard for early years practitioners is not related to professional training alone. Nursery school teachers may receive the same rates of pay as other teachers but they still tend be regarded less favourably. Almost every aspect of the care and education of small children is consistently undervalued. Even the new university degrees in early childhood studies were regarded at first with some suspicion as potentially lacking academic rigour, though this initial perception soon changed as the demanding interdisciplinary content of these degrees and the quality of the students taking part began to convince even the most sceptical. These academic early childhood programmes, now running in more than a score of institutions, offer a ray of hope, for they are currently producing a fresh generation of well-educated and thoughtful potential professionals.

All the same, the number of graduates in early childhood studies is still relatively low. Most preschool staff remain woefully ill-educated for the job. Combined with low pay and inadequate working conditions this has serious consequences. Frequent staff turnover is one. A survey of private nurseries (Penn, 1995) found that as many as 90% of staff in certain nurseries changed their jobs within a year, with an average of 32% in the entire sample. Similar figures were found in America, though in this case staff with longer and higher-level training had very much lower turnover (Whitebook et al., 1989). Morale and enthusiasm would almost certainly be higher with a better-educated and better-remunerated workforce. Certainly this proved to be the case in Penn's recent comparison of similar nurseries in Spain, Italy and England. In the former two countries she also found staff engaged in lively theoretical debate – a practice typically absent in England (Penn, 1997).

Similar evidence comes from Scandinavia, where in the late 1960s and 1970s the growth in the proportion of women in paid employment generally led to a dramatic expansion of preschools. Combining both care and education, these institutions foster well-educated professional adult staff enthused by a strongly principled approach. Additionally all staff are expected (and funded) to take part in continuous study and personal development, and the same is true in Italy. In Britain, by contrast, the recent *Draft Framework for Qualifications and Training in the Education, Childcare and Playwork Sectors* (QCA, 1998) appears seriously limited in its ambition. Narrowly focused on imparting basic techniques and emphasising training rather than education, it avoids any mention of professional teaching qualifications, the early childhood studies degrees, or indeed any other degrees.

A further limitation of the *Draft Framework* concerns children with disabilities, many of whom are found in early years settings – indeed the numbers are expected to increase. One authority writing on behalf of Mencap (Dickins, 1999) argues that staff need more specialist knowledge and regrets that such training is missing from the document, claiming that it should be mandatory if the government is to implement adequately its other directive, the new *Programme of Action* (DfEE, 1998).

Interactions – the mesosystem

Three areas of interaction between groups will be considered here, respectively the interfaces between parents and professional workers, between professionals themselves within a multidisciplinary centre, and between the many groups now brought together in Early Years Development and Childcare Partnerships. The meaning of the word 'partnership' deserves spelling out. It is used very imprecisely and far too often. In dictionary terms it refers to shared decision-making between equals, though unequal power relationships often mean that in practice one side of the partnership may not see it that way.

Parents and professionals

Gillian Pugh's detailed examination of this relationship (Pugh, 1989) places the variations on this theme on a continuum that ranges from minimal involvement through to active managerial roles and participation in decision-making. Along this continuum one can identify several intermediate forms of engagement. First the participation of parents in their own child's education starting at birth and long before a child reaches an organised preschool. How far parents are seen to be educators of their own children once organised schooling begins will vary, with some educational bodies going to great lengths to ensure this continues. Second is parental involvement through helping in group-learning settings in preschools or schools themselves. Helpers in these situations may not necessarily feel at all like partners, but more like a useful pair of hands. Furthermore parent helpers from ethnic minority groups, or parents who have had poor school experiences themselves, may find the school atmosphere unwelcoming. The responsibility lies with the school to create an environment where everyone feels 'at home'.

A third form of participation sees parents serving as governors or on committees, but unless the paid professionals go out of their way to engage them actively, these parents may feel confined to a minor role. It is true that few parents, however 'expert' with regard to their own children, will have the detailed knowledge ideally required to participate fully. In any case the role carries a heavy burden, as attested by the difficulty schools have in recruiting parent governors.

Community playgroups are run more democratically, but given the rapid return to paid employment by many women, this kind of involvement has reduced.

Interprofessional working

For 20 years or so a few innovative multidisciplinary centres have been experimenting with ways of working with staff from differing professional backgrounds (Makins, 1997). This admirable and practical approach to serving communities is now being promoted by the government through Centres of Excellence, 28 of which have been specified as pilot projects. In addressing the concept of partnership between professionals – who may be social workers, teachers, health visitors, nursery nurses, and specialists such as speech therapists – projects have had to take into account many issues. Each of these professionals starts out with a different initial training which has its own priorities and views of children, parents and childrearing. Pay and conditions, such as hours and holidays, often vary so that individuals from some professions may not feel as fully valued as others. To create a truly cohesive partnership between colleagues will require much work and understanding (Leathard, 1994).

Early Years Development and Childcare Partnerships

The Early Years Development and Childcare Partnerships based in local authorities are a worthy idea. The government has given them the task of bringing together the diverse strands of the preschool sector. All providers are potential members, whether private, community, voluntary, local authority, or any other organisation with an interest in the early years. Inevitably this results in a very large number of people attending meetings and being kept informed. Voluntary workers especially, like school parent governors, can find themselves faced with extremely heavy and responsible duties. Substantial government funding will, it is hoped, enable good practice to develop, but this is an experimental layer of decision-making and is likely to be uneven in its success. How far groups such as childminders feel truly represented by such an organisation is a question for research.

Quality experience – the microsystem

In trying to examine the quality of the daily experience of children in preschool settings one must go beyond the minimum, measurable requirements of state registration – like sufficient space, safe and healthy environments, appropriate adult/child ratios, good and well-maintained equipment. Many local authorities have therefore turned to the Effective Early Learning Project whose ten-point framework includes necessary practicalities as well as 'Child Involvement' and 'Adult Engagement' (Pascal & Bertram, 1997).

Vastly different demands may be made of children. In order to consider some possible microsystems (in other words children's daily experience), three different curricula for three- and four-year-olds are analysed below, the High/Scope, Montessori and the Reggio Emilia approaches. A curriculum for babies and toddlers is treated separately.

The curriculum will be taken to include all that takes place, planned and unplanned, in an educational setting, including the 'hidden curriculum' (that is, the ethos of the group, the social relationships, and attitudes towards gender, race and disability). In each case the curriculum will be considered in four dimensions – its underlying principles, content, organisational structure, and adult involvement. Through this discussion the consequences of particular ideological frameworks for the daily experience of children can be demonstrated. Each of these internationally valued approaches has been documented by the educationalists concerned; see Hohmann & Weikart (1995) for High/Scope; Hainstock (1978) or others for Montessori; and Edwards *et al.* (1998) for the Reggio philosophy and practice.

1. Principles

The High/Scope approach, developed in Illinois, USA, in the 1960s, was the result of experimental teaching by graduates using the Piagetian perspective that the essential role of a child's active hands-on engagement with the environment is the main route to cognitive development. Two further principles were incorporated, those of children selecting their activities and then reflecting on the consequences (in other words, becoming autonomous) and of children taking responsibility for their actions.

In the Montessori approach, evolved in Rome in the 1920s, Maria Montessori drew on her work with children with learning disabilities and street children. The underlying belief is of the innate human drive to understand the world through sensory exploration, so that children unfold 'like a flower' given an appropriate structured environment and a unique form of adult support.

The Italian town of Reggio Emilia is the home of the third approach which, from around the 1960s, has gradually become internationally known through its exhibition The Hundred Languages of Children. The roots of the work stem from parent-run schools set up in response to experiences of Fascism and World War II. The principal perspectives here are of children as competent, questioning citizens and co-constructors of their worlds (see the earlier *Children* section). The 'Hundred Languages' refer to the multitude of ways in which children might engage with ideas.

All three approaches declare a belief in the potential of children and their active participation in conceptualising their world. The actual practices, however, are very different.

2. Content

High/Scope formulates over 50 'Key Experiences' which include curriculum topics such as language, but which specially emphasise mathematical and logical concepts. These Key Experiences provide the mental framework for the adult educators, who aim to ensure that the 'experiences' become a reality, whereas for the children the content will appear like a play environment with traditional activities such as a home corner, painting, construction, and so forth.

Unique structured equipment is at the heart of the Montessori method. Didactic, self-correcting materials such as stacking bricks and interlocking shapes, or sensory activities in the form of matching sounds, are worked through *independently* by each child. The sequence is carefully controlled, each stage increasing in difficulty. Children's learning about the real world is also given priority. They are expected to become independent and self-sufficient, and acquire physical skills such as pouring, lacing and polishing. Montessori's belief that purely imaginative play was an escape into fantasy, and hence 'childish', led to its exclusion far as possible.

In the Reggio approach the content takes the form of themes or projects with the aim of engaging deeply in fundamental conceptual ideas. The children explore their topic in depth, asking questions, forming hypotheses, and using such forms of representation as drawing, painting, model-making, tape-recording, photography and computers to document the stages of the project. The visual and written record is then available to everyone, including parents, and serves as a form of reflection and evaluation for children and staff. A further contrast with the other two approaches is the employment of practising artists in all the schools to work with the children.

3. Structures

The word structures here means organisation of time, people, space and materials. In all three curricula the materials needed for play, construction and art work are easily available and accessible to the children. As a general rule, children will be expected to select independently whatever is necessary for the task in hand. The time dimension in a High/Scope session is most clearly structured using the format of 'Plan, Do, Review'. On arrival each child tells an adult what they propose to do in the session, then carries out the plan (which might be 'to play at mummies and daddies in the home corner') and finally in a small group talks about it. Other small-group activities give children opportunities for skill development or storytime.

In a Montessori session the self-correcting equipment represents the highly structured element. Children use it at their own pace, the assumption being that they will select the material which is at the stage they are ready for, and move on when proficient to the next piece of equipment.

In the Reggio approach the time allowed is notably as long as necessary for the task in hand; a project might last a day, a week, or a year. Children work in small groups with a teacher or an artist, often developing themes that show the school as linked into the wider community, as for example in collaboration with local carpenters in the making of a new table (Reggio Children, 1997). Although the High/Scope and Montessori methods also pay great attention to the layout of space, with materials attractively available, the Reggio approach explicitly states that the environment is another teacher. Consequently the architectural design of buildings and internal areas has been given high priority (Reggio Children, 1998).

4. Adult roles

This dimension may be the most significant element affecting children's experience. Commitment to the educational philosophy involved, as well as engaged enthusiasm and sense of self-esteem, are usually evident among practitioners in all these three ways of working, and in both High/Scope and the Reggio approach team-work is vital.

High/Scope teachers aim to foster problem-solving and encourage the children to take responsibility. At the start of the session the teacher listens to the children's choice and then, while they are engaged in their play, continues to pose thought-provoking questions or make suggestions. The session concludes with a small-group, adult-led review of the activities just engaged in.

Montessori staff have a very distinctive prescribed role. The key is the prepared classroom. The teacher selects and organises equipment according to the Montessori method, making it available and attractive before the children's arrival. The teacher's role, once the children are in action, is then passive: to stand back and give the minimum assistance, talk as little as possible and intervene only when really necessary.

In a Reggio classroom the adult role is diverse, but more egalitarian than in the other approaches. Planning is a co-operative experience without hierarchies. Children, artists, teachers and parents take part on an equal footing. Essentially the adults are expected to challenge the children intellectually, to make them visualise what *might or might not happen*, and to hypothesise generally. The focus is on children's thinking, with teachers acting as prompters, facilitators and recorders, creating documentation of the whole learning cycle.

A curriculum for babies

Babies are a special case, and the issue of their day care is now receiving more attention. In the USA the influential *Carnegie Report* (Carnegie Corporation of New York, 1994) highlighted research about the high susceptibility of the brain in the first year to environmental hazards of all kinds including the psychological stresses of parents. Among the recommendations was the provision of good quality day care for babies as well as support for parents (Phillips, 1995).

The microsystem for babies, whether they are in a home or centre-based setting, presents the same essential elements as for older preschool children. If the adults believe that all that is required is safety, cleanliness, warmth and food, important as these are, a baby is being denied the rights for development as a thinking, friendly, communicating individual. The foundations for early learning in *Quality and Diversity in Early Learning* might be used as a starting point (applicable to older children too): Belonging and Connecting, Being and Becoming, Contributing and Participating, Being Active and Expressing, and Thinking, Imagining and Understanding (Early Childhood Education Forum, 1998, p11–16).

In addition to this theoretical framework a few practical points need to be added. Current legislation says nothing about the quality of the environment, yet bright demanding colours are over-used, and noisy echoing large rooms or small cramped spaces are all too common (Penn, 1996). The structure of the environment should also take into account the number of babies in the space. A maximum of six is now recommended, with an adult: baby ratio of 1:3 to reduce the noise and anxiety created by crying (Penn, 1997). Human relationships are centrally important, not merely between the baby and her 'key person', but equally with other babies. The degree of communication between infants has been much underestimated, but its strength and potential is clearly shown in a recent training video and accompanying text (Goldschmied & Selleck, 1996). Similarly other chapters in the present book emphasise the early competence of babies, reinforce our understanding and thus encourage us to think seriously and positively about their strengths.

Concerns for the future

After years of stagnation, governmental policies for young children are at last bringing about a quiet revolution. An effort is being made to create unstigmatised services offering free half-time nursery places for all children over three whose parents want them, though parents still have to pay for the rest of the day. Centralised control of education and care for children from birth, with inspection made the responsibility of the Department for Education and Employment, carries both risks and potential. And while such exciting innovations as the Centres of Excellence and Sure Start are making progress in targeted areas, problems nevertheless remain.

The quality of services across the country will inevitably continue for some time to be seriously uneven, especially in terms of buildings and staffing. Many preschools (previously playgroups) struggle in inconvenient, unsuitable buildings with multiple users. Still more important, staff training has up to now been so varied and often inadequate that the quality of pedagogy which children will encounter is at present unacceptably diverse. Moreover, staff will be required to work effectively with all children, including children at risk or those with special needs, with their parents too and with other professionals in the community. The challenging and complex preschool stage demands high levels of professionalism but so far government plans for raising the standard of educational qualifications, both at initial and in-service levels, are quite inadequate for early childhood services that do justice to this foundational period.

Chapter 9

Child Agency and Primary Schooling*

Andrew Pollard

Introduction

In this chapter there are two major themes. The first concerns the 'agency' of primary school age children – their capacity to interpret experience and to act. The second relates to the structures of the schooling system, in particular the National Curriculum and assessment, that shape the experience of children as 'pupils'. Seen more analytically, we have the 'identity' and 'self' of the child, and the school context and educational challenges to which they must respond. How do children cope?

This approach reflects two central tenets of the new sociology of childhood. For instance, Corsaro (1997) proposes that children are 'active agents who construct their own cultures', and that childhood is a structural form or part of society – the nature and conception of which varies historically. This is in stark contrast to some previous approaches that have positioned children as being deficient, passive and dependent for psycho-biological reasons, or as being in need of socialisation and induction into the norms of mature, responsible, adult society. Nor can we treat 'childhood' as being homogeneous, for there are many childhoods in our complex, multi-dimensional society. However, whilst the concept of childhood denotes a particular period of developmental time for each individual, it is also a manifestation of the expectations and arrangements that family, community or nation adopt. These take cultural forms, as reflected in the media and social relationships, and structural forms, as illustrated by national educational requirements.

I will be particularly concerned with children as 'pupils', with the ways in which new features of the national educational system are beginning to define and impact on childhood, and with children's responses.

*I would like to acknowledge, with thanks, Cassell's permission to reproduce and edit some material from Pollard, A. (1996) *Reflective Teaching in the Primary School* and from Pollard, A. & Filer, A. (1999) *The Social World of Pupil Careers*. I am also grateful to the editors for their comments on a draft of this chapter.

The agency of children in their childhoods

As we have seen, it is a fundamental precept of the new sociology of childhood that children should be seen as active, thinking, rational individuals (James & Prout, 1990). As Mayall (1996b, p2) puts it: 'the standpoint is to conceptualise children as agents, with specific views on the institutions and adult groups they interact with'. Thus we appreciate that each of the four million primary school pupils in the UK has a unique 'biography', and the ways in which they feel about themselves, and present themselves in school, will be influenced by their previous cultural, social and material experience. Factors, such as gender, social class, race, language development, learning styles, health and types of parental support, are so numerous and so complex in their effects that, although broad generalisations about patterns of advantage and disadvantage can be made, it is foolish to generalise in specific terms about their ultimate consequences.

As an example of child agency, let us consider the perspective of Harriet regarding her primary school. Harriet came from a middle-class family and was rather bored by her formal education, and tended to disengage with it. However, she had a strong sense of humour and a divergent imagination, which was fostered through her relationship with her 'best friend', Hazel. In Year 3, as 7–8 year olds, they enjoyed imaginative playground games as an alternative to schoolwork – and they described an example of this to my colleague Ann Filer:

AF	What do you like playing in the playground?
Hazel	We like to play Dragons and Unicorns.
Harriet	And back fights. You sit with backs together and push against one another.
Hazel	Play fights. You jump over each other like a tiger does.
Harriet	We like cute wasps and bees.

[The children tell of finding and naming snails and children from another class stepping on 'their' snails. They recognised the pattern on the shells they said, so they know it was theirs.]

(Friendship group interview, July 1991, Year 3)

These activities were looked upon with a mixture of amusement and amazement by their more conventional peers, but for Harriet and her friend they were an independent source of enjoyment.

Two years later, Harriet had formed quite critical views of some of the other children, regarding them as 'pratts' and 'snobs'. As she put it:

AF	How are some (children) snobs?
Harriet	They say 'I'm better than you' (. . .) Showing off. Their hair, their body. Like this [Harriet flicks her hair]. Sally Gordon always tries to make her hair curly and nice for all the boys in school.
AF	Do others show off their hair?
Hazel	Mary and Sarah and all that group.
Harriet	[Harriet demonstrates how Sally walks to 'show off' her body].

Hazel   And they like to make themselves all tidy with shiny shoes and little squeaky voices.
AF   So your group is different.
Harriet   Yes. We're normal.
Hazel   No, we're not normal. Some people say we're crazy. They bring in Barbie books and dolls and trolls.
Harriet   And silly little pencils with trolls on and Barbie pencil cases.
AF   So you don't go in for that sort of thing.
Hazel   No. I just use any pencil that works.

(Friendship group interview, January 1993, Year 5)

In this conversation, the two girls distinguished themselves from the mainstream girls' friendship groups and the stereotypical body and style consciousness endorsed by the majority of girls at the school. Harriet, moreover, did something similar in relation to her classroom identity and in opposition to the competitive 'goodness' that characterised the strategies of the larger and more conventional girls' group.

AF   Can you tell me how you think some children get to do well in school?
Harriet   By being teacher's pet. Someone like Sally Gordon. Gets everything right.
AF   Do the friends that children have make a difference to how well they do in school?
Harriet   Well Mary and Sally, they are two people who really suck up to each other but if Mary gets ahead, Sally will rush to finish to get with her. Sally might say 'Well it wasn't me that did that picture' if it wasn't good, 'it was Mary', because she doesn't want to get told off.

(Pupil interview, June 1993, Year 5)

By Year 6, Harriet was bored and unhappy at school and did not like her teacher. She explained her general position to Ann Filer, and became quite animated at the thought of her teacher being promoted.

AF   What can you tell me about Year 6, Harriet?
Harriet   I don't like it.
AF   Why's that?
Harriet   It's boring. Work's too hard.
AF   You've been managing well, haven't you?
Harriet   Yes, but I don't like it. I don't like Mrs Chard.
AF   She likes you.
Harriet   I don't think so.
AF   I think she's got quite a soft spot for you.
Harriet   (No response)
AF   She's going to be a head teacher, isn't she.
Harriet   Oh gawd! I'm glad I'm not going to be in her school. No one will like her except the girlie girls (. . .) She thinks I'm a pain in the neck 'cos she keeps calling me one. My chatting.
(. . .)
Harriet   This is the worst year. And Mr Brown's class and Miss Scott's.
AF   What were the best bits?
Harriet   When I ran away from school but it wasn't good when Mrs Davison came to pick me up. I thought I was going home to lunch and Mum wasn't there so I went on my own and I thought this is great because no-one can find me and pick me up and I hid in the garden. It's in my file. (She laughs) I expect it will be reported to Halberton (Grammar School) that I might run away.

AF   Were there any good years?

Harriet Miss George's, Miss King's, Miss French's. I liked the teachers and they liked me.

(Pupil interview, June 1994, Year 6)

These snippets from the story of Harriet's pupil career, recounted in full detail over the seven years of her primary schooling in Pollard & Filer (1999), provide just a brief glimpse of her perspective, her strategic thinking and her actions. In a nutshell, though influenced by the expectations and pressures of her family, peers and teachers, Harriet formed her own opinions, with the particular support of her best friend. She provides an example of the agency of all children – though not all children express themselves so vividly. Indeed, child agency is manifested in many ways and this is a reflection of the diversity of the challenges and situations that children face in the modern world. We cannot forget that poverty and financial insecurity grew considerably in the 1980s and 1990s and the family circumstances in which children develop are becoming increasingly diverse. There are thus many childhoods being experienced simultaneously as young people engage with the world they find around them. There is also considerable risk and uncertainty in modern circumstances – but children do have views about these events, situations and dilemmas which they experience. They have rights and take actions which both respond and contribute to situations – thereby, they express their agency.

Blyth (1984) has offered a simple but powerful model of children's learning which generalises across the diversity of children's lives. It occurs through the interaction of children's own development and experience. This interaction is basic to survival and has, Blyth argues, underpinned human development for millions of years. In this scenario, modern forms of curriculum and schooling are seen as society's 'planned interventions' into this fundamental process. They are the social constructions and products of a particular historical period and set of social, economic, cultural and political circumstances and decisions. They reflect particular perceptions of children and of childhood, and also values and priorities for the future – 'the ways things are, and what they ought to be'.

An interesting feature of this analysis is that, when considering learning at the basic level of the interaction of development and experience, the child is clearly and inherently seen as being active. Progressively, as he or she develops, the child must make sense of new experiences, and in so doing will also contribute to the experiences of others. It is only when the socially created 'planned intervention' of curriculum and schooling is introduced that the child is repositioned as 'pupil' and becomes viewed, in terms of the education system, as deficient. We may conclude that children have their own integrity and agency, but that children's interactions within the family or in school settings are likely to be powerfully structured by wider adult understandings of what they should, or should not, do.

These ideas have been explored further though the Identity and

Learning Programme, a detailed, longitudinal study of social influences on the learning of 19 children as they progress through 12 years of schooling (from age four to 16) (Pollard & Filer, 1996; 1999). Analysis of classroom teaching/learning episodes has been complemented by study of the influences of the parents and siblings, schools and successive teachers, and of friendships, peers, youth, media and techno-cultures. Narrative case studies of pupils' learning over time show the enormous complexity of intellectual, affective, pedagogic, social, cultural and linguistic factors involved in pupil learning.

In *The Social World of Children's Learning* (1996) and *The Social World of Pupil Careers* (1999), Ann Filer and I have told the stories of children growing up through successive cycles of experience which spiral on and on through life. We have represented the factors which affect children in Figure 9.1.

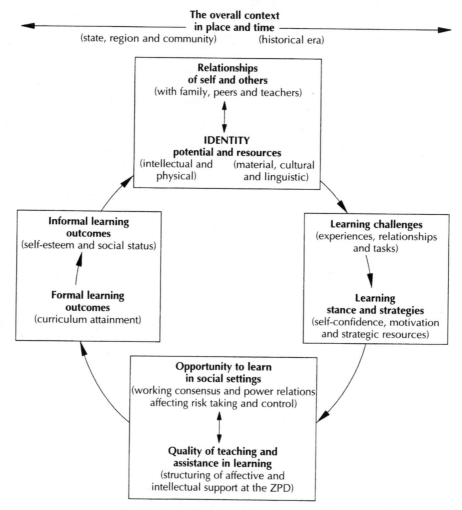

Fig. 9.1 A model of learning, identity and social setting.

The overall socio-historical context in place and time is crucial since it denotes the wider economic, political, social and cultural factors within which childhood is set. It is then posited that child identity is a product of relationships between the self and significant others, as mediated by intellectual and physical potential, and by material, cultural and linguistic resources. In other words, 'self identity' makes personal sense of, and embodies, social relationships, capabilities, opportunities and experiences. Given this foundation, children engage with new learning challenges, and do so with varying degrees of self-confidence, motivation and strategic resources. They are active. In the classroom setting, they face two major constraints. First, the 'opportunity to learn' relates to power relations and to the risks that are involved in learning. Is there a danger of humiliation if they get things wrong? Are there opportunities for experimentation? Is the teacher supportive, appreciative and fair? Second, there are concerns about the quality of teaching. Are clear tasks set and appropriate explanations offered? Is support provided at appropriate points, particularly when the understanding of children needs to be extended beyond their previous capabilities?

These classroom factors hinge on the relationship between teachers and pupils. A 'working consensus' represents recognition of the needs, rights, activity and dignity of the other (Pollard, 1985). The self of each party is respected in what teachers often call a 'good relationship'. Crucially for pupils and their sense of fulfilment, this means that their right to appropriate agency is accepted, and they negotiate aspects of classroom life that are important for them. The academic outcomes of such classroom processes are found in the form of curriculum attainments, perhaps in English, maths or science, but there are other informal learning outcomes too. These take the form of reinforced or undermined self-esteem and social status, which in turn roll forward to inform each child's sense of identity.

This model highlights the way in which identity and self-confidence affect each child's engagement with learning. Classroom performance is, in these terms, as much a product of the child's learning disposition and of social factors as it is the result of effective instruction. Indeed, we believe that the two sets of factors are inextricably linked together: the child and the teacher; the learner and the curriculum; emotion and cognition; the social context and the instructional context.

Extrapolated over time, we see a spiralling process as each child engages with successive teachers. The agency of the children is expressed in the term 'strategic biography' which maps their social and academic careers through school life.

But what exactly is the nature of the 'planned intervention' of the National Curriculum that our particular society has decided to introduce? Universal elementary education goes back to the Forster's Education Act of 1870 and has been through many manifestations since. However, the 1990s saw an exceptional period of curricular prescription and ancillary requirements. These are the result of critique, discussion, political lobbying, media comment, committees, Parliamentary debates, ministerial decisions and the implementation plans of numerous government agencies and schools. The National Curriculum is a social construction – it is our society's intervention in the fundamental interaction between children's development and their experience.

The National Curriculum and assessment system

The National Curriculum and its assessment system are undoubtedly the most significant developments in educational provision in recent years. I consider them in some depth here, because they now impose a fundamental framework around the school lives of young children.

In 1988, for the first time, the UK Parliament set out aims for educational provision in state-maintained schools. The Education Reform Act stated that the curriculum must be:

> 'balanced and broadly based; promote the spiritual, moral, cultural, mental and physical development of pupils at the school and of society; and prepare pupils for the opportunities, responsibilities and experiences of adult life.'

A clear structure for the education system in England and Wales was introduced and Figure 9.2 clarifies the relationship between 'key stage', 'pupil year' and pupil age. It also indicates the way in which assessment takes place at the end of each key stage. The extension of the primary years into those of secondary education is included because a key aspect of the National Curriculum is the expectation of continuity in the learning experiences provided between schools at transfer points.

In England, the Education Reform Act established ten subjects as the basis of the National Curriculum for children aged between five and 11, and it also required that pupils should receive appropriate religious

Age of pupils	Pupil year	Key stage	School	Assessment
5 or under 6 7	Reception Year 1 Year 2	Key stage 1	Infant school	 At age 7
8 9 10 11	Year 3 Year 4 Year 5 Year 6	Key stage 2	Junior school	 At age 11
12 13 14	Year 7 Year 8 Year 9	Key stage 3	Secondary school	 At age 14
15 16	Year 10 Year 11	Key stage 4	Secondary school	 At age 16

Fig. 9.2 Age of pupil, school year and key stage.

education. In Wales, Welsh provided an additional subject and in secondary education, pupils must also study a foreign language. Scotland and Northern Ireland have related, but independent and significantly different, structures.

The foundation subjects of the National Curriculum are thought to cover the range of knowledge, skills and understanding commonly accepted as necessary for a broad and balanced curriculum for individual pupils. Of these foundation subjects, English, mathematics and science are also identified as core subjects, without knowledge of which it is thought other learning cannot take place effectively. Indeed, competence in language, numeracy and scientific method has been regarded as being necessary throughout the curriculum and in all aspects of adult life. The other foundation subjects are now design and technology, information and communication technology, history, geography, art and design, music, physical education and Welsh, in non-Welsh-speaking schools in Wales. Additionally religious education remains a statutory requirement.

The National Curriculum is supported by a statutory framework of 'subject orders' which set out 'common requirements', 'programmes of study' and 'attainment targets'. Further, pupil attainment for each attainment target is described by 'levels of attainment'.

Common requirements apply to each of the 'subject orders'. They cover issues such as access to the curriculum for all pupils, the use of spoken and written language (including grammatically correct sentences and correct spelling and punctuation), provision of opportunities to use information technology and, in Wales, opportunities to apply knowledge and understanding of Wales.

Programmes of study set out essential knowledge, skills and processes which need to be covered in each subject by pupils in each stage of schooling. These are minimum statutory entitlements. Programmes of study are intended to be used by schools in constructing schemes of work.

Levels of attainment identify points of knowledge, skill and understanding for each subject, against which pupil attainment can be assessed. Most pupils are expected to reach Level 2 at the age of seven, and Level 4 at the age of 11.

Attainment targets are defined from within programmes of study to represent the knowledge, skills and understanding which pupils are expected to master as they progress through school. Attainment targets are used in assessment procedures.

Level descriptions indicate the type, quality and range of work which a child 'characteristically should demonstrate' in a subject to be deemed to have reached a particular level.

Religious education has particular status and the Standing Advisory Council on Religious Education (SACRE), made up of representatives of local faiths in each education area, advises on the content of religious education and collective worship. The 'agreed syllabus' that they produce must be 'in the main Christian' whilst 'taking account of the other principal religions of the UK'.

The content and goals of the curriculum are thus very precisely described and teachers and schools within the state-maintained system have only limited scope for interpretation and use of professional judgement. Children attending mainstream schools in England and Wales therefore now experience a relatively standard curriculum, wherever they live.

Assessment has also become more and more important in primary education. This has occurred for two reasons. The first, and by far the most significant, has been the concern of successive governments to introduce ways of 'measuring' educational outputs. This has been seen as a means of informing parents about the progress of their children and as a way of comparing school performance. Such output assessment data are known as 'summative', and the 'SAT' tests which children take at the age of seven and 11 are of this type. The results of these tests must be reported to parents and are often published in the form of league tables.

The second reason for the growth of assessment derives from teachers, who have increasingly come to realise the value of more continuous assessment in informing the process of their teaching. Thus, as a course of study or a lesson progresses, a teacher gathers evidence of pupil responses and adjusts the learning programme to meet pupil needs. Teachers are thus able to engage more directly and accurately with the development of the learner's thinking and understanding. Process assessment data of the sort required by these processes are known as 'formative'.

The basic difference in the aims of summative and formative assessment produces serious tensions – for instance, comparison versus support, product versus process, government versus professional control. Many assessment experts suggest that the effectiveness of one form of assessment is likely to undermine the effectiveness of the other (Harlen *et al.*, 1992). In particular, when summative testing is emphasised, there is a tendency for teaching to be narrowly directed towards whatever the tests measure. A broad and balanced curriculum is thus distorted (e.g. Gipps, 1990; Broadfoot *et al.*, 1991), and this is a serious concern in relation to the primary school curriculum which is becoming increasingly focused on basic skills.

Since 1997 and the election of a Labour government, there has been a particular emphasis on the development of literacy and numeracy within the National Curriculum. Highly structured programmes have been introduced across all schools in the form of the 'Literacy Hour' and 'Numeracy Hour', whilst there has been some relaxation of expectations in relation to coverage of the content of other curriculum areas. From September 2000 the results of a curriculum review will begin to be implemented. This established a new rationale for the National Curriculum and reinforced the importance of basic skills in numeracy, literacy, information and communication technologies, citizenship and personal and social education, whilst the arts and humanities inevitably receive less prominence.

There are a number of advantages which a national curriculum provides in support of children's learning. For instance, aims and objectives for each stage of children's education are clearly stated and these provide a helpful clarification of what both children and teachers are expected to do. After all, research has consistently shown that the lack of clarity in teaching and learning aims is a very significant inhibitor on pupil progress. Second, parents have the opportunity to know and understand what is being taught and may be able to support their children more effectively. Third, curriculum continuity can be provided between schools, and curriculum progression can be ensured both from class to class and on transfer between schools. These are very significant advantages compared with the uncoordinated provision of the past.

However, despite these structural clarifications, there is a fundamental problem in realising the educational potential of children. How can a specified curriculum, at one and the same time, address national concerns and set out a national framework for curriculum content and progression whilst also remaining flexible enough to draw on the particular interests, experiences, learning styles and physical and intellectual capabilities of individual children?

The truth, of course, is that no national curriculum can meet these objectives equally effectively. There has to be a trade-off – and children are inevitably on the receiving end of whatever decisions are taken. In the case of the National Curriculum, the prescriptive approach that has been established by successive governments may have a number of weaknesses concerning the psychology of learning. First, the specification of subject matter may, or may not, articulate with children's previous experiences or interests, so motivation may be compromised. This has enormous significance for the development of positive dispositions to learn and the notion of 'lifelong learning'. Second, the curriculum may be over-specified. For instance, psychologists such as Bruner (1977) point out that children can learn most things at most ages if they are taught in an appropriate and meaningful way. Some children thus experience and become interested in things which the National Curriculum does not anticipate – and teachers may not be able to follow up those interests. Third, we now know that children do not often learn in a simple, linear way, with a step-by-step progression as some behaviourist psychology might have had us believe. Perhaps learning may be better represented by a spiral model, where children meet a concept, fact or skill and then encounter it again later when they develop their understanding further. Indeed, Vygotskian learning theorists suggest that children learn most effectively when they are able to 'make sense' of some experience, particularly when they are supported by more experienced or knowledgeable teachers, parents or peers (Tharp & Gallimore, 1988). Fourth, the increasing emphasis on assessment outcomes affects children and their approach to learning. There is evidence that young children are becoming increasingly instrumental – seeking merely to get high scores rather than to develop deeper understanding (Pollard & Triggs, 2000). This could undermine the development of a positive self-identity as a learner and of 'learning mastery' (Dweck, 1986). Clearly such psychological processes have serious implications when considering the consequences of the National Curriculum.

An over-prescribed curriculum can thus have unintended consequences regarding children's learning. However, primary school teachers are well aware of this, and it is not generally the case that the National Curriculum has caused a reversion to 'old fashioned', didactic teaching methods. It is recognised, however, that tapping children's interests and imagination in the context of the National Curriculum requires particular skill and empathy from teachers. The challenge is to be able to motivate children with subject knowledge itself, and a great deal of attention is now being paid to developing more effective ways of teaching.

Many teachers aspire to build, progressively, from children's existing knowledge, understanding and skill and then to use formative assessment to judge how to support them further. An idealised model of 'good practice' has been developed (Pollard, 1996) which children may experience in primary schools in one form or another. It suggests that there may be five key stages of a teaching/learning session. First is 'orientation' – arousing children's interest and curiosity. Second is 'elicitation/structuring' – helping children to find out and clarify what they think. Third is 'intervention/restructuring' – encouraging children to test, develop, extend their ideas or skills. Fourth is 'review' – helping children to evaluate the significance of what they have done. Finally, 'application' – helping children to relate what they have learned to their everyday lives.

Skilful teaching of this sort is increasingly understood in primary schools, and is a far cry from the 'chalk and talk', transmission models of the past, in which children were expected to be entirely passive and simply 'read, mark and learn' the material presented to them. Indeed, for those with a wholehearted understanding of children's capabilities, it is possible to take the process even further by involving children more actively in the teaching-learning process. One excellent approach is through 'pupil self-assessment'. This is a process through which children learn to monitor and evaluate their own learning strategies and achievements. In psychological terms, self-assessment contributes to processes of 'meta-cognition' – the key capacity of being able to stand back from a learning experience and to make an open, personal evaluation so that future actions can be adjusted. This is, as Vygotsky (1978) put it, a form of 'self-regulation' and for pupils it heralds the development of independence as external support for learning provided by teachers, parents and others becomes less necessary. Children may thus be encouraged to share aims and plan personal targets, to review and record their achievements, and to help report progress. The outcome of such processes of self-assessment cannot be assured but, even when the learning targets are very specific, pupils' sense of ownership of their learning progress tends to increase and they become more active learners as they see how they can achieve their personal objectives.

Coping with schooling

We have focused on the agency of primary school aged children, and seen how the new sociology of childhood can illuminate our understanding of this. It is perhaps ironic that, at the same time as this new emphasis has developed, the national educational system has become more prescriptive than at any other period in recent history. How then do children reconcile themselves to this new situation? How do they cope?

The first thing to be noted is that it is difficult to generalise, for there are considerable differences to be found among girls and boys, able and less able, working and middle class, north and south, black and white, etc. The actions and perspectives of children will reflect their socio-cultural influences and economic circumstances.

However, there are some characteristic strategies which essentially relate to the structural and cultural position of pupils and to their capabilities (Pollard, 1985; Pollard & Filer, 1999). Some children may decide that the easiest way to cope with school is to try to conform to teacher expectations. As long as the work is not too challenging, this is a very low-risk strategy – although there is a possibility of being labelled a 'keener', 'swot' or 'goodie' by peers. Teachers know that compliance can be obtained in this way and this fact may have enabled children to 'drift' through their schooling. However, with growing pressure to meet 'performance targets', teachers feel increasingly obliged to challenge pupils further. If children are confident and reasonably able, they may attempt to negotiate with their teacher so that work expectations are ameliorated. Ann Filer and I have called this strategy 'redefining' and it is often attempted by children who have a good relationship with their teachers.

For children who find it difficult to meet the demands of the National Curriculum and its assessment system, the situation may be hard. If they maintain their attempt to comply, they may suffer the indignity of receiving low assessment grades and being placed in low teaching sets or groups (for these are increasingly being used). On the other hand, if they become disruptive, they may graduate from minor reprimands towards more serious trouble. In recent years there has been a significant increase in pupil exclusions from primary schools – a phenomenon that was almost unheard of before the introduction of the National Curriculum. For instance, in 1995–6 the number of exclusions from primary schools in England increased by 18%, from 1400 to 1600. Of these, 95% were boys. Children from African-Caribbean families were also disproportionately represented and exclusion remains closely related to patterns of social disadvantage – poverty, homelessness, parental break-up or illness, and bereavement. There is evidence that the growth in exclusions is related to the increasing pressure on schools to 'perform' in published achievement 'league tables'. The Mental Health Foundation (1999, p31), for instance, notes that:

> 'the potentially negative impact of a narrowly focused academic definition of "raising standards" can be seen in recent research showing evidence of increasing pupil distress in primary school.... We believe that there is a pressing need to increase the emphasis of schools towards children's emotional well-being.'

It may be that the increased specification and control of National Curriculum requirements has introduced more pressure than some teachers and pupils can cope with.

One of the largest recent studies of the impact of the National Curriculum and assessment in the 1990s was the Primary Assessment, Curriculum and Experience (PACE) project (Pollard *et al.*, 1994; Pollard & Triggs, 2000). This focused on the primary school experience of a national sample of the first full cohort of pupils to have been taught through the National Curriculum. Their responses and behaviour in relation to curriculum, pedagogy and assessment were documented annually. In the first phase of the study the PACE team found that children were to a large extent being 'protected' from the effects of a reformed curriculum which their teachers saw as inappropriate and potentially damaging to centrally important teacher–pupil relationships. Teachers seemed to be 'mediating change' and, in particular, moderating the impact of the revised assessment procedures on their pupils. Much of what was reported then reflected the constants of classroom life, characterised by Jackson (1968) as 'crowds, praise, power'. As the children moved on into Key Stage 2 pupils seemed to be becoming progressively instrumental and concerned to satisfy the requirements of their teachers. Whilst the children were younger, they had placed high priority on being active in their classrooms; now they were concerned with being successful. There was a gradual tightening of the frame of classroom life, both in terms of the three basic dimensions of curriculum, pedagogy and assessment, and on the children's construction of themselves as learners.

Of course, children also have to cope with the 'hidden curriculum' of schooling. It consists of the many things that are 'picked up' during school activities but which are not a designated part of the official curriculum – the role and status of the teacher and of the learner; attitudes towards learning and to school; the ways boys or girls 'should' behave; differences 'because' of being black or white, middle class or working class. The hidden curriculum is implicit within routine school procedures and curriculum materials. It may be unrecognised and is often unexamined. Such implicit messages can have a profound effect on the self-image of children, upon their images of school and their attitudes to other social groups.

Children thus have to learn to cope and survive in classroom situations in which they may well feel insecure. Children's culture and the support of their peer group are considerable resources in this because they provide alternative arenas for activity, alternative sources of value and alternative judgements of worth. Thus a boy who is disaffected from his schoolwork may take pride from being the best footballer in the playground, and a girl who feels nervous about contributing in lessons may feel much more comfortable in the company of her friends. Self-esteem and social status thus have a quite different source for potential fulfilment and the official criteria of the school and adult world are challenged by the independent currency of children's own perspectives, criteria and priorities.

'Breaktime' is of particular importance in providing the major time and setting in which pupil culture develops, and a recent study by

Blatchford (1998) provides a good overview of its value. Children liked the opportunity to socialise with their friends, relax from work and play games. Breaktime games and children's friendships and social networks are closely interconnected and can be traced back to the attitudes and characteristic strategies that children adopt towards school work. However, more than this, the playground provides a setting with relatively light adult supervision which gives children scope to act spontaneously and independently. The defining characteristic of child culture, as Opie & Opie wrote (1959), is that it is the children's own – and playtime is rather similar. Thus, whilst teachers might characterise it in terms of enabling children to 'let off steam' and relax, there is actually a great deal more going on. It provides experiences that mirror those of adult society, enabling children to play out roles, relationships, activities, strategies, groups, laughter, tragedy, success, failure, conflicts, fights, alliances, resolutions, etc. These issues are engaged with in semi-autonomous ways – between the 'bells' and requirements that mark the school day, but with minimal adult supervision. The agency of children thus has more scope, and the construction of meaning is often more immediate and engaging to children than anything which may be facilitated by adults in classrooms or at home. Sometimes learning to be 'sensible', as defined by an adult, is not enough – and it is more important to have learned for oneself.

Unfortunately, there is pressure on the use of time in primary schools and there is some evidence that the length of breaktimes is reducing. For some children, this may bring some relief, for research suggests that around a quarter report being 'bullied' at some point in their primary school careers. This usually takes the form of name-calling, being hit, gestures, extortion or exclusion from a friendship group – and mostly takes place in playgrounds or on the journey between home and school. Involvement in occasional bullying is quite widespread, though boys are responsible for most of it, and girls very rarely bully boys. Children who are less able, who had special needs or who come from a minority ethnic group are particularly vulnerable.

Conclusion

In this chapter we have focused on the agency of children and on the demands of national educational structures. Both are of vital importance in education, for the goal is to harness the interests, energy and motivation of children as they are inducted into and contribute to the knowledge, norms and values of our society. This suggests that school education should be based on balanced consideration of teaching and curriculum and learning and learners. A simple way of expressing the key educational process is:

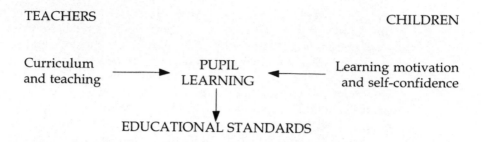

In the 1990s it appears that the drive for higher measured standards and 'performance' may have begun to create an imbalance. The education system has become increasingly organised and prescriptive, thus offering entitlements – but in so doing, it risks undermining motivation and failing to recognise diversity. This is not an easy dilemma to manage. However, whilst the media and politicians debate and prescribe on the issues, children experience the direct consequences whenever they take on the role of 'pupil'.

Chapter 10

Technologies and Environments: New Freedoms, New Constraints

Julie Selwyn

Each year millions of children die in the developing world through environmental causes, with malnutrition being the biggest killer (UNICEF, 1998). The vast majority of deaths are not caused by random acts of nature but because of political choices about how economies are managed. In any year there are at least 30 wars going on around the world. The UN estimates that between 1988 and 1996 two million children were killed in armed conflict and a further six million seriously injured. Many more were affected as family members were killed or injured or families became displaced and refugees. In the last 30 years, the distinction between civilians and soldiers has blurred and the number of civilian casualties has risen from 5% to 90%.

The UN has voiced concern that in recent wars such as in Bosnia and Rwanda, children have become the deliberate targets for military attack. The military have taken the view that the civilian population is quickly demoralised by losing its children and once dead there will be no future generation to seek revenge. Children in Northern Ireland have also suffered as a consequence of the 'troubles' (Cairns, 1996), and, as in other conflicts, they too became the target for acts of violence. A programme of research funded by the UN culminated in the Machel Report (1996) which made recommendations about the measures required to protect children and the actions needed to promote physical and psychological recovery after armed conflict. The report recognised that the effective implementation of the UN Convention on the Rights of the Child (United Nations, 1989) would go a long way towards protecting children.

Although this chapter generalises, it is important to keep in mind that each child's experience and perception of their own lives will be very different. Every child shares something called a 'childhood', but each child's experience of it is in some way unique. Children entering Britain as refugees, those born to traveller families, those in boarding schools, the victims of terrorism, or those homeless in B&B accommodation will all have different experiences. Other children in Britain may be working either in their parents' businesses or caring for siblings, allowing parents to work (Pettitt, 1998). Racism (Troyna & Hatcher, 1992), bullying and poverty detrimentally affect many children's lives.

This chapter will focus on children's lives in Britain, although we must remember that international events have an impact (e.g. such as pollution blown from Europe or decisions made by the European Commission). The chapter is divided into two main sections: outside and inside the home. We begin by examining the amount of freedom children have to move around their neighbourhoods and communities. The rise in car ownership has had one of the biggest impacts on children's lives in the last two decades. Parental fears for safety have restricted children's movements and this has delayed the development of certain skills and affected the making of friendships. Increasing traffic plays another role, creating pollution and adversely affecting health. The interconnections between increased traffic, pollution, lack of exercise, diet and health will be explored. The second section moves inside the home to look at children's use of the media and concerns expressed about the detrimental effect of TV, the newer media and advertising. This chapter highlights some of the contradictory influences in children's lives but children are also active participants and cope with the pressures by shaping their worlds in unexpected ways.

Outside the home

Despite some adult disapproval, Enid Blyton's books are as popular as ever. Her adventure stories with children playing away from home, solving mysteries, outwitting the baddies (adults) and returning home to bask in glory continue to enthral each generation of readers. Yet the environment which she describes, one where children 'played out,' spending hours away from adult supervision, largely disappeared during the 1970s. Hillman *et al.'s* (1990) two surveys demonstrated a continuing decline in children's unsupervised activities and in the extent of their independence. The proportion of 7–8 year olds going to school on their own fell dramatically from 80% in 1970 to 9% in 1990. Parents explained that fear of traffic accidents was the primary reason for curtailing freedom. In the 1990s, 'stranger danger' became a major concern for parents. Yet out of 20 million children in Britain, ten are murdered by strangers each year; a figure unchanged in the last twenty-five years (Lindon, 1999).

Freedom of movement for girls and boys has been curtailed as fears of paedophiles and abusers have swept the nation. Adults increasingly monitor children in Western societies. The publicity material for a surveillance system to stop children wandering too far from crèches at 'Tesco Extra' sells itself by claiming 'it can monitor kids as well as merchandise' (Bright, 1999). Children also internalise this fear and in effect adopt a self-imposed curfew (Davis & Jones, 1997). On their own outside the home, children are often perceived as being up to no good and potential troublemakers (Ward, 1978) or at risk and neglected by their parents. One of the contradictions in children's lives is how air travel has opened up the world but fears of traffic and strangers have closed immediate neighbourhoods and communities. The opportunity to travel has allowed many children to visit and see other countries and for others (e.g. some

Asian children) to stay in regular contact with relatives. It is ironic that with this greater freedom has come such a loss of freedom at home.

'Responsible parents' do not take risks with their children's safety and escort children everywhere. Lindon (1999) argues that society has developed 'the precautionary principle' where the adult obsession with risk drives them to remove every possible source of danger. This may be doing more harm than good by preventing children working out their own strategies to deal with difficulties. Lack of experience in being on one's own leaves children unprepared and perhaps lacking the resilience to cope in the adult world. Hillman (1993) has expressed concern that such a situation has been allowed to develop with so little comment on the consequences for children's development. Drawing on research evidence, he states that an important element of children's maturation is an environment which enables children to have opportunities to take initiatives, develop a sense of adventure, exercise body and mind and develop social and emotional coping skills *whilst on their own*. The restrictions placed on children's freedom to move around independently affect all these areas of development.

Garbarino (1992) sees the neighbourhood as a place for exploration, social interaction and the setting for the physical and emotional development of the child. He refers to the neighbourhood in which a child lives as the 'child's turf'. At first, the 'turf' extends not much beyond the front door but gradually as the child develops, the turf widens to encompass more of the neighbourhood. Children's relationship with their neighbourhood changes during the early years. Initially it is explored with parents but from about the age of six, children state they prefer being with their best friend playing outside; what Moore (1986) calls ' the best friends duet'. Wheway & Millward's (1997) survey of primary-aged children found that children liked to 'hang about', meeting up with friends in a spontaneous way in their home area, often using the street as the place to congregate. In a study comparing four different types of neighbourhoods, Berg & Madrich (1980) asked four-year-olds what they wanted from their neighbourhood. All the children were very concerned that they should be able to meet and make friends, but only in some neighbourhoods was this able to happen. Children wanted 'to hang about' seemingly doing 'nothing' in their neighbourhoods. This provided them with the opportunity to explore, interact with peers, and play favourite games. Children like to climb trees, build dens, swing, and slide but there are fewer opportunities for children to interact with their environment.

Studies (Southworth, 1993) have shown that children's most valued places are rivers and lakes or small pockets of nature in urban environments even when they have little experience of them. Moore (1986) believes that interactions with nature are important for child development but this is difficult to evidence. We do know that some environments provide richer opportunities for physical and fantasy play than others but the presence of nature may be more than just aesthetic. Spencer (1989) suggest that this may be important in understanding a child's sense of place, of rootedness to an area, of having an individual place in history and be linked to the development of identity and self. All humans have an innate capacity to appreciate nature and this is particularly true for children. Drawing on a range of material including autobiographies, Tuan (1978) notes how important childhood recollections of places and nature are to adults. He gives as an example the feeling of hugging a tree and being able to explore its branches; an experience not always possible in today's man-made play environments. Children need to experience the natural world to:

- Develop knowledge, e.g. awareness of the seasons, weather;
- Develop skills, e.g. of looking after plants, climbing, running;
- Shape attitudes towards the environment and the patterns evident in nature.

The patterns in nature are not only pleasing and beautiful but we are becoming more aware of the importance of patterns (fractals) in understanding our world. At the simplest level, fractals are irregular shapes that appear the same whatever the scale, e.g. snowflake. These patterns have influenced the development of new mathematical models such as chaos theory and can be seen repeated throughout the universe in cells, plants and weather patterns. Without access to the natural environment, children are less connected to nature and the whole biosphere.

Playgrounds

One of the responses to fears for children's safety has been to set aside specific outdoor spaces for children's play. Hillman (1993) argues that playgrounds should be called 'learning spaces' to emphasise the importance for children's development, but provision in Britain is very limited, with little regulation compared to other European countries. Facilities are particularly limited for disabled children, rural children and for those living on housing estates. New housing estates have often been built without any community facilities and this includes places for children. Instead, children are seen as a threat to the environment rather than being included in the planning of the spaces. The land set aside for playgrounds is often unwanted and attracts a very low financial subsidy. All too often, playgrounds are on a flat boring piece of land sometimes with fixed equipment such as rings or slides. Despite the adventure playground movement (Benjamin, 1992) playgrounds with little scope for imaginative play continue to be built. Frequently playgrounds are vandalised, badly littered or fouled by dogs (Titman, 1991).

Children are escorted to playgrounds and are watched by their carers so that children's opportunities for privacy and exploration are severely limited. Over 20 years ago Altman & Wohlwill (1978) commented that there was a lack of academic interest in the concept of privacy and children. Studies that have been done (Wolfe in Altman & Wohlwill, 1978) found that although the meaning of the word privacy changed with age, all children, whatever their culture, attached importance to having some privacy. This area of children's lives continues to receive little attention in the literature. Recently large indoor play areas have been developed. These have benefits in that parents can supervise in the warmth but offer children little opportunity for exploration and experimentation. Play is controlled with supervisors patrolling giving an illusion of security but these centres further segregate children both from the natural world and from adults. They are also expensive and exclude those without money or transport to get there.

Although the design of neighbourhoods may make it difficult for children to meet, children use spaces in imaginative ways. If one thinks of how teenagers use indoor shopping centres, sitting around or hanging over the rails to watch and catch the attention of their peers, younger children too use spaces in ways that are different from that intended. Our local park is designed with dense bushes around it, to keep the dogs out and the children in. Visit it at any time and there will be groups of children not on the play equipment but having 'adventures' in the bushes. The children act out dramas often based around 'baddies' and 'goodies' and in the process create some privacy for themselves.

Exercise and health

As we have seen, parents (whenever possible) escort their children and this has a major impact on children's freedom and is very expensive. During 1990, 1 356 000 hours were spent in Britain escorting children. The cost of this was estimated at £10–20 billion annually (Hillman, 1993). Car travel and the reduction in free play have also reduced the amount of exercise taken by children. The government's policy statement *Raising the Game* (Department of National Heritage, 1995) placed a firm emphasis on increasing the amount of sports in schools. It aimed to re-establish sports as 'one of the great pillars of education'. The report concentrated on developing competitive team sports and associated healthy exercise and vigorous sport. However, competitive sport is disliked by a sizeable number of children, particularly girls, and participation drops rapidly after leaving school (OPCS, 1995). Other organisations such as the World Health Organization stress the need for learning about incorporating regular exercise into daily life and most importantly generating an enthusiasm for exercise which will continue after education ends. Patterns of exercise are set in childhood and a number of studies have shown that as a nation we do not take enough exercise (Allied Dunbar National Fitness Survey, 1992). Only 1% of children in Britain cycle to school compared with 60% in the Netherlands and once at school British children take part in less physical activity than almost all their European counterparts (Armstrong & McManus, 1994). Sedentary children become sedentary adults, with increased risk of heart disease and other health problems.

Having a car can also be enabling, allowing families, for example, to visit relatives who may live some distance away. Not all children though have access to transport. Public transport is limited, particularly in council estates and rural areas, and there are access difficulties for disabled children. The government states that it is committed to reducing our dependence on the car and has begun to outline proposals for change. In the White Paper 'A New Deal for Transport: Better for Everyone' (1998), 'home zones' were one of the suggestions for improving the environment. These have been a feature of European neighbourhoods for more than 25 years. In Holland, for example, pedestrians and cyclists have legal priority over cars in home zones. In Britain, the idea is to give quiet residential streets back to the people who live in them by lowering speed limits, adding trees and plants and removing the distinction between the road and the pavement. The government is intending to evaluate six pilot schemes but critics believe the scheme does not go far enough. Councils are expected to fund these changes from within their own budgets and therefore the likelihood of change is limited. There are other schemes being evaluated such as 'safe routes to schools'. Changing our car-dominated culture is going to be very difficult when driving a car is seen as an expression of individual freedom.

Road traffic accidents are also one of the main causes of death (either as a passenger or a pedestrian in an accident) for children over the age of five. The Health of the Nation (Department of Health 1992), the national strategy for improving health, set a target of 33% reduction in child mortality from unintentional injury by the year 2005. Death rates have declined since 1985 for each of the leading causes of death (traffic accidents, fire and flames, suffocation and aspiration) but the decline is significantly lower for some children. For example, as we have seen, the number of miles cycled and walked has reduced and this explains the decline in pedestrian deaths but the rate of decline for children from poorer families has been much smaller. The injury rate for children in social class V is five times higher than that of children in social class I.

Inequalities in health are long standing. Evidence on social inequalities played an important part in the pressure to set up the welfare state. Subsequent reports (e.g. Whitehead, 1992; Acheson, 1998) have had a significant impact on the debate about the priorities in health and the links between poverty and ill health have become well established. Children living in households dependent on benefits often live in poor housing, are more likely to be ill, to have accidents inside and outside the home, to die younger and to have poor health as adults. Yet, the 1998 UN Human Development report ranked Britain as twelfth in the world in terms of income but with one of the highest levels of poverty in the developed world (Howarth et al., 1999). Children in poorer families are less likely to travel by car and therefore have to walk or cycle. They are the ones most likely to be in traffic accidents (Woodroffe et al., 1993). There are also gender differences in the mortality rate (depending on the cause of death), with boys more likely than girls to die from accidental death. For example, the ratio is 1:1 for traffic accidents but 5:1 for cycle deaths. The death rate continues to decline with the Health of the Nation target within reach. However, this has been achieved largely by the reduction of children's freedom of movement and ignoring inequalities.

DiGiuseppi and colleagues (1997) conclude that government targets will be met but as a nation, we are missing the point. There may be important societal costs by increasing future health problems due to, for example, lack of exercise and pollution and widening socio-economic disparities in child death rates.

One of the success stories in children's health over the last 30 years has been the reduction in acute diseases and in some cases eradication. There have also been dramatic improvements in the treatment of diseases such as cancer, with many more children now surviving. However, whilst the death rate has declined, the rate of chronic illnesses has increased. For example, diabetes in childhood:

- 2 in 10 000 in 1946
- 6 in 10 000 in 1956
- 12 in 10 000 in 1970
- 18 in 10 000 in 1997

There is a genetic component to this illness but that does not explain the increase. Asthma, autism and other illnesses also appear to be increasing. The cause of the apparent increase is hotly debated with pollution and diet implicated as important factors in changing patterns of health.

Diet

Although eating patterns differ across cultures, there are trends in consumption. Snacking is common, with children aged between one and eleven years obtaining approximately a third of all calories from snacks. Children eat less regularly, eat less as a family group, and more frequently in front of the TV set, either alone or with siblings or friends. Visits by children to fast food restaurants have increased and the food sold, burgers, pizza, etc., are typically high in saturated fats, cholesterol and calories. High calorie diets have been linked to increasing obesity in childhood and the risk of developing cancer as an adult (James et al., 1997). 'Children welcome' is a common sign outside many restaurants which appear in good food listings but even here, the assumption is that children's menus should contain only burgers, chicken nuggets and fish fingers. There is an assumption that children will not enjoy the experience of eating out and instead need to be entertained with crayons, clowns, etc., sometimes in their own segregated area. This is a very different view from that taken by most other European countries.

There is also a converse trend. Some parents through either religious, health or moral reasons adopt a vegetarian/vegan diet. Planned vegetarian diets are very healthy but there has been an increase in Vitamin D deficiency in vegetarian children and malnutrition in children whose high needs for energy exceed those of adults, commonly called 'muesli malnutrition' by the popular press. The health fears sparked by food scares have caused many parents to buy organic food. The majority of baby food now sold in this country is organic but at present the cost of buying the week's shopping is prohibitive except for the wealthiest families. Parents are concerned about the quality of food and the apparently increasing pollution.

Pollution

Children are far more vulnerable to pollutants than are adults for a number of reasons.

(a)   Children have a larger surface area in relation to their weight and have higher metabolic rates.

(b)   Children process calories and oxygen faster so that a resting child under three inhales twice as much air as a resting adult per unit of weight.

(c)   Children's bodies and organs are growing rapidly; they have little body fat to store pollutants and organs are sensitive to chemicals. Their height also means they are closer to the ground where concentration of some pollutants (e.g. from traffic) is greatest.

(d)   Children's habits and activities increase their exposure. Babies tend to put everything they pick up into their mouths and this increases the risk of hand to mouth contamination.

(e)   Poorer children are at greater risk as their bodies tend to be smaller and thinner and therefore their bodies find it more difficult to deal with pollutants. They are also more likely to be living near the busiest roads or in industrialised neighbourhoods.

(Adapted from Timberlake & Thomas, 1990)

There are a large number of pollutants in the environment and children come into regular contact with them. The following are some of the ways pollutants are absorbed into children's bodies.

Air

The air children breathe, particularly in urban environments, regularly exceeds international guidelines on safe levels of pollutants such as carbon monoxide, nitrogen oxide and ozone. To date, the link between air quality and the increase in asthma remains unproven but air quality does aggravate established respiratory problems and diseases. Asthma is now the most common chronic disease in childhood and it is estimated that one in seven children in Britain is affected (National Asthma Campaign, 1998). Passive smoking is the most important indoor air pollutant. Children whose parents smoke are two and a half times more likely to become smokers themselves (Charlton, 1996). The Royal College of Physicians (1992) has summarised the effects of passive smoking on children and concluded that parental smoking is responsible for 17000 hospital admissions per year of children under five. Children of smokers are more likely to suffer from respiratory diseases and as adults have a greater risk of lung disease and cancer. There are also other consequences such as absences from school due to smoking-related illness (e.g. coughs lasting longer) which has an adverse affect on children's educational attainment.

Water

The water children drink may contain lead and other pollutants such as nitrates caused by overuse of fertilisers and pesticides (Rosenbaum, 1993). There are no safe levels of lead in the environment as even small quantities affect cognitive development and lead has been linked to higher levels of aggression and hyperactivity (Timberlake & Thomas, 1990). In Britain, large numbers of homes have lead pipes. Although a Royal Commission in 1983 recommended the replacement of lead pipes there has been little progress, primarily due to householders having to bear the expense. Again, children from poorer homes are more likely to be drinking contaminated water.

Radiation

Radiation is always present in our environment, but the increase in electrical appliances and gadgets has also resulted in increased non-ionising radiation. Safety limits for these gadgets are unknown but their presence in the home has raised concerns for children's health. The Chernobyl disaster in 1986 resulted in more than 250 000 children in northern Britain exceeding the annual recommended level of radiation, placing them at increased risk of developing cancer. Other concerns have been the effect on children who live or play near overhead power cables. There is some evidence that they are linked with the development of cancer in childhood (Olsen et al., 1993).

The dumping of pollution is common on sites where children play, in rivers or on beaches where children swim. All children in Britain are exposed to pollution, but, for children living in poverty, their environment is one that is likely to reinforce their vulnerability. For the first time Friends of the Earth have linked pollution data with potential health threats and displayed the data on their Internet site (http://www.foe.-co.uk/factorywatch/). It shows that in 1996 10 000 tonnes of chemicals were released into the air by Britain's worst factories. Many of these factories are in areas where mortality and morbidity rates are higher than the rest of the country. The poor are often blamed for their own ill-health. The publication of pollution maps (*Observer*, 30/5/99) highlights the importance of understanding all the factors which contribute to significant inequalities in health and contribute to children's developmental pathways.

Inside the home

During the last 30 years, there have been significant improvements in children's homes. There is less overcrowding and most (but by no means all) families have access to hot water, an inside lavatory and bath. Parents fearful for their children's safety have been able to encourage children to play inside as smaller families and larger homes have created more space. Bedrooms are used for far more than sleep–they contain computers, game consoles, TVs, video recorders as well as toys. The use of bedrooms for play is often seen as representing the restrictions on children's freedom. If children are playing in the bedroom, parents know the children are 'safe' and can relax. Cunningham (1995) argues that what may seem to be a reduction in freedom has given girls more freedom to join in with the game culture. The move of games from arcades in the street to personal game machines in bedrooms has given girls the freedom to join in what was once a male preserve. Increasing number of girls are playing on games machines although there are gender differences in the types of games preferred.

Many children have easy access to information (through technology) although this too is determined by gender and class. In a survey of 1300 children aged 6–17, half of all six-year-olds had a TV in their room which was two or three times more likely than their European counterparts (Livingstone & Bovill, 2000). The survey revealed gender and class differences with boys twice as likely as girls to have a PC. Although working-class children had TVs and game machines only 2% had access to the Internet in comparison with 14% of the middle-class children. Access to the Internet is and will be of increasing importance but worldwide those who are poor, female or from an ethnic minority are likely to find themselves excluded (UN Human Development Report, 1998 at *www.un.org/esa/socdev/family*).

Is the media a harmful force in children's lives?

There are tensions around both old and new media. The 'effects' of TV and electronic games have dominated discussions about young children's use of the media. Generally TV has been seen as harmful, being blamed for making children fat, for the inability to read, for increasing violence, for brainwashing and corrupting innocent minds and most other social problems. Claiming harmful effects for the media is not new. Bazalgette & Buckingham (1995) note the earliest concern of this kind was probably voiced by Plato who wanted to ban the dramatic poets from his ideal republic on the grounds they would damage impressionable minds! The construction of the child in these debates holds childhood to be a time of innocence, a time not to be corrupted by an exploitative media. As we have seen in previous chapters, this view of childhood does not match the reality of many children's lives and fails to acknowledge that children are active participants within their own environments.

We know little about the way young children watch and use the media. We do know they use the media in very different ways and the uses and meanings they give seem to be determined by the context within which they are living. Cairns (1996) found that children living in Northern Ireland had found out and made use of a confidential telephone helpline from information they had gained from TV. In addition, 600 000 young children rang Childline within the first ten years it was in operation after publicity through various media (Childline, 1996). Children learn about their world from the TV and can put the knowledge to good use. A survey of British businessmen in 1989 found that the main reason for their growing concern over environmental issues was that their own children constantly reminded them about green issues and pollution (Timberlake & Thomas, 1990, p58).

There are other reasons for lack of research. First, young children comprise a specialist audience and children's programmes form a minor part of TV production. Second, preschool children are absent from rating figures which to a large extent determine programming. Third, information often comes from parents and may not be accurate. Some studies have used observation as the method to watch how young children view TV and this kind of research informed the makers of *Sesame Street*. We do know that babies begin to show limited sporadic attention to the TV before they are one and that children as young as one or two begin to imitate TV models. Between two and three years old there is an increase in the hours watched and attention paid to TV programmes. By three to five, the majority of children can watch TV quite attentively with boys and only children watching more than girls and siblings (Plomin *et al.*, 1990; Bazalgette & Buckingham, 1995).

Research, although culturally specific, suggests that the ability of children to understand the content of television programmes is strongly linked to cognitive development. Children build on skills already learnt. TV can add to these skills and influence physical behaviour, verbal communication and cognitive abilities. There have been concerns (Ward, 1997) that language is delayed in the homes of preschool children where the TV is on as background noise. However, Ward found that parents who played and talked with their children for as little as 20 minutes a day were able to reverse the effects of previously noted language delay. This would seem to demonstrate not the effects of TV on development but the importance of the quality of the relationship between the carer and the child.

Lealand (1998) studied the viewing patterns in New Zealand of 78 children under five. She found that many other activities were occurring whilst the television was on. Children ate, drank, slept, read, played with toys or siblings, drew, and talked to others, to themselves and to the TV. The most frequent activity was talking, with girls more likely than boys to talk back to the TV. Far less common were periods of intense silent attention. Yet this model of the hypnotised child dominates discussion of the TV.

Another concern is that children copy characters from their favourite TV shows. Children as young as four are able to recognise that cartoons are not real, but, as Hawkins (1995) noted, children do more than this. They watch cartoons, particularly those where the characters are human, and assess how the events depicted match their own view of the world. TV programmes provide children with the symbols they need to act out dramas. Examination of the use of stories by children (Bettelheim, 1978; Rustin & Rustin, 1987) highlights their importance in resolving unhappiness and loss. Bettelheim (1978, p5) was struck by the impact of stories on children with emotional and behavioural difficulties, even when the story had a violent content.

'For a story to truly hold the child's' attention, it must entertain him and arouse his curiosity. But to enrich his life it must stimulate his imagination: help him to develop his intellect and to clarify his emotions: be attuned to his anxieties and aspirations: give full recognition to his difficulties while at the same time suggesting solutions to the problems that perturb him.'

Rustin & Rustin (1987) argued that children are particularly interested in common story themes of separation or crises of conscience, when they are separating from their parents by entering school or joining group cultures and these aid identity formation.

Perhaps this is why children watch so many soaps. Surprisingly the majority audience for children's TV is the elderly and the unemployed (Bazalgette & Buckingham, 1995) whereas many children watch programmes thought of as adult entertainment. The award-winning Harry Potter book (Rowling, 1998) had to change its cover from bright primary colours to one more subdued, to prevent embarrassment of adult readers. Holland (1996) believes that the media are helping realign children's and adult's values, shaping and reflecting the boundary between childhood and adulthood. Many adults want to stay young for as long as possible. Children's TV is made by adults and may reflect adult wishes and desires far more than those of their audiences. Quality TV is important but whose definitions of quality should count? Children's, parents' or programmers'?

There are also contradictions in that children's TV has always had a space for children's voices. In the vanguard were *Blue Peter* and other programmes such as *Child's Eye* which demonstrated that children could interview politicians very effectively. These are examples of high quality children's TV programmes but old cartoons fill much of the schedules. Quality programmes are expensive to make. Barker (1989) questions the ubiquitous nature of US cartoons. Is their popularity because they speak to all children across cultural boundaries (the idea of children sharing a common culture) or is it due to lack of choice and clever marketing?

The 'effects' of the media are more complex than the polarised views often presented. Livingstone & Bovill's (2000) study of the use of leisure time of children reports that there is no evidence to support the moral panics about addiction to computer games or mindless watching of TV. However, 'effects' studies do not take an ecological view. We still do not know enough about how the context in which the child lives interacts with use of the media.

Are children important consumers?

Children have become consumers from a very early age, as every parent knows with the tyranny of the party bag. The children's market is a relatively recent development with the arrival of designer clothes and make-up targeted at the youngest children. Advertisers see children as having 'pester power'- the ability to persuade their parents to buy. Although when asked children demonstrate concern about the environment (Cullingford, 1994; Qualter *et al.*, 1995), they are also targeted by advertisers and encouraged to consume more and more. Warner (1989) claims it is the marketing man's dream to make every child an expensive child and there is considerable pressure on parents.

In 1990, Sega and Nintendo were virtually unheard of but by 1993 they had achieved market dominance and were in 60% of children's homes with 80% of all children playing regularly. It is a massive market and to put it into some kind of context, Nintendo makes more money than the whole of the American film industry (Cunningham, 1995). The success of games machines has led to films being made into games and cross-licensing of products, so that there are connections between toys, films, television programmes and games marketed at children. In the early 1980s, manufacturers began to target girls by introducing characters (e.g. My Little Pony, Care Bears) in a new type of TV programme. The belief was that girls would watch boys on TV but boys would not watch girls. Although the toy market had expanded rapidly, giving boys more complex and exciting construction toys, there was little available for girls. The new programmes did not have a strong story line but were made specifically to sell products to girls (see Seiter's (1995) feminist analysis of the attempts to ban this kind of programme). It is illuminating that those supporting programmes of this kind argued they were empowering as they enabled young children to be consumers and gave girls their own programmes. Is it empowering to be a consumer? Are these programmes an attempt by multi-nationals to link advertising, enjoyment and product purchasing in the minds of very young girls whom they see as future shoppers and housewives, adults who will turn to 'retail therapy' (shopping) to relax?

This recent targeting of girls as consumers may not be as straightforward as it seems. Children interact with their environment and the 'lifespan' of products is short. The Spice Girls offered girl power for a short period before their audience moved on and My Little Pony is no longer a 'must have'. Children use products in their own ways often not as the manufacturer intended. Perhaps the biggest effect is pressure on parents who see providing toys as a measure of their love for their children. For parents on low incomes this frequently means getting into debt and eating poorly themselves. Children living in poor families quickly learn to reduce their expectations, anxious about their families not having enough money. Shropshire & Middleton (1999) describe a process where children learn to be poor.

Conclusion

There are many contradictory forces within society that affect children's lives. Children can expect to live longer than any previous generation but the rate of chronic disease continues to increase. Children appear to be more welcomed in what were once adult-only environments (e.g. the pub) but are often segregated from adults once there, corralled into separate play areas. Children have a much wider range of activities and opportunities such as sporting holiday breaks and clubs, but only if their parents can afford to pay. Community facilities, such as libraries, are under threat of closure while expensive 'pay to play' areas continue to be built. More choice does not necessarily mean greater access and for many poor children their access is limited. Children in Britain are increasingly monitored by parents and by other adults through closed circuit video cameras, and through other electronic surveillance systems. When asked, children state that they resent these restrictions and prefer outdoor activities to indoor passive activities (Livingstone & Bovill, 2000). Given choice, children want to be outside playing with friends.

Chapter 11
Family Stress and Family Support

Margaret Boushel and Hilary Burgess

'Any set of social and economic arrangements which is not founded on the acceptance of individual responsibility will do nothing but harm. We are all responsible for our own actions. We cannot blame society if we disobey the law. We simply cannot delegate the exercise of mercy and generosity to others.'
(Margaret Thatcher on the welfare state)

'Family life is the foundation on which our communities, our society and our country are built. Families are central to this Government's vision of a modern and decent country. But families are also under considerable stress. Family life has continually changed – and changed for good reasons as well as bad. But what families – all families – have a right to expect from government is support.'
(Foreword by Jack Straw MP to Supporting Families, Home Office 1998)

For the last 20 years, 'the family' has been at the forefront of political debate in Britain. Statements such as those above provide some insight as to how politicians see families and their views about the role of the state in supporting them.

In Chapter 12, the economic relationship between the state and the family will be examined. In this chapter, we concentrate on the ways in which the state and other organisations, through the activities of child welfare professionals, provide support to families experiencing stress. We begin by considering the sources of stress in families and what is known of their impact and outcomes for children. Then we consider recent government child and family support policies, outlining the circumstances in which the state identifies families in need of support and the ways in which this will be provided. The role of other agencies and support systems is also summarised. To illustrate the discussion, we explore examples of stresses and professional responses in relation to healthcare provision, support for minority ethnic families and parenting skills support. Finally, we identify some central principles underpinning effective professional interventions.

Family stress

All families experience periods of stress from time to time. The reasons underlying these are as varied and diverse as life itself and to understand them we need to consider both structural and individual stresses. They may be grouped under several broad and interconnected headings – structural factors, life events, interpersonal stress and individual factors. As we shall see below, in each area, children's and parents' vulnerability to stress may be of a permanent or temporary nature.

Structural stressors

Parenting and family life must be assessed in its context (Garbarino, 1982; Pugh *et al.*, 1994), including financial resources and environmental conditions, such as housing. Poverty is central to the stress experienced by many families, with lone parent families and some minority ethnic groups especially vulnerable. Structural explanations of need suggest this arises from inequalities of power and status, reflecting the structure of society itself. In relation to income, for example, unemployment, wage levels and benefit levels interact and directly affect levels of need. The correlation of poverty with a number of other factors, such as poor health, poor housing and low educational achievement, has been repeatedly demonstrated (Kumar, 1993). In turn, these have been shown to contribute to problems such as domestic violence and child abuse. The organisation of society also results in inequalities in relation to gender, race and disability. For example, many minority ethnic groups have been shown to be disadvantaged in relation to employment, education, housing (Platt & Noble, 1998), reflecting both patterns of immigration and structural racism within British society. Recent efforts within Europe and by the new Labour administration in the UK to counter 'social exclusion' indicate a growing recognition of the impact of structural factors on social needs.

Social change stressors

Although 80% of children live in households with two parents, parental divorce or separation is increasingly likely. A growing proportion of young children (around 3% according to Clarke, 1996) live in re-constituted or step-families. Lone parents now head one in five families with dependent children, though, for many, single parenthood is a transitional state until a new partnership is forged. Whilst the rate of teenage pregnancies has fallen, Britain still has the highest rate in Europe (about three times higher than that in France or Holland). Marriages and partnerships between partners of different ethnic backgrounds are becoming more common, so that now more than 25% of all minority ethnic children under the age of four are of dual heritage (Berrington, 1995, p204). Families are smaller and the role of the extended family has declined, disrupted by the increasing absence of close geographical links and by the restrictions created by the growing participation in employment by women of all ages. Thus, the nature of family life, and the task of parenting has, for many, become more complex.

Changing employment patterns and the availability of affordable childcare are significant in understanding stress in family life. The proportion of mothers in paid employment rose from 40% in 1983 to 62% in 1998. However, mothers with degree-level education, whether partnered or alone, are far more likely to be employed than less well-educated lone parents (79% compared to 21% in 1998). Although there are differences in employment rates between minority ethnic groups (Platt & Noble, 1998), in general, lone parents find it far more difficult to earn enough to keep a family (Land, 1999). A recent study of parenting (Ferri & Smith, 1996) emphasised also the difficulties faced not only by families with no wage earner (often larger families), but also by those where one or both parents worked long hours. Despite changes in the labour market, women are still the primary carers for the majority of children. Moreover, women are more likely to be poor, especially those who are single parents. It is hardly surprising then that women are the prime users and recipients of welfare services (Abbott & Wallace, 1992).

Life-course events as stressors

Recurrent 'life-course' events, such as birth, adolescence, death or the transition to parenthood, commonly cause stress. However, contemporary writers emphasise the varying configurations such events take in different families, thus moving away from the concept of a standard or 'normal' pattern of development (see Berk, 1998). Moreover, the experience of families is shaped by the social context in which they live; hence the concept of nigrescence, which analyses black identity confusion and change (Cross, 1992). Of particular significance here is the transition to parenthood, which entails a reconfiguration of the partnership between parents, as roles, expectations and relationships change. The birth of a child may heighten existing conflicts, lower satisfaction with the partnership and alter the economic relationship between parents (Cowan & Cowan, 1992).

Meanwhile adverse life events such as illness, disability, accidents and unemployment frequently lead to stress and problems for children and their families. In particular, the impact of disability on family life is becoming better understood, both where children are disabled (Robinson & Stalker, 1998) and where disabled parents lack sufficient support, so that children take on a role as 'young carers' (Aldridge & Becker, 1995).

Interpersonal relationships as stressors

Interpersonal problems commonly identified in contemporary Western society include fractured family relationships, family violence and social isolation. All have an impact on parenting capacity (Belsky & Vondra, 1989). A lack of support in close relationships is strongly implicated in parenting difficulties (Quinton & Rutter, 1988). Moreover, a parent's room for manoeuvre may be constrained where access to material and social resources is controlled by the other partner or when that partner is a perceived source of risk to the parent or child (Boushel, 1994; Boushel & Lebacq, 1992). Graham notes this paradox in her study of mothers of preschool age children, when she describes the 'absolute poverty and relative power' of lone mothers in the allocation of scarce resources (Graham, 1987 in Brannen & Wilson, 1987, p57). Conversely, supportive partners have been shown to be the major influence in mitigating the effects of adverse childhood experiences and parenting difficulties (Quinton & Rutter, 1988).

Grandparents and friends can help parents cope with the physical and emotional demands of parenting and provide role models and advice, including the identification or modification of protective strategies (Garbarino, 1982; Cochran *et al.*, 1990). As with partners, the social circle may also be a negative influence. In Dibble & Straus's (1980) study, advice sought from third parties sometimes reinforced parents' own use of physical punishment, rather than diminishing it. Informal support systems may also be overburdened and become unable to meet the demands placed upon them (London Borough of Lambeth, 1987), or parents may lack the skills necessary for making positive relationships with friends and relatives.

Studies also suggest that some children have individual characteristics which make them more difficult to parent or which are not a good 'fit' with their parent's personalities (Werner, 1990). Thus, a combination of the inherited factors, psychosocial experiences and environmental circumstances of both parent and child makes each child's childhood and their parenting a unique and more or less satisfying event for all concerned.

Individual experiences and characteristics

At an individual level, adverse childhood experiences may affect the ability of adults to manage in partnerships or as parents. As Belsky & Vondra point out, 'at least under certain stressful conditions, developmental history influences psychological well being, which in turn affects parental functioning and, as a result, child development' (1989, p168). The concept of a cycle of deprivation or abuse (or intergenerational transmission) has been largely discredited due to its deterministic assumptions (Rutter, 1985). However, more subtle recent analyses show how, for example, parenting is particularly problematic where there is an intergenerational lack of good experiences of parenting (Hills, 1995). Recently, developing understanding of the human genome has lead to explanations which include genetic susceptibility to certain conditions or problems (such as attention deficit disorders, alcoholism, mental ill health, and potentially more complex issues such as poor parenting). With the proviso that deterministic causality is not assumed, it is likely that the concept of genetic vulnerability will increasingly be linked with environmental and social explanations to further our understanding of particular stressors (Plomin, 1994).

Risk and resilience

Where parenting takes place in very stressful circumstances the sources of risk to children may encompass a broad range of threats to health and development (Garbarino, 1982). These might be grouped loosely as follows: first, physical and developmental risks. These include health risks and accidents inside or outside the home (Avery & Jackson, 1993), and risks such as racism and bullying (Boushel, 1996). A second group of risks arises through the lack of warm, secure relationships and a boundaried home environment (Gibbons *et al.*, 1995). These are known to lead to conduct or emotional problems in children that often have long-term consequences (Rutter & Rutter, 1993). Third is the risk of physical or sexual abuses or neglect. The risks include, therefore, those likely to cause immediate harm to a child's health or development and those where harm is more likely to have an impact in the longer term.

Resilience has been defined as 'normal development under difficult conditions' (Fonagy *et al.*, 1994, pp231–57) and the capacity of parents and children to cope successfully with stress is a growing area of interest for social scientists. We know that harm to children, whether 'accidental' or 'non-accidental', is the result of complex interactions between individual vulnerabilities, environmental weaknesses and specific events (Garbarino, 1982; Department of Health, 1995b). Research in fields such as developmental psychopathology has begun to focus on those factors that help protect children in risky contexts (Quinton & Rutter, 1988; Cicchetti & Carlson, 1989; Rutter & Rutter, 1993).

The availability of material resources can clearly mitigate stress, for example by purchasing childcare, by having holidays or meeting additional dietary requirements arising from illness. Conversely, Westlake & Pearson found that mothers living in an impoverished area of Newcastle understood and shared professional concerns about health risks to children, but 'they simply did not have the time, financial or emotional resources to act on their knowledge' (1997, p148). Of central importance also are the emotional supports available to families. For example, it has been shown that the extent of maternal depression is correlated with families where parents have poor relationships with each other and where community support is weak (Cooper & Murray, 1998).

Personal expectations and perceptions of different events also play a part in our capacity to deal with stressful circumstances, along with problem-solving skills, temperament and personality. Successful coping has been associated with life experiences and 'street-wise' skills rather than measured intelligence, although it too plays a part (Clausen, 1991; Ceci & Bronfenbrenner, 1994). These skills are particularly important when options are very limited, as has been shown for the effects of 'planning behaviour' in the escape from childhood disadvantage (Quinton *et al.*, 1993). Prior parenting experiences are also relevant. Parenting difficulties are associated with poorer understanding of risks and less knowledge of developmental need (King & Fullard, 1982). Child abuse is often associated with unrealistic and age-inappropriate expectations of children's behaviour, problems that are exacerbated when the parent lacks the advice and support of more experienced women (Crockenberg, 1981). There are significant differences, too, in how well we are equipped psychologically to survive adversity. Resilience is likely to be influenced by the parent's self-esteem and mental state (Perris *et al.*, 1994). Depression and low-self esteem are associated with feelings of power-lessness in the face of risk and adversity, and a tendency to accept blame which can lead to less effective action. For example, mothers who blame themselves have been shown to deal less effectively with their partner's sexual abuse of their children (de Young, 1994).

Many parents show remarkable resilience and ingenuity. Mothers try to manage inadequate resources to ensure that children are cared for as well as possible (Graham, 1993; Dowler & Calvert, 1995; Westlake & Pearson, 1997). Coping strategies included borrowing money, going without food themselves and taking other risks with their own health (such as by smoking, drinking alcohol and eating 'unhealthy' foods) – 'short-term coping mechanisms which gave them space, or a sense of "reward", to enable them to cope with the day-to-day duties' (Westlake & Pearson, 1997, p147). Child protection agency and domestic violence refuge records indicate that women have consistently approached child welfare agencies for support when concerned about their ability to protect children, particularly when the risk has been from adults within the home (e.g. Gordon, 1989; Mullender & Morley, 1994). Child welfare professionals easily underestimate or ignore these strengths. However, restrictions on resources limit the range of strategies that are open to parents, and the possible consequences of adversities – for example, in mental distress or disorder – may reduce the coping capacities of those who would otherwise organise things well. Parents also may be wary of seeking formal support for a number of reasons, such as fear of racism (Mama, 1989) or the likely financial, social and emotional costs involved (Hooper, 1992).

This range of explanations is important to bear in mind when we move on to look at support services, since our ability to provide these appropriately and effectively is framed by our ability to understand the causes and impact of family stress.

Child and family welfare services

Who provides support to families under stress?

The key players in the provision of child and family welfare services are the state, the independent sector and the informal sector, comprising the local community and the family itself. The concept of the 'mixed economy of welfare' reflects a move away from a position where the state was expected to provide the majority of services, acknowledging the shifting boundaries between these domains over time (Finlayson, 1990).

Much support comes from families themselves, both within the group of people who live together and from extended family links. For example, grandmothers provide a great deal of informal support and childcare. The British Attitude Survey of 1995 showed that although extended family contact is decreasing, 53% of women saw their mothers at least weekly and 8% saw them daily (McGlone *et al.*, 1996). Beyond the family, the local community is a potential source of support through informal arrangements between neighbours and friends. However, families and the local neighbourhood may also be unsupportive, because of their abusive behaviours, through racism or simply the lack of capacity to assist.

Independent sector organisations contributing to child and family welfare may be voluntary or private. Voluntary provision ranges from local, relatively unstructured groups relying on unpaid activists or volunteers to large national childcare organisations such as Barnados, NCH Action for Children, the NSPCC and the Children's Society. The value of their services depends on their accessibility and appropriateness. Black voluntary organisations often play a key role by offering family support in the context of the ethnic community's broader needs and concerns, since many are holistic and develop within local communities (Sudbury, 1998). In recent years, the role of private organisations in child and family welfare has increased, particularly in relation to preschool daycare.

The third source of family support is the state. Its role comprises measures for enabling and supporting families, and measures for surveillance, control and protection. State intervention is planned and delivered both nationally and locally. Some state services, such as health and education, are 'universal' (provided to all as a right, regardless of income, and free at the point of delivery). Others, including many social services, are 'residual' or 'targeted' (focused specifically on those identified as in greatest need). The extent to which the state should intervene in family life, and when this becomes state interference, is an enduring question in child and family welfare (Fox Harding, 1991). This boundary is interpreted differently in different countries and cultures, is subject to change over time, and is likely to be contested.

Levels of intervention

The model developed by Hardiker *et al.* (1995) provides a useful framework for thinking about the aims of child and family welfare services. Three levels of intervention are defined.

(i) *Primary level interventions*, where the aim is to strengthen families and prevent problems arising through the provision of universal services or services geared to vulnerable groups (e.g. health, transport and environmental provision and anti-poverty measures).

(ii) *Secondary level interventions* which aim to address at an early point identified difficulties within families, for example by provision of daycare, family centres, respite care, befriending networks or counselling services. It is at this level that voluntary sector initiatives have tended to predominate but the state also has an important role to play in their provision both centrally and locally.

(iii)   *Tertiary level interventions* which are concerned with individuals or families where there are advanced or chronic problems and who may be perceived as problematic or in need of rescue or protection.

In Britain, tertiary level child protection interventions increasingly have dominated state child and family welfare services since the 're-discovery' of child abuse in the late 1970s and 1980s. However, the surveillance role expected of social workers has made families afraid that their children will be removed and social work intervention, not surprisingly, is seen as stigmatising. Such a legacy is hard to overcome if the state is also to work effectively at tertiary and secondary levels. Moreover, research studies indicated that the focus on child protection meant that many families in need of support are filtered out of the system (Department of Health, 1995b). Along with other concerns this has led to a call for the 'refocusing' of state welfare services towards a more supportive service that acknowledges adversity and builds on child and family strengths.

Inter-agency planning, co-ordination and practice

Given the wide range of state and independent sector agencies providing family welfare services, there is clearly a need for co-ordination. In Britain, there has recently been a trend towards strategic national planning, with identified goals and national standards linked to a requirement for local planning. In England and Wales the Children Act (1989) requires local authorities to draw up inter-agency Children's Services Plans to co-ordinate and develop provision in a given locality. Since 1997 local authorities have also been required to draw up Early Years Development Plans. Health Improvement Plans must be drawn up jointly between health authorities, trust, primary care groups, local authorities and voluntary agencies. 'Modernising Health and Social Services' (Department of Health, 1998c) sets national priorities, goals and standards, with designated lead agencies in either health or social services or a requirement to co-operate. In some other European countries, notably Sweden and Norway, co-ordination has been taken one step further, with the creation of ministries dedicated to the welfare of children or children and families at governmental level (see Chapter 12).

The emphasis in these national strategies is on holistic, child-centred, 'joined up' services focusing on need and outcomes. The priority is to ensure that children are protected from abuse, to raise the quality of state care, improve the life chances of children 'in need' and support young people leaving care. To achieve this, the Quality Protects Programme was launched in 1998, setting out eight national objectives for social services departments. The Home Office consultation paper Supporting Families (1998), published during the same period, emphasises the need to increase early years provision and parenting support. It proposed an enhanced role for health visitors, a national parenting helpline and the development of Sure Start. The latter is a major new initiative designed to enhance the physical, psycho-social and educational development of children under four years of age living in disadvantaged communities and redress the social exclusion of their parents.

An ecological approach

Bronfenbrenner's ecological model, described in the Introduction, enables us to conceptualise the multiple influences and participants in the welfare of children and their families. Services may be provided for a number of individuals or groups within this network; for example, to the child or parents alone, to mothers, fathers or to groups within the community. However, to target interventions effectively we need to consider which factors have the most important influence on children's longer-term safety and proper development, taking account of the impact of poverty, racism, sexism and disability – the child's 'protective environment'. A review of cross-cultural and cross-national research indicates that four factors are particularly relevant (Boushel, 1994).

(i)   *How children are valued:* Children who are valued are less likely to be abused and more likely to be provided with supports that enhance their physical, social and psychological development.

(ii)   *How women and carers are valued:* Carers, whatever their gender, need what Rutter has called 'permitting circumstances' (Rutter, 1974 in Pugh *et al.*, 1994) to care well for children, including the necessary financial, social and emotional supports. Nevertheless, there is a potentially significant tension between a focus on children's needs and the needs of parents, which needs exploration in both policy and practice developments.

(iii)   *Social interconnectedness:* Positive social networks provide advice and help with childcare tasks, encourage greater consensus and closer monitoring of acceptable parenting practices and provide opportunities for adult stimulation, support and development. Children's networks provide stimulation and support and introduce them to other models of adult behaviour.

(iv)   *Protective safety nets:* These include both formal and informal sources of protection such as particular family members, trusted adults in the community or in local agencies, and can operate at primary, secondary or tertiary levels. Like other support services, to be effective they need to be *accessible* and *acceptable*. From an ecological perspective, each of the four factors needs to be considered in relation to three contexts – the family, the extended family and community, and the state (Boushel, 1994).

Building effective services

Family support services usually are developed in response to needs identified by professionals, politicians, or those who experience the need.

Often it is assumed that the service provided will meet the need identified within the resources available. However, some initiatives, although well intentioned, fail to do so, or have unintended outcomes that outweigh the benefits, such as some aspects of current child protection services. Greater attention is now being paid to the effectiveness of services – their accuracy in identifying needs, to the processes used in meeting them, and to the long- and short-term outcomes for the children and families. This concern with effectiveness is apparent in a range of welfare services, including health, social work and education (e.g. Cochrane Collaboration, NHS Centre for Reviews and Dissemination, Department of Health, 1995b).

Evaluating the effectiveness of services is not without problems. The impact of some interventions may only be adequately researched over many years. Many family support programmes are multi-dimensional, so it is hard to distinguish which elements or combinations of elements are the most successful. Nevertheless, some common themes emerging from the research include: the need for services to take greater account of the wider context of family life and pressures on parents; the need to hear and respect both parents' and children's understandings of their difficulties and needs; and the need for greater clarity in the way resources and professional interventions are targeted and their impact on the problem identified.

To help illustrate some of the issues discussed, in the following sections we take some specific examples of child and family welfare services and explore their range, focus and capacity to strengthen the child's protective environment.

Child health promotion and support

The first example is the range of services provided to all preschool children by health visitors. These underline the importance of ensuring a healthy childhood and offer support with parenting at this stage in the life-course. Health visitors are specially trained nurses, based in general practice, who visit parents and children soon after a baby's birth, and maintain an advisory role to parents until the child is of school-going age and beyond. This is a service that has many of the characteristics of a 'mainstream' or primary-level intervention yet raises issues about focus, resource allocation, effectiveness and acceptability that are important to consider in relation to all child and family welfare services.

In terms of primary intervention, it is increasingly clear that child and maternal health is best promoted through interventions which encourage breast-feeding, positive parenting, accident prevention, immunisation, nutrition and dental care, and which mitigate the impact of postnatal depression (Sinclair *et al.*, 1997, p29). The UN Convention (Article 24) emphasises the need to focus on primary healthcare, whilst the third report on UK child health services (Hall, 1996) and the NHS Guide to Good Practice (Department of Health, 1996) gave renewed attention to this area. The Hall report identified the tasks of child health promotion as identifying needs, providing emotional support and education, preventing and detecting disorders and health problems, providing practical help and developing community-based projects (p21).

Child health surveillance services have a slightly different function. According to the Patient's Charter (Department of Health, 1996), they are provided 'to help you bring up your child and pick up any problems with growth or development' (p5). They include the physical examination of new babies at birth by a paediatrician and a home visit by a health visitor within the first couple of weeks of the new baby's arrival home. The identification of and support for mothers with postnatal depression is an important aspect of the health visitor's role at this point. There is usually also an opportunity to attend 'baby' clinic sessions providing further developmental checks at about six and 18 months and again in the preschool period. These developmental checks commonly include assessments for hip displacement, hearing loss and abnormalities in growth.

There is considerable local variation in the range and quality of child health surveillance and support programmes. Child health visitor staffing levels vary and are diminishing: a survey of 70 of the 196 NHS trusts by the Health Visitor's Association found a one-third cut in staff numbers (1993). Current approaches to child health surveillance have been questioned for other reasons. The 1994 Audit Commission report recommended that, whilst continuing to provide a universal service, at a local level health visitors should use measures of deprivation to shift the balance of their work towards vulnerable families. The 1996 Hall report expressed concern about both the effectiveness of some of the developmental checks used and about the standard of their implementation. It was suggested that routine assessments for specific problems should only be made when the assessment used was known to be effective and when identification of the problem would be followed by prompt and effective treatment, as is the case with hip displacement. The benefit of hearing tests was questioned, and doubts raised about other developmental checks except where the child's medical history or parental observation suggests there may be a problem. The 1996 report emphasised the importance of heeding and responding to parental perceptions of developmental problems and of targeting attention towards families known to be vulnerable (Hall, 1996).

Studies of effective health promotion projects suggest that they have certain characteristics in common: they are highly rated by parents; the aims are clear and the benefits tend to be modest; they do not 'overload parents with too many messages' and may need to stimulate parental interest before providing information; and they must take account of the complex and diverse impact of poverty and deprivation (Hall, 1996, Chapter 2). The latter may affect parents' ability to give priority to their child's health and to find and access acceptable services.

One such primary care initiative is the Child Development Programme (Barker *et al.*, 1994). Specially trained health visitors visited new mothers on a monthly basis for a year, working with them on health promotion and childrearing strategies. Later, the Community Mothers programme developed, in which health visitors trained local women to provide the programme to new mothers. Both initiatives appear to have been effective in promoting immunisation, good nutrition and positive parenting behaviours (Johnson *et al.*, 1995).

These services are designed with concerns about the child and mother at their core. However, the way they are organised and delivered may also help strengthen or limit the child and mother's social networks and the child's protective safety net. There are many examples of small-scale initiatives by health visitors, acting alone, with other professionals, or with parents to set up parenting classes, support groups, mother and toddler groups and so forth, to improve child and maternal health and development whilst also strengthening their wider protective environment. The focus on vulnerable groups, however, raises the profile of the health visitor's role in child protection surveillance and intervention and has left many concerned that they will lose parental trust, on which they have traditionally built their interventions.

Support services for minority ethnic communities

Social networks connect families with the wider community. In Britain, family isolation has often been viewed as the result of 'personal difficulties in making and sustaining social relationships in the community' (Department of Health, 1988, p59). For some, this may be a primary factor, but we need to consider other reasons. For example, families experiencing racism, or whose main language differs from that spoken around them will have greater difficulties in avoiding social isolation. Building effective and acceptable services for minority ethnic families requires an understanding of the complexities of institutional, cultural and interpersonal racism, and the way in which this affects children's 'protective environments'.

Whilst legislation alone cannot eliminate discrimination, it can provide an important backdrop to secondary level intervention. The Race Relations Act 1976 makes it an offence to incite racial hatred or discriminate on the basis of race in a range of areas. The Children Act 1989 (Schedule 2) gives local authorities a duty to take into account a child's race, language and religion when providing social work services. However, immigration legislation means that some children are deprived of the support of family, whilst the 1998 Education Reform Act, by specifying that Christianity be given a special place in the school curriculum, makes it harder to provide opportunities for children to value and understand other faiths.

Racism significantly affects the everyday experiences of many black and minority ethnic families. Many studies record the racist attacks experienced by adults and children, which range from spitting and physical assaults by adults and children to arson, vandalism and written and verbal abuse (see Boushel, 1996). It is not surprising that mothers may restrict children's freedom to play outside because of these racist attacks or that mothers of mixed-parentage children chose or have social isolation thrust upon them in mainly white areas (Currer, 1991 in Graham, 1993, p.98; Hartcliffe and Withywood Black Support Group, 1993; Tizard & Phoenix, 1993), often with an impact on their psychological health (Banks, 1996).

The consequences of such abuse and isolation can be far reaching. Studies undertaken in the late 1980s showed that children of African-Caribbean/white background were two and a half times more likely than other children to experience state care, and the risk increased for those living in areas with a small black population (Bebbington & Miles, 1989). More recently, Baldwin & Carruthers (1998, pp36–7) found that in a disadvantaged area, a quarter of black parents, compared to 5% of white parents, had never requested a childcare service and twice as many black as white parents had not used such a service. Of those who had requested a service, twice as many black as white parents had had their request refused. Children do not readily inform parents or other adults of racist incidents and their experiences are less well documented. Their willingness to seek help depends on how they think the information will be received and dealt with (Troyna & Hatcher, 1992; Tizard & Phoenix, 1993). Racism is experienced as most hurtful during primary school years, when children find it difficult to understand and rebut (Tizard & Phoenix, 1993).

Secondary level interventions can be effective in redressing these inequalities. Black and other minority ethnic networks provide support in sharing ideas about children's specific health and physical care needs, about English and language of origin classes, about ways of helping children value themselves and their racial and cultural heritage, and about ways of resisting and dealing with racism. Some parents may need professional help to establish informal local black and mixed-parentage networks. For white mothers in multi-racial families, dealing with racism may be a new and traumatic experience. Parents and children may value help in developing age-appropriate, non-violent responses to racist abuse (Wilson, 1987; Tizard & Phoenix, 1993). Staff in health and welfare services may be well placed to provide information about the community and local services, to put minority ethnic families in touch with one another and to ensure that services are meeting their needs.

Children's friendships with others of similar ethnic origins can provide important peer support for oppressed groups. However, since there is also a connection between levels of racism and patterns of inter-racial friendship, schools and early years agencies can play an important role by promoting positive inter-racial friendship and co-operation. Racism and racial attacks can be reduced by positive policies about appropriate behaviour from children, staff and parents (Troyna & Hatcher, 1992). The evidence suggests that black and minority ethnic families generally welcome support from professionals of all ethnic backgrounds, once professionals have built up trust by demonstrating commitment and a willingness to understand and respond to the issues these families are facing.

Parenting support

In our final example, we consider the interventions designed to increase confidence and skills in parenting. For many of the reasons already discussed, it cannot be assumed that parents of young children have developed adequate childrearing skills before becoming parents themselves, nor that sufficient support and advice will be available through informal family and friendship networks to make parenting a manageable and fulfilling task. Parenting difficulties are associated with poverty and social stress, as well as factors in the parent's own background that mean that s/he has lacked sufficient opportunities to develop a sense of self-efficacy, an empathic understanding of young children's needs, and the skills necessary to protect and enhance children's healthy development.

Some studies have considered how parents (usually mothers) deal with perceived risks, including risks from their own behaviour and that of others. In an early study, Graham explored mothers' anger towards their babies, and the ways they tried to protect their baby from the risk they felt themselves to present because of their tiredness or frustration. These included leaving the baby to cry, drowning out the noise by turning up the radio or putting her head in the airing cupboard (Graham, 1980). More recently, Roberts et al. (1995), in a study of 280 households on a Glasgow council estate, detail some of the inventive ways in which mothers dealt with the threat of 'accidental' injuries and some of the constraints they face as they tried to reconcile the competing demands created by unsafe environments, limited resources, their other household responsibilities and their children's wishes to explore.

Failure to explore the risks perceived by parents and the protective strategies they have already developed may lead both to inadequate assessments of their capacity to protect their children and to increased parental disillusion and disempowerment (Fisher et al., 1986; Boushel & Lebacq, 1992). If the concept of partnership is to be translated into practice and some of these problems alleviated, we need to understand more about how successful parenting is undertaken in difficult circumstances, and of the informal and formal supports that can strengthen the parenting capacity of those who are experiencing difficulties. Understanding and building on parents' own efforts, their existing supports and perceived needs is also important because access to professional services is limited and the duration of formal interventions is often brief (Department of Health, 1995b).

The 1994 Report of the All-Party Parliamentary Group on Parenting and the International Year of the Family included recommendations about education, preventive work with families, reform of the benefit system, provision of childcare, and strengthening the role of fathers and mothers through family-friendly employment practices. These are primary level state interventions, which reflect the extent to which children and parents are valued in society. Many of these are now being put into place by the current Labour Government, along with secondary and tertiary level interventions to support families, as outlined in the Green

Paper 'Supporting Families'(Home Office, 1998). The Children Act 1989 (Schedule 2) also gives local authorities a specific duty to provide or arrange for the provision of parenting support where children are deemed to be 'in need'.

A common approach to the provision of parent support has been through the development of services based in 'family centres'. These centres may take many different forms: some are locally based, open to all parents with young children and offering a wide range of activities and services for both children and parents (e.g. toy libraries, literacy schemes, mother and toddler groups, community education projects). Others are 'targeted' on families where parenting difficulties have been identified by professionals, and where the emphasis is on the development of improved parenting skills (Smith, 1996; Cannan & Warren, 1997). At present, most parents using family centres are women; their preference is for community-based, non-stigmatising services which provide for their own as well as their children's needs and for their needs as parents (Smith, 1996).

Many centres offer 'parenting skills' programmes. These vary in the extent to which they emphasise parenting skills, relationships and behaviours and in their structure, with most having more than one focus (Barlow, 1997). Group-based programmes that include 'a combination of relaxation, cognitive restructuring and problem-solving skills' have so far been shown to be most effective (Macdonald & Roberts, 1995; Barlow, 1997). There is evidence that parent education, support and training programmes may be effective in reducing or preventing child abuse and neglect, although the nature of the programme and the workers' skills are significant variables (Smith, 1996). However, there are some kinds of families for whom parent support and education is unlikely to be a sufficient response (Macdonald & Roberts, 1995).

An important challenge in this area of family support is parental take-up of these services. As we have seen, some parents may feel unwelcome or be less likely to have this provision offered to them because of their ethnic background. For other parents, the difficulty is that the service or the way in which it is provided is seen as stigmatising. There are also major problems in involving male parents, although some initiatives such as fathers and couples groups have been successful in this respect. The timing of parenting skills interventions also needs further exploration. The emerging evidence suggests that interventions very early in a young child's life may be most successful, which is why the new Sure Start initiative will focus on children under four and their families. However, interventions with school-age children and young people also need further exploration and evaluation.

Improving child and family welfare services

Having highlighted the complexity of the stresses that affect families and the supports available to them, we conclude this chapter by suggesting the ways in which child and family welfare services might be improved in the future. First, we would argue the central importance of recognising the normality of parenting problems, and how changes in society affect the resilience and coping strategies of parents. Given this, the state needs to play a central role, putting in place the primary-level interventions that prevent problems from worsening. The state should also ensure that adequate secondary and tertiary level supports are available, through direct provision and also by facilitating the contributions of the independent sector and of families and communities. Work across these sectors must be co-ordinated. Where there is a risk to children or parents from abuse, the tensions between compulsory intervention for protection and support need to be reconciled and balanced. The services provided need to be effective in meeting the needs of children and their parents (both mothers and fathers). Finally, the importance of participation by families in the way services are planned and delivered locally must be recognised. In summary, support must be available, accessible and acceptable to families and it must be effective.

Chapter 12

The Child as Citizen

Hilary Land

Introduction

Children in Britain today are growing up in circumstances which are very different from a generation ago and government policies, priorities and structures do not fully reflect this. Family life has changed dramatically for a substantial and growing minority of children. The decline in marriage has been accompanied by the growth of cohabitation, lone parenthood and divorce, followed by re-marriage or cohabitation again. The first step into the labour market is more difficult to make, especially for the unqualified young man, and once in work it is more difficult to earn 'a family wage'.

In 1968, 1.4 million children lived in poor households. By 1995, this had increased to 4.3 million with most of the increase occurring since 1979. 'The child poverty rates have increased in Britain very much more than in any other country for which we have data' (Bradshaw, 1999, p21). The number of low wage earners claiming means-tested family credit has increased five-fold since 1979. Unemployment is more widespread and throughout the 1990s a quarter of all children were living in families with no earner. This compares with one in twelve in 1979. Altogether, over half of the 4.3 million poor children in 1996 lived in households with no one in paid work, and over a third of children in Britain were growing up in families dependent on means-tested benefits. The gap between their standard of living and that of the family on an average income has been widening. By the mid 1990s the disposable income of the richest 20% was seven times greater than that of the poorest 20%. This compares with a four-fold difference only a generation ago.

Central and local government systems for delivering the various health, education and welfare services have changed along with the methods of funding them. The legislative frameworks within which each operates have been radically altered in the past ten years, but not necessarily in ways which have been consistent, either with each other or with reforms in family law. The new Labour Government at least recognises the need for 'joined-up thinking' in policy making but has so far only taken small steps to achieve this. Some changes have strengthened the ability of health and welfare professionals, as well as of parents, to take into account and to act in 'the best interests' of the child. However, others have failed to do so, and leave little time or space for either the voices of the children themselves, or of their parents, to be heard and considered. Children – even young children – are now often seen in the media more as 'villains' needing punishment than as 'victims' needing protection. The introduction of curfews for young children and electronic tagging of toddlers are examples of measures which betray adults' fear of children out of control and therefore either a danger to others or to themselves.

This chapter will examine the extent to which children and childhood are visible in the many policy debates which affect their lives, and will discuss what needs to change if children and their interests are to have both a higher priority in the allocation of resources and a voice in the policy making process. As Chapter 7 describes, under the Children Act 1989 children do have certain rights to have their views heard but in many other areas of policy and practice children must remain silent. Nevertheless, children are slowly inching their way up some of the policy and research agendas. They are beginning to be taken more seriously as individuals in their own right, both in the measurement and analysis of social issues and social problems as well as in developing policies to improve their welfare. One reason for this is the UN Convention on the Rights of the Child to which Britain is a signatory. Some countries have developed innovative mechanisms and practices in order that policies become more sensitive to children. These will be drawn on to illustrate ways in which policies and practices in Britain might be developed in accord with the objectives of the UN convention. First, however, this chapter will discuss some of the other evidence of a growing concern to increase the visibility of children and will explore the challenges this poses for the ways in which policy makers and researchers think about children and childhood.

Children and their economic and family circumstances

The interaction of economic and family circumstances is complex and the picture given when the unit of analysis is the household or family is different from that when the unit of analysis is the child. For example, the proportion of households comprising a couple family with dependent children has fallen from 38% of all households in Britain in 1981 to only 25% of all households in 1996–97. Couple families with no children now outnumber those with children (ONS, 1998a, p42). The proportion of households comprising families with three or more children has fallen from 9% to 5%. However, when children are the focus it is clear that although the number of larger families has declined, nearly a third of children are still growing up with at least two siblings (see Fig. 12.1 below). This compares with just over two-fifths 30 years ago. Conversely, the proportion of children in lone parent families has increased three-fold. The risk of poverty is greater among lone parents and families with three or more children.

Great Britain	1972	1981	1991–92	1996–97
Couple families				
1 child	16	18	17	17
2 children	35	41	37	37
3 or more children	41	29	28	26
Lone mother families				
1 child	2	3	5	5
2 children	2	4	7	7
3 or more children	2	3	6	6
Lone father families				
1 child	–	1	–	–
2 or more children	1	1	1	1
All dependent children	100	100	100	100

Source: ONS, 1998a, p46 Table 2.10

Fig. 12.1   Percentage of dependent children living in different family types.

Much is made in the media and by politicians of the fact that by the early 1990s nearly one in five children were living in a one-parent family household, compared with one in ten 30 years ago. However, the average length of time spent as a single mother is three years and as a divorced mother is five years. Therefore, on the one hand these figures under-estimate the number of children who, for part of their childhood, will spend time living with one parent alone. On the other hand focusing on these figures detracts attention from the fact that at any point in time the vast majority (four out of five) children are living in a family with two parents. In a growing number of families one parent will be a step-parent. In 1991, there were half a million step-families with one million step-children and natural children living with them.

A number of comprehensive reviews of the extent and nature of inequalities among families with children, using a wide range of statistics gathered from various government departments, have been published by non-statutory and charitable trusts in recent years. For example, in 1995 Barnardos published *All Our Futures*, which collated and analysed the impact of public expenditure and fiscal policies on Britain's children and young people. This detailed and comprehensive review concluded that although conditions have generally been improving for children and young people:

'There are marked inequalities of outcomes for children according to their ethnic origins, according to the part of the country or type of neighbourhood they live in, and most notable of all, according to their social class background or the economic position of their families.'

(Holterman, 1995, p160)

The measures of wellbeing of children examined showed that:

'Children from poor homes have lower life expectancy and are more likely to die in infancy or childhood; they have a greater likelihood of poor health, a lower chance of high educational attainment, a greater risk of unemployment, a higher possibility of involvement in crime and of enduring homelessness. Girls from poor homes are at greater risk of teenage pregnancy.'

(Holterman, 1995, p160)

The report drew attention to the evidence that showed that whilst at any one time only a minority experienced worsening conditions, the risk of these problems being experienced throughout large sections of society was growing. The author recommended that there be a greater willingness to spend more on public services for children and to give higher priority to 'promoting a social and economic environment in which all children can reach their full potential' (p165). An analysis of child poverty over the past 30 years in Britain found that children are more likely to be counted among the poor than in the 1960s. The authors also concluded:

'...shifts in the economic position of children or indeed between households with and without children have gone largely unrecorded. Part of the reason for this is the lack of empirical work in economics (and even in social policy) that attributes a key role to children who are frequently modelled only in terms of their effect on parental or household outcomes.'

(Gregg et al., 1999, p164)

In order to understand the dynamics of poverty and inequality it is also important to look at changes over the life course of individuals. In other words, how do experiences in childhood affect the circumstances and life chances when adult? This in turn will have an impact on their children's futures. A recent study on the effects of childhood disadvantage concluded: 'family financial distress during the childhood years displays an important association with subsequent economic success or failure and that this is a key factor underpinning intergenerational transmissions of economic status' (Machin, 1999, p20). Using longitudinal data from the National Child Development Study of a cohort of individuals born in 1958, Kiernan found that low educational attainment was the most powerful single factor associated with becoming a young parent. She also found that teenage mothers and young men who became fathers before age 22 were likely to come from families with low socio-economic status where financial hardship was reported (Hobcraft & Kiernan, 1999). A poorly paid part-time or even full-time job does not offer an escape from poverty to the man or woman with a family to support. Acceptance of part-time employment is more likely to make sense if there is already a full-time earner in the family. The growth of two-earner families has been accompanied by a growth in no-earner families. Gregg suggests 'the collapse in the availability of work to work-poor families ... is not related to the characteristics of the individuals. It is not an underclass story. It is the changing nature of work on offer in the labour market to those who are out of work, relative to the needs of those kinds of families' (Family Policy Studies Centre, 1994, p13).

The new Labour Government recognises that there are many jobs in the bottom end of the earnings distribution which do not pay a 'family wage', i.e. a wage sufficient to support a wife and one or two children. The Working Families Tax Credit (WFTC) which was introduced in 1999 will increase the resources going to working parents. It is estimated that over 1.4 million families will benefit from this in the first instance and it will cost £5 billion annually. The New Deal programmes aim to make unemployed people more employable by improving their education, training and work experience. Low income and unemployment reduces the possibility of marriage as an option (the 1991 Census showed that couples with children from social class 5 were more likely to be cohabiting and less likely to be married than couples from social classes 1 and 2) (Haskey, 1996, p22), and puts marriages at risk of breakdown and divorce.

Growing concern about child poverty has been one of the reasons for the higher profile which children are beginning to have in the policy and research agendas. Previous Conservative Governments refused to treat the concept of poverty seriously despite endorsing the agreement reached at the Copenhagen Summit on Social Development in 1995, which included a commitment to make greater 'public efforts to eradicate absolute poverty and reduce overall poverty substantially'. The Labour Government however has pledged to abolish child poverty over the next 20 years. In the Beveridge lecture in spring 1999 the Prime Minister announced 'our historic aim that ours is the first generation to end child poverty for ever and it will take a generation ... We have made children our top priority because as the Chancellor said in his Budget "they are 20% of the population but they are 100% of the future".' The definition of poverty to be used is a relative one, i.e. the poor are those living in households with an income less than half that of the average household. The WFTC is to be one of the key mechanisms for redistributing resources from childless households to those with children.

Children in the research and policy agendas

In a review of sociological and policy perspectives on children and childhood, Brannen (1999) identified a total of four major policy concerns, including the extent of child poverty, which have been driving the research agenda in Britain in recent years. These are first, concern about the growth of the lone parent family which is interpreted to signify the break up of the 'traditional' family and the growth of irresponsible parenthood. Second, concern about the growth of poverty among children at international as well as the national level. Third, the debate about children's rights manifest in particular in the 1989 UN Convention on the Rights of the Child and fourth, concern about the future of coming generations and the balance between young and old. The last is underpinned by what Saporiti (1994) calls the re-discovery of 'sociography', which he argues uses a coherent set of demographic social and economic statistics and indicators which take the child as the unit of observation and childhood as the unit of analysis (p19).

Brannen also argues that policy concerns have driven the social science research agenda in Britain particularly in the last 20 years. These concerns have not however carried equal weight and as a result there has been more funded research on the social problems arising from family break-down or malfunctioning than on inequality and poverty. The latter raise unacceptable political questions which challenge the dominant economic orthodoxies, i.e. they draw attention to the inadequacies of the market. For similar reasons there has been considerable reluctance to examine the more negative interactions between the functioning of the labour market and family life. The new Labour Government *is* concerned about child poverty, as mentioned above. However, the Chancellor of the Exchequer's belief that employment is the route out of poverty makes it unlikely that research on the negative aspect of the growing insecurity and 'flexibilisation' of the labour market on children and their welfare will be generously funded. Daycare policies have been developed with the focus on the needs of mothers in employment rather than on the welfare of children *per se* or, despite the rhetoric, how employment might better fit the needs of families. The shift of responsibility for under five-year-olds from the Department of Health to the Department of Education and Employment should be seen in this context. The renewed interest in citizenship, Brannen argues, however, is consistent with liberal theories which place less emphasis on the responsibility of the state and more on families and individuals. The other side of the coin of individual rights is individual responsibility. It also goes with a research agenda which emphasises children's agency and children's perspectives. Nevertheless, this is very different from an agenda heavily influenced by child development and socialisation theories which in turn have drawn heavily on paradigms from medicine and education. In this respect Britain has a great deal to learn from Scandinavian researchers. Brannen concludes:

> 'Once childhood is considered a status rather than a transitory period and once children constitute a visible social group, it is possible to value children's productive contribution to the social, economic and emotional division of labour through their activity in school, households and elsewhere. Children also become visible as consumers and clients of services.'
>
> (Brannen, 1999, p149)

'Attending to the voice of children has acquired a certain respectability in the last few years. It is a slower process, however, to obtain research evidence to increase our knowledge of children's perspectives on the social institutions in which they live and play their part in constructing' (Mayall, 1996b, p22). Too often children are included within 'parents and children' and the parent (usually the mother) speaks on behalf of the child(ren). This of course assumes their interests and perspectives coincide. Teenage children have been researched and interviewed more extensively, especially in relation to health-related behaviour, e.g. smoking and drinking. Using younger children as informants is less common but with sensitivity and proper safeguards and with parents' consent it can be done. For example, a recent study of the expenditure patterns of families with children not only interviewed the adult responsible for the housekeeping but also interviewed all children over the age of five (Middleton *et al.*, 1997). An Economic and Social Research Council funded research study, in progress at the time of writing, has successfully involved children as young as eight in a study of children's understanding of and attitudes towards domestic violence. A study conducted by Gingerbread (1999), a lone-parent organisation, interviewed children in two childcare centres about what they liked and disliked about their mothers going to work. They included children aged between three and ten years and their comments were very revealing. For example, an eight year old said, 'She's happier when she's got a job' and a six year old said, 'She has to work too hard'. As Mayall argues, research can teach adults what children know and think about the services they use. In addition, children's active involvement in, for example, their own healthcare has a positive outcome on the maintenance and promotion of their own health and wellbeing (Mayall, 1996a, p25).

Failure to treat children in their own right can have very serious consequences. Following a number of tragic cases of children dying as a result of being given drugs tested only on adults, the issue was debated in Parliament in spring 1999. During the debate it was reported that 25% of all drugs given to children in hospitals were not licensed for that purpose and that 36% of all children in hospitals received drugs in that way. Moreover, among newborn babies admitted as patients in hospital the situation was even worse: 65% of all treatments were not licensed for children and 90% of all these baby patients received such treatments (House of Commons Debates, 19 April 1999, col. 669). The European Union established guidance on the clinical investigation of medical products on children. This came into effect in September 1997 but compliance is only voluntary and the Parliamentary Under-Secretary of State for Health concluded the debate by stating that the Government 'expect that the pharmaceutical industry will take heed of the European guideline and be prepared to work with us' (col. 678). The US Government is tougher. From April 1999 it is compelling pharmaceutical companies to provide information about the effects of their drugs on children if such a use is likely (col. 671).

The UN Convention on the Rights of the Child

Worldwide, there have been developments towards an increasingly unified children's legislation in all jurisdictions and this has inevitably increased the visibility of children. Britain is among the 187 of the 190 UN member states which, since 1990, have voluntarily ratified the UN Convention on the Rights of the Child. The Convention is a wide ranging treaty addressing general principles such as non-discrimination, best interests of the child, the right to life, survival and development as well as respect for the views of children. The Convention places a duty on governments to ensure its implementation, to make its principles known both to adults and to children and to make reports on progress towards implementation widely available. A child includes all those under the age of 18 years. In January 1996, the Parliamentary Assembly of the Council of Europe adopted a European Strategy for Children which seeks to make children's rights a higher political priority within the member states included within the Council of Europe.

This growing international recognition of the need to address the failure of government structures and policies to safeguard and promote the welfare and rights of children has yet to be fully incorporated into British government practices, priorities and policies. The UN Committee on the Rights of the Child, the only international monitor of the implementation of the Convention, has reviewed government structures for children in over 50 countries, including Britain. Their reports highlight the lack of adequate co-ordination in every country.

However, compared with many other countries, Britain has done less to give a higher priority to the best interests of children throughout the political agenda in a consistent way. There have been some encouraging developments at both central and local government level in planning and co-ordinating services for children, particularly in health and the social care of children 'in need', but in other policy areas much less progress has been made. Indeed in some recent legislation, for example the Education Act 1993, the Government failed to take account of the Convention. The policies for homeless families introduced in 1996, which gave local authorities the ability to offer homeless families temporary rather than permanent accommodation as was previously the case, may be in breach of it. The UN Committee, which is reviewing again the British Government's progress towards implementation of the Convention in 1999, is not however seeking uniformity in approach but rather, to use their own words, that 'the Convention should be the main bench-mark and inspiration of action'.

Parliament has not passed legislation which specifically incorporates the provisions of the Convention because the Government holds the view that no such legislation is necessary: existing legislation already incorporates both its principles and standards. The UN Committee on the Rights of the Child in their 1995 review came to a different conclusion. They drew attention to the ways in which the principle of 'the best interests of the child' had not been applied consistently in health, education and social security legislation. They identified specific issues in which the rights of children could be in conflict with those of their parents and were concerned about the disadvantages experienced by children from minority ethnic groups and gypsy and traveller children. They also regretted the lack of effective and independent co-ordinating mechanisms for discussing and monitoring the implementation of the rights of the child. They noted with concern the increasing number of children living in poverty and the rate of divorce and the number of single-parent families. 'These phenomena raise a number of issues including as regards the adequacy of benefit allowances and the availability and effectiveness of family education' (para. 16). (By 'family education' they mean education for parenthood which should begin while children are still in school.)

In August 1999 the British Government submitted their second report to the UN Committee on the Rights of the Child. The report emphasised the Government's commitment to ending child poverty within a generation and drew attention to the national childcare strategy Sure Start, to increases in child benefit and to the new Working Families Tax Credit. However policies concerning the very low age of criminal responsibility (10 years in England and Wales), child curfews for children under 10 and the rise in the number of children (12 to 14 years old) serving custodial sentences in secure training centres are likely to be of concern to the UN Committee when it examines the report in 2002. The Government is committed to consulting on whether the law allowing for the 'reasonable' punishment of children should be reformed but at the time of writing the consultation paper had not been published (Harker, 1999).

Tax and benefit reforms

The Labour Government is making major reforms to the welfare state. Changes in tax and benefit systems raise a number of important issues. First, there are important concerns which have always been associated with social security systems about the effect of the benefit system on claimants' incentives to take up paid employment, as well as, once in employment, to increase their earnings. Today, with more divorce and diverse family and household circumstances, not only are there concerns about 'poverty' and 'employment' traps but also about trapping people in particular household or family situations, especially if these are believed to be disadvantageous for children. Parity between children irrespective of marital status of their parents has become a very important issue again in the debate about how and to what extent the state should share with parents the cost of children.

The second issue arising from the very different marriage and child-bearing patterns of the 1990s concerns the question of how the cost and care of children should be shared between parents – both natural parents and step-parents, none of whom may be (and may never have been) married to each other. In contrast to previous policies based on the pragmatic view that men were more likely to support the women and children with whom they were living than those whom they had deserted, the Child Support Act 1991 is based on the view that the claims of natural children for maintenance have priority over the claims of step-children, irrespective of the marital status of any of the parents and irrespective of living arrangements. The controversy this has aroused shows that this is an issue over which there is little consensus. The review of child support, which has just been completed at the time of writing, is still based on the principle that the biological father is primarily responsible for the maintenance of his children. Whilst there is widespread support for the view that parents are responsible for their children, at least until they are of school-leaving age, and that those able to contribute to their support should do so, there remains the question of how this responsibility should be shared by the state on behalf of the wider community, whether or not state support should be limited to those with incomes below a certain level and how an adequate level of income is best guaranteed to children in all circumstances. The 1998 budget indicates that the government wants to target resources for children in poorer families but is ambivalent about the place of universal tax-free child benefit. In other words children's rights to claim resources from the state are increasingly contingent on the economic circumstances of their parents, i.e. their claims arise from poverty not citizenship.

The broader impact of social and economic policies on children

The needs and rights of children can be addressed and met not only within the tax and benefit systems but also in a wide range of public services. As the Barnardos' Director of Child Care wrote in the Foreword to the report already cited (Holterman, 1995):

> 'It has perhaps been less well recognised that policies that do not have children as their main focus may nevertheless have an impact on children's welfare, and can thereby contribute to, or detract from the well-being of children. Across a wide range of fields, such as energy, transport, taxation and employment, government policies have an impact on children and young people. As children are not their main focus, these may be overlooked or underestimated.'

It is therefore important that the impact on children of policies across all government departments is monitored and procedures for co-ordination examined.

Currently there is much room for improvement within central government, for outside the Department of Health, there has been little evidence of policies affecting children being based on strategic thinking or even necessarily based on sound evidence on the effectiveness of particular initiatives. The Sure Start programme is a welcome initiative in this respect because it takes a broad perspective on the context in which children live and evaluation is built into the programme. However, this programme will only reach 5% of all children under three years old.

In some areas of government there is little acknowledgement of the impact of their policies on children. For example, although the primary objective of housing policy had long been 'to bring a decent home within reach of every family' (Department of the Environment (DoE), 1993), it is disquieting that the DoE did not respond to the request from the Department of Health on behalf of the Gulbenkian Foundation for information on the content of their work affecting children and the arrangements for co-ordinating with other departments. Overall housing conditions in Britain have continued to improve, but housing tenures have become more polarised and affordable rented accommodation harder to find. This has had a particular impact on young people and lone parents who are dependent on this form of tenure. Homelessness has increased dramatically during the 1980s so that by the early 1990s there were about 200 000 children in homeless families. A study of lone parents in 1995 found nearly a third had experienced homelessness in the previous 10 years. As Chapter 10 shows, poor housing in general puts children at risk of accidents, respiratory disease and infections. Stress and behavioural problems are linked to over-crowding and high flats. Lack of outdoor play space (on which there is no data in the English Housing Condition Survey) restricts the physical activities on which children's full development depends.

It is crucial to see and understand children in the context of their families, their homes and the environment in which they live, but, as argued above, it is also necessary to collect statistics which take the child as the unit of analysis and include those not living within private households. There is insufficient information collected which can be interpreted to reflect the situation of children, let alone information which is child-specific. The annual budget is analysed in terms of its impact on different household and income groups, but not, as it is in some countries, in terms of its impact on women or of its impact on children. In 1996 both Norway and Sweden published a children's annexe or supplement to their annual budgets. The Office of National Statistics' report Focus on Children, published for the first time in Britain in 1996, is a very slim volume and only includes children up to the age of 16 years and illustrates the paucity of official data on children, their lives and changing circumstances. It is also very expensive so is not going to be widely read by the general public. Indeed, it is unlikely to find its way into many public, university or school libraries. The Report of the Registrar General's decennial supplement for England and Wales, The Health of our Children, was published in 1996 and is an excellent collection of essays. However, it had a very short print run and at the time of writing was not available.

Co-ordinating policies

Functional divisions within government and between budgeting systems which do not offer any incentives to collaborate and share financial responsibilities for joint provision hamper co-ordination – the integration of education and social services for preschool children has been hindered for years by these divisions. In some policy areas there is a tendency for departments to shift responsibility for particular problems from one to the other, for example, between local authority housing and social service departments. The escalating problem of school exclusions is an example of the unintended consequences of changes in the Department of Education and Employment's budgeting systems. These changes are picked up – eventually – by social service departments and the police at great cost to individual children and their future prospects, as well as to future taxpayers. Section 27 of the Children Act 1989 and Section 166 of the Education Act 1993 are being used to establish greater co-ordination in some local services for children, but as the Children's Rights Development Unit's latest report (1994, p39) makes clear, criticism must be levelled against:

> 'government which lacks any detailed, principled strategy for children; in which different departments give mixed and contradictory orders and messages through legislation and ministers; which promotes local flexibility in guidance but often prevents it in practice because of rigid departmental boundaries and funding mechanisms.'

This is not to suggest that there is no existing recognition of the need for better co-ordination of services. As the Gulbenkian Foundation's Inquiry's 1995 consultations within central government found (Children's Rights Development Unit, 1995), in addition to the planning and co-ordination of children's services to which the Department of Health is already committed, there is also 'a great deal of individual commitment to further co-ordination and co-operation' (p5). However, since then, the Home Office has taken more responsibility for children, or rather *parenting*, and the Department of Education and Employment is the lead department for the under fives. The Department of Health therefore has a weaker role with respect to children's services.

Effective government structures for children

Compared with most government departments the voluntary sector in Britain has been more active in gathering information on governmental arrangements for co-ordinating policy on children and implementing the Convention in other countries, as well as consulting with government departments and government bodies within Britain.

The Gulbenkian Foundation has taken a leading role through the establishment and funding of the Children's Rights Development Unit in 1992. In order 'to review the full implications of the Convention for all areas of law, policy and practice affecting children in the UK, and propose action needed for compliance' (Lansdown & Newell, 1994, pxii), the Unit has consulted and worked collaboratively with a wide range of over 180 organisations, both statutory and non-statutory, as well as with professional organisations and individuals concerned with children. They also held some consultation sessions with children and young people themselves. Together with the Association of Metropolitan Authorities, in 1995, the Unit published 'Checklist for Children: local authorities and the UN Convention on the Rights of the Child' which focused on the implications of the acceptance of the UN Convention for local authority priorities and practices. In 1995 the Foundation set up an inquiry into effective government structures for children and reported in 1996. It presented a picture of current government structures for children based on evidence provided by central government departments and collated by the Department of Health. As well as considering various proposals for changing government structures and considering the case for a Children's Ombudsman or Children' Rights Commissioner, the authors of the report surveyed central and local government structures for children already introduced in other countries.

Overseas experience

There are a number of models and structures in place in various countries across the world. Some examples include Norway which was the first country to establish an independent office of a Children's Ombudsperson – *Barneombud* – in 1981. The Barneombud now receives funding from the Ministry of Children and Family Affairs, created in 1991. This ministry has three departments covering kindergarten affairs, family and gender equality issues; general child and youth policy; and consumer affairs. The Barneombud is consulted formally by government as part of the consultative 'hearings' process, which are conducted by Norwegian ministries prior to presenting legislative proposals to Parliament. Although its creation was initially controversial, by the end of the 1980s, five out of six Norwegians thought it should continue.

The Barneombud's balance of work has shifted from investigating individual cases towards pursuing issues of principle and policy change. Changes to which they have contributed include new regulations concerning the rights of children in hospital, raising the age at which young people can be imprisoned in adult prisons, legislative recognition of the rights of children to know both their parents and a requirement that the boards responsible for regulating local planning have a special official responsible for monitoring plans for their impact on children.

New Zealand has had a Ministry of Youth Affairs since 1989, responsible for policy advice on issues concerning young people aged 12–25 years, and an office of Commissioner for Children established under the Children, Young Persons and Families Act 1989. The Commissioner investigates individual complaints as well as enquiring into and reporting on laws and practices concerning the welfare of children and young persons.

Portugal has an inter-departmental commission composed of representatives of the Ministries of Education, Health, Solidarity and Social Security and Justice. In addition there is a High Commissioner for Equality and Family Matters and an Ombudsman whose function is to protect citizens including children against bad administrative practices.

Denmark has had an inter-departmental committee on children since 1989 and it now involves senior officials from 15 ministries chaired by a permanent secretary in the Ministry of Social Affairs. There is a Ministerial Committee on children which meets two or three times a year to discuss proposals from the inter-departmental committee. In 1995, Denmark established a National Council for Children's Rights for a trial three-year period. One of its tasks has been to establish direct consultation with children from different social environments and age groups. There has been consultation on issues such as children's use of television and videos, their participation in local community decision making and physical punishment. The Minister of Social Affairs in 1996 invited children under 15 years to write to her about their concerns. The most common message from the 3000 letters received was that they wanted their parents to spend more time with them.

In Canada, at the federal level there is no single department for children but there is a multi-department initiative to address the wellbeing of children, especially young people at risk and their families. This is co-ordinated by the Children's Bureau in the Department of Health. The Bureau co-ordinates policies consistent with the principles of the UN Convention and advises ministries and federal government bodies. It has about 20 permanent staff and also appoints specialist advisers. Some provincial governments have appointed an ombudsman (British Columbia) or a Children's Advocate (Alberta).

The European Union

Across the European Union there are some potentially exciting developments. For example in 1998 a project called 'Children are European Citizens too' was launched. This had financial support from the Directorate General V of the European Commission. They have organised a number of seminars which have included children aged 11 and 12 years old, as well as key decision-makers. The report (Ruxton, 1999) based on these seminars calls for the incorporation of the UN Convention into EU law as well as establishing structures and procedures which will give children's perspectives a higher profile. Some EU countries have made considerable progress in giving children a voice. For example, in France, children or youth town councils have become involved in regional and local policy making. In Britain, Ministers for Children were designated for Scotland and Wales in 1997 in conjunction with devolution, but there are few initiatives for England. In November 1998 the Government launched a national Children's Parliament on the Environment under the auspices of the Department of the Environment, Transport and the Regions. This involved school children aged 10 and 11 in debating and essay competitions on the theme 'Sustainable Development'. Ten of the winning children presented a five-point Action Plan to the Prime Minister at Downing Street in the summer of 1999. It is not clear how this will be fed into the final policy-making process.

Conclusion

There is then a wealth of ideas and evidence on how government structures and practices at all levels of policy formulation, implementation and evaluation might be changed and developed in order to provide children with the services to meet their basic needs, to more fully establish the rights of children and young people to care and protection, as well as to be active participants in society on every level. Proposals for a Select Committee on Children, a Minister for Children with a Children's Unit in the Cabinet Office and an Independent Office of Children's Rights Commissioner or Ombudsperson have been put forward and considered but none have yet been implemented. As the Audit Commission concluded in their report Seen but not Heard (1994), 'Experience so far suggests that total commitment from the top to a joint approach is crucial to success'. More broadly, the sociologist John O'Neill's (1994, p99) warning must be heeded:

'Each nation must accept responsibility for its own harshness towards children and youth and for its failure to strengthen the civic commons that has for half a century softened the discomforts of class-based poverty and prejudice. If we ever lose sight of the civic commons that is at risk in the debate of the welfare state, we truly risk returning to that state of nature where life is short, nasty and brutish.'

Appendix

Table of theorists' contributions

Theorist date	Country	Source of evidence	Age range
Erik Erikson 1902–1994	Born in Germany; emigrated to USA	Teaching experience; psycho-analysis training; anthropological studies	Life-span
John Bowlby 1907–1980	England	Psychiatrists training; research on displaced children from WWII; prison studies	Predominantly birth to ten
Jean Piaget 1886–1980	Switzerland	Biologist; observation of own three children; investigative interviews of Swiss children	Birth to puberty
Lev Vygotsky 1896–1934	Russia	Child psychologist and educationalist; anthropological studies across Russia	Birth to puberty
Urie Bronfenbrenner 1917–	USA	Psychologist; cross-cultural studies, especially in USA, Russia and China	Life-span
Alfred Adler 1870–1937	Austria; lived in USA	Psychoanalyst training, clinical work with all ages	Life-span
Michael Rutter 1933– and colleagues	England	Psychiatrist; review of longitudinal studies	Life-span

Major contribution	Cognitive	Affective	Social	Physical	Moral
Stage theory of psycho-social development		✓	✓		
Attachment theory, its significance for mental health		✓	✓		
Stage theory of child's construction of knowledge	✓				✓
Social construction of knowledge especially the contribution of culture and language	✓	implicit	✓		
An ecological framework of human development using a systems approach	✓	✓	✓		
View of people as socially connected, creative and goal-orientated		✓	✓		
Pathway concept of development; diverse influences, e.g. genetic and environment	✓	✓	✓		

References

Abbott, L. & Pugh, G. (1998) *Training to Work in the Early Years.* Open University Press, Buckingham.

Abbott, P. & Wallace, C. (1992) *The Family and the New Right.* Pluto Press, London.

Acheson, D. (1998) *Inequalities in Health.* Department of Health, London.

Alanen, L. (1994) Gender and generations: feminism and the 'child question'. In: *Childhood Matters: Social Theory, Practice and Politics* (eds J. Qvortrup, M. Bardy, G. Sgritta. & H. Wintersberger), pp27–42, Avebury, Aldershot.

Aldridge, J. & Becker, S. (1995) The rights and wrongs of children who care. In: *The Handbook of Children's Rights: Comparative Policy and Practice* (ed. B. Franklin), pp.119–30, Routledge, London.

Allied Dunbar National Fitness Survey (1992) *A Report on Activity Patterns and Fitness Levels.* Sports Council and Health Education Authority, London.

Altman, I. & Wohlwill, J.F. (eds) (1978) *Children and the Environment.* Plenum Press, New York.

Alwash, R. & McCarthy, M. (1991) Accidents in the home among children under 5: ethnic differences or social disadvantage? *British Medical Journal,* **296**, 1450–52.

Anderson, M. (1980) *Approaches to the History of the Western Family 1500–1914.* Cambridge University Press, Cambridge.

Andersson, B.-E. (1989) Effects of public day care: a longitudinal study. *Child Development,* **60**, 857–66.

Andersson, B.-E. (1992) Effects of daycare on cognitive and socio-emotional competence of thirteen-year-old Swedish school children. *Child Development,* **63**, 20–36.

Andrews, A.B. & Ben-Arieh, A. (1999) Measuring and monitoring children's well-being across the world. *Social Work,* **44**(2), 105–15.

Aries, P. (1962) *Centuries of Childhood.* Jonathon Cape, London.

Armstrong, N. & McManus, A. (1994) Children's fitness and physical activity: a challenge for physical education. *British Journal of Physical Education,* **25**(1), pp20–26.

Arnold, E. (1997) Issues of reunification of migrant West Indian children in the United Kingdom. In: *Caribbean Families: Diversity Among Ethnic Groups* (eds J.L. Roopnarine & J. Brown), pp243–58, Ablex Publishing Corporation, Greenwich, CT.

Astington, J.W. (1994) *The Child's Discovery of the Mind.* Fontana Press, London.

Atkinson, R.L., Atkinson, R.C., Smith, E.E. & Bern, D.J. (eds) (1993) *Introduction to Psychology,* Harcourt Brace Jovanovich Inc, FLA.

Audit Commission (1996) *Counting to Five: the Education of Children Under Five.* HMSO, London.

Avery, J.G. & Jackson, R.H. (1993) *Children and their Accidents.* Edward Arnold, London.

Badinter, E. (1981) *The Myth of Motherhood.* Souvenir Press, London.

Baldwin, N. & Carruthers, L. (1998) *Developing Neighbourhood Support and Child Protection Strategies: The Henley Safe Children Project.* Ashgate, Aldershot.

Ball, C. (1994) *Start Right: The Importance of Early Learning.* Royal Society for the Encouragement of Arts, Manufacturers and Commerce, London.

Bandura, A. (1989) Social cognitive theory. In: *Annals of Child Development* (ed. R. Vasta), **6,** 1–60. JAI Press, Greenwich, CT.

Bandura, A. (1997) *Self-efficacy: The Exercise of Control,* Freeman, New York.

Banks, N. (1996) Young single white mothers with black children in therapy. *Journal of Clinical Child Psychology and Psychiatry,* **1,** 1.

Barker, D.J.P. (ed.) (1992) *Fetal and Infant Origins of Adult Disease.* British Medical Journal, London.

Barker, D.J.P. (1997) Fetal nutrition and cardiovascular disease in later life. *British Medical Bulletin,* **53**(1), 96–108

Barker, M. (1989) *Comics: Ideology, Power and the Critics.* Manchester University Press, Manchester.

Barlow, J. (1997) *Systematic Review of the Effectiveness of Parent-training Programmes in Improving Behaviour Problems in Children Aged 3–10 Years.* Health Services Research Unit, Oxford.

Baron-Cohen, S. (1995) *Mindblindness.* A Bradford Book, MIT Press, Cambridge, MA.

Barrett, J. (1998) New knowledge and research in child development, Part 1. *Child and Family Social Work,* **3,** 267–76.

Barrett, J. (1999) New knowledge and research in child development, Part 2. *Journal of Child and Family Social Work,* **4,** 97–107.

Barron, S.L. and Roberts, D.F. (eds) (1995) *Issues in Fetal Medicine.* Macmillan, London.

Barton, C. (1999) A v United Kingdom: The thirty thousand pound caning – an 'English vice' in Europe. *Child and Family Law Quarterly,* **11**(1), 63–73.

Baumrind, D. (1967) Child care practices anteceding three patterns of pre-school behavior. *Genetic Psychology Monographs,* **75,** 43–88.

Bazalgette, C. & Buckingham, D. (1995) *In Front of the Children.* British Film Institute, London.

Bebbington, A. & Miles, J. (1989) The background of children who enter local authority care. *British Journal of Social Work,* **19,** 349–68.

Bee, H. (1995) *The Developing Child.* HarperCollins, New York.

Behlmer, G. (1982) *Child Abuse and Moral Reform in England, 1870–1908.* Stanford University Press, Stanford, CA.

Belsky, J. (1984) The determinants of parenting: a process model. *Child Development,* **55,** 83–96.

Belsky, J. & Vondra, J. (1989) Lessons from child abuse: the determinants of parenting. In: *Child Maltreatment* (eds D. Cicchetti & V. Carlson), pp153–202, Cambridge University Press, Cambridge.

Benjamin, J. (1992) Play and participation. *Streetwise,* Autumn issue, **12,** 2–8.

Beresford, B. (1994) *Positively Parents: Caring for a Severely Disabled Child.* HMSO, London.

Beresford, B. (1995) *Expert Opinions: A National Survey of Parents Caring for a Severely Disabled Child.* Policy Press, Bristol.

Berg, M. & Medrich, E.A. (1980) Children in four neighbourhoods: the physical environment and its effect on play and play patterns. *Environment and Behaviour*, **12**, 320–48.

Berk, L. (1994) *Infants and Children: Prenatal Through Early Childhood*. Allyn & Bacon, Boston, MA.

Berk, L. (1998) *Children through the Life Span*. Allyn and Bacon, Boston, MA.

Berrington, A. (1995) Marriage patterns and inter-ethnic unions. In: *Ethnicity in the 1991 Census* (eds D. Coleman & J. Salt), pp.178–212, OPCS.

Berry, J.W., Dasen, P.R. & Saraswathi, T.S. (eds) (1997) *Handbook of Cross-cultural Psychology, Vol. 2, Basic Processes and Human Development*. Allyn & Bacon, Needham Heights, MA.

Berry, J.W. & Sam, D.L. (1997) Acculturation and adaptation. In: *Handbook of Cross-cultural Psychology, Vol. 3, Social Behaviour and Applications* (eds J.W. Berry, M.H., Segall & C. Kağitçibaşi), pp291–326, Allyn & Bacon, Needham Heights, MA.

Berry, J.W., Segall, M.H. & Kağitçibaşi, C. (eds) (1997) *Handbook of Cross-cultural Psychology, Vol. 3, Social Behaviour and Applications*. Allyn & Bacon, Needham Heights, MA.

Bettelheim, B. (1978) *The Use of Enchantment: The Meaning and Importance of Fairy Tales*. Penguin, Harmondsworth.

Bjorklund, D.F. & Bjorklund, B.R. (1992) *Looking at Children: An Introduction to Child Development*. Brooks Cole Publishing Co., Pacific Grove, CA.

Blair, T. (1999) The Beveridge Lecture, 8 March, Toynbee Hall, London.

Blatchford, P. (1998) *Social Life in School*. Falmer Press, London.

Blenkin, G. & Yue, N. (1994) Profiling early years practitioners. *Early Years*, **15**(1), 13–22.

Blyth, A. (1984) *Development, Curriculum and Experience in Primary Education*. Croom Helm, London.

Blyth, E. (1995) The United Kingdom's Human Fertilisation and Embryology Act 1990 and the welfare of the child: A critique. *The International Journal of Children's Rights*, **3**, 417–38.

Bolak, H. (1997) When wives are major providers: culture, gender and family work. *Gender and Society*, **11**(4), 409–33.

Bornstein, M.H. & Lamb, M.E. (1992) *Developmental Psychology: An Advanced Textbook*. Erlbaum, Hillsdale, NJ.

Botting, B. (ed.) (1996) *The Health of our Children, The Registrar General's decennial supplement for England & Wales*. HMSO, London.

Boulton, M.J. & Smith, P.K. (1994) Bully/victim problems in middle school children: stability, self-perceived competence, peer perceptions, and peer acceptance. *British Journal of Developmental Psychology*, **12**, 323–9.

Boushel, M. (1994) The protective environment of children: towards a framework for anti-oppressive, cross-cultural and cross-national understanding. *British Journal of Social Work*, **24**, 173–90.

Boushel, M. (1996) Vulnerable multiracial families and early years services: concerns, challenges and opportunities. *Children and Society*, **10**, 305–16.

Boushel, M. & Lebacq, M. (1992) Towards empowerment in child protection work. *Children and Society*, **6**(1), 38–50.

Boyle, M. (1997) *Re-thinking Abortion*. Routledge, London.

Bradley, B. (1989) *Visions of Infancy*. Basil Blackwell, Oxford.

Bradley, R.H. & Caldwell, B.M. (1982) The consistency of the home environment and its relation to child development. *International Journal of Behavioural Development*, **5**, 445–65.

Bradshaw, J. (1999) Child Poverty in Comparative Perspective. Paper given at Conference 'Developing Poverty Measures: Research in Europe Defining and Measuring Poverty', Bristol, July.

Brandon, M. & Lewis, A. (1996) Significant harm and children's experiences of domestic violence. *Child and Family Social Work*, **1**, 33–42.

Brannen, J. (1999) Reconsidering children and childhood: sociological and policy perspective. In: *The New Family* (eds E. Silva & C. Smart), Sage, London.

Brannen, J. & Wilson, G. (eds) (1987) *Give and Take in Families: A Study of Resource Distribution*. Allen & Unwin, London.

Bright, M. (1999) Parents make kids too soft to survive. *The Observer*, 1 August, p12.

Broadfoot, P., Abbott, D., Croll, P., Osborn, M., Pollard, A. & Towler, L. (1991) Implementing national assessment: issues for teachers. *Cambridge Journal of Education*, **21**(2), 153–68.

Bronfenbrenner, U. (1974) The origins of alienation. *Scientific American*, **231**, 53–61.

Bronfenbrenner, U. (1979) *The Ecology of Human Development*. Harvard University Press, Cambridge, MA.

Bronfenbrenner, U. (1997) The ecology of developmental processes. In: *Handbook of Child Psychology, Vol. 1: Theoretical Models of Human Development* (ed. R.M. Lerner), Wiley, New York.

Bronfenbrenner, U. & Ceci, S.J. (1994) Nature-nurture reconceptionalized in developmental perspective: A bioecological model. *Psychological Review*, **101**, 568–86.

Browne, K. & Herbert, M. (1997) *Preventing Family Violence*. Wiley, Chichester.

Browne, K. & Saqi, S. (1988) Approaches to screening for child abuse and neglect. In: *Early Predicting and Prevention of Child Abuse* (eds K. Browne, C. Davies & P. Strattan), pp57–86, Wiley, London.

Bruce, T. (1991) *Time to Play*. Hodder & Stoughton, London.

Bruner, J.S. (1977) *The Process of Instruction*. Harvard University Press, Cambridge, MA.

Bruner, J. & Haste, H. (1987) *Making Sense: The Child's Construction of the World*. Methuen, London.

Buchan, W. (1796) *Domestic Medicine*. Balfour, Auld & Smellie, Edinburgh.

Burman, E. (1994) *Deconstructing Developmental Psychology*. Routledge, London.

Butler, I. & Williamson, H. (1994) *Children Speak*. Longman/NSPCC, London.

Cadogan, W. (1784) *Essay on the Management and Nursing of Children*. John Knapton, London.

Cairns, E. (1996) *Children and Political Violence*. Blackwell, Oxford.

Calder, P. (1996) National Vocational Qualifications in Child Care and Education: an advance? *Early Child Development and Care*, **126**, 39–50.

Calder, P. & Fawcett, M. (1998) Early Childhood Studies Degrees. In: *Training to Work in the Early Years* (eds L. Abbott and G. Pugh), Open University Press, Buckingham.

Campbell, B. (1997) So, what price motherhood now? *The Observer*, 5 May.

Cannan, C. & Warren, C. (eds) (1997) *Social Action with Children and Families: A Community Development Approach to Child and Family Welfare*. Routledge, London.

Carnegie Corporation of New York (1994) *Starting Points: Meeting the Needs of our Youngest Children*. Carnegie Corporation of New York, New York

Ceci, S.J. & Bronfenbrenner, U. (1994) Cognition in and out of context: a tale of two paradigms. In: *Development Through Life: A Handbook for Clinicians* (eds M. Rutter and D. Hay), pp239–59, Blackwell Science, Oxford.

Central Statistical Office (1994) *Social Focus on Children.* HMSO, London.

Chamba, R., Ahmad, W., Hirst, M., Lawton, D. & Beresford, B. (1999) *Minority Ethnic Families Caring for a Severely Disabled Child.* Policy Press, West Sussex.

Chapman, S. & Lupton, D. (1994) *The Fight for Public Health: Principles and Practice of Media Advocacy.* BMJ Publishing Group, London.

Charlton, A. (1996) Children and smoking: the family circle. *British Medical Bulletin,* **52**(1), 90–107.

Chasanoff, I. (1992) Cocaine polydrug use in pregnancy: two year follow up. *Pediatrics,* **89**(2), 284–9.

Childline (1996) *Talking with Children about Child Abuse.* Childline, London.

Children's Rights Development Unit (1994) *UK Agenda for Children.* Children's Rights Development Unit, London.

Children's Rights Development Unit (1995) *Making the Convention Work for Children.* Children's Rights Development Unit, London.

Chugani, H. (1996) Functional brain reorganisation in children. *Brain Development,* **18**(5), 347–56.

Cicchetti, C. & Carlson, V. (eds) (1989) *Child Maltreatment: Theory and Research on the Causes and Consequences of Child Abuse and Neglect.* Cambridge University Press, Cambridge.

Clarke, L. (1996) Demographic change and the family situation of children. In: *Children in Families: Research and Policy* (eds J. Brannen & M. O'Brien), pp66–83. Falmer Press, London.

Clausen, J.S. (1991) Adolescent competence and the shaping of the life course. *American Journal of Sociology,* **96**, 805–42.

Cloke, C. & Davies, M. (eds) (1995) *Participation and Empowerment in Child Protection.* Pitman Publishing, London.

Cochran, M. (1993) *International Handbook of Child Care Policies and Programs.* Greenwood Press, Westport, CT.

Cochran, M. (1995) European child care in global perspective. *European Early Childhood Education Research Journal,* **3**(1), 61–72.

Cochran, M., Larner, M., Riley, D., Gunnarsson, L. & Henderson, C. Jr (1990) *Extending Families: The Social Networks of Parents and their Children.* Cambridge University Press, Cambridge.

Cockett, M. & Tripp, J. (1994) *The Exeter Family Study.* University of Exeter, Exeter.

Cole, M. & Cole, S. (1993) *The Development of Children.* Scientific American Books, New York.

Cole, G.D.H. & Filson, A.W. (eds) (1967) *British Working Class Movements: Select Documents 1789–1875.* Macmillan, London.

Collins, N.L. & Read, S.J. (1994) Cognitive representations of attachment: the structure and function of working models. In: *Advances in Personal Relationships, Vol. 5: Attachment Processes in Adulthood* (eds K. Bartholomew & D. Perlaman). Jessica Kingsley, London.

Cooper, A., Hetherington, R., Baistow, K., Pitts, J. & Spriggs, A. (1995) *Positive Child Protection: A View from Abroad.* Russell House Publishing, Lyme Regis.

Cooper, P. & Murray, L. (1998) Postnatal depression. *British Medical Journal,* **316**, 1884–6.

Cooter, R. (ed.) (1992) *In the Name of the Child: Health and Welfare 1880–1940.* Routledge, London.

Corker, M. & French, S. (1999) *Disability Discourses.* Open University Press, Buckingham.

Corsaro, W.A. (1997) *The Sociology of Childhood.* Pine Forge Press, London.

Coveney, P. (1957) *The Image of Childhood, The Individual and Society: A Study of the*

Theme in English Literature (first published as *Poor Monkey*). Penguin, Harmondsworth.

Cowan, C.P. & Cowan, P.A. (1992) *When Partners Become Parents*. Basic Books, New York.

Cowan, P.A. (1997) Beyond meta-analysis: a plea for a family systems view of attachment. *Child Development*, **68**, 61–3.

Crokenberg, S. (1981) Infant irritability, mother responsiveness, and social support: influences on the security of infant-mother attachment. *Child Development*, **52**, 857–65.

Cross, W.E. (1992) *Black Identity: Theory and Practice*. Temple University Press, Philadelphia, PA.

Cullingford, C. (1994) The attitude of children to their environment. *Cambridge Journal of Education*, **24**(1), 7–19.

Cunningham, H. (1991) *The Children of the Poor: Representations of Childhood since the Seventeenth Century*. Oxford University Press, Oxford.

Cunningham, H. (1995a) *Children and Society in Western Society since 1500*. Addison Wesley Longman, Harlow, Essex.

Cunningham, H. (1995b) Moral Kombat and computer game girls. In: *In Front of the Children* (eds C. Bazalgette & D. Buckingham), British Film Institute, London.

Cutting, A.L. & Dunn, J. (1999) Theory of mind, emotion, understanding, language, and family background: individual differences and interrelations. *Child Development*, **70**(4), 853–65.

Dahlberg, G., Moss, P. & Pence, A. (1999) *Beyond Quality in Early Childhood Education and Care*. Falmer Press, London.

Dallison, J. & Lobstein, T. (1995) *Poor Expectations, Poverty and Undernourishment in Pregnancy*. NCH and the Maternity Alliance, London.

Daniel, B., Wassell, S. & Gilligan, R. (1999) *Child Development for Child Care and Protection Workers*. Jessica Kingsley Publishers, London.

Davidoff, L. & Hall, C. (1987) *Family Fortunes.* Hutchinson Educational, London.

Davin, A. (1978) Imperialism and motherhood. *History Workshop*, **5**, 9–65.

Davin, A. (1996) *Growing up Poor: Home, School and Street in London 1870–1914*. Oram Press, London.

Davis, A. & Jones, L. (1997) Whose neighbourhood? Whose quality of life? Developing a new agenda for children's health in urban settings. *Health Education Journal*, **56**, 350–63.

Dawson, G., Frey, K., Panagiotides, H., Osterling, J. & Hess, D. (1997) Infants of depressed mothers exhibit atypical frontal brain activity: a replication and extension of previous findings. *Journal of Child Psychology and Psychiatry*, **38**(2), 179–86.

Daycare Trust (1995*) Reaching First Base: Meeting the Needs of Refugee Children from the Horn of Africa – Guidelines for Good Practice*. Daycare Trust, London.

Department for Education and Employment (1996) *Desirable Outcomes for Entry to Statutory Schooling*. DfEE Publications, London.

Department for Education and Employment (1998) *Meeting Special Educational Needs – a Programme of Action*. DfEE Publications, London.

Department for Education and Employment (1999a) *Sure Start: Making a Difference for Children and Families*. DfEE Publications, London.

Department for Education and Employment (1999b) *Early Learning Goals*. DfEE Publications, London.

Department of Health (1988) *Protecting Children: A Guide for Social Workers Undertaking a Comprehensive Assessment*. HMSO, London.

Department of Health (1992) *The Health of the Nation: strategy for health in England.* HMSO, London.

Department of Health (1994) *The National Food Guide.* The Stationery Office, London.

Department of Health (1995a) *Breastfeeding: Good Practice Guidance to the NHS.* HMSO, London.

Department of Health (1995b) *Child Protection: Messages from Research.* HMSO, London.

Department of Health (1996) *The Patient's Charter: Services for Children and Young People.* Department of Health, London.

Department of Health (Brazier report) (1998) *Surrogacy: Review for Health Ministers of Current Arrangements for Payments and Regulation.* The Stationery Office, London.

Department of Health (1998a) *Why Mothers Die, Report on Confidential Enquiries into Maternal Deaths in the United Kingdom 1994–1996.* The Stationery Office, London.

Department of Health (1998b) *Health and Personal Social Services Statistics for England.* The Stationery Office, London.

Department of Health (1998c) *Modernising Health and Social Services, National Priorities Guidance 1999/0–2001/2.* Department of Health, London.

Department of National Heritage (1995) *Sport: Raising the Game.* HMSO, London.

Department of Social Security (1998) *Households Below Average Income 1979–1996/7.* Stationery Office, London.

Department of Social Security (1999) *A New Contract for Welfare: Children's Rights and Parents' Responsibilities,* Cm 4349. The Stationery Office, London.

Department of the Environment (1993) *Annual Report: The Government Expenditure Plans for 1993–4 to 1995–6.* HMSO, London.

Department of Trade and Industry (1992) *Home and Leisure Accident Research Data.* Consumer Safety Unit, London.

Department of Transport (1995) *National Travel Survey Report,* HMSO, London.

De Casper, A.J. & Spence, M.J. (1986) Prenatal maternal speech influences newborns'perception of speech sounds. *Infant Behaviour and Development,* **9,** 133–50.

De Casper, A.J., Lecaneut, J.P., Busnel, M.C., Granier-Deferre, C. & Maugeais, R. (1994) Fetal reactions to recurrent maternal speech. *Infant Behaviour and Development,* **17,** 159–64.

De Vries, J.I.P., Visser, G.H.A. & Prechtl, H.F.R. (1984) Fetal motility in the first half of pregnancy. In: *Continuity of Neural Functions from Prenatal to Postnatal Life* (ed. H.F.R. Prechtl), pp46–64. Spastics International Medical, London.

Dibble, U. & Straus, M. (1980) Some social structure determinants of inconsistency between attitudes and behaviour: the case of family violence. *Journal of Marriage and the Family,* February, 71–82.

Dickins, M. (1999) Programming for special educational needs. *Coordinate,* March, 70.

Di Giuseppi, C., Roberts, I. & Leah, L. (1997) Influences of changing travel patterns on child death rates from injury: trend analysis. *British Medical Journal,* **314,** 710–13.

Donaldson, M. (1978) *Children's Minds.* Penguin, Harmondsworth.

Dosanjh, J.S. & Ghuman, P.A.S. (1997) Child-rearing practices of two generations of Punjabi parents. *Children and Society,* **11,** 29–43.

Dosanjh, J.S. & Ghuman, P.A.S. (1998) Child-rearing practices of two generations of Punjabis: development of personality and independence. *Children and Society,* **12,** 25–37.

Douglas, G., Murch, M. & Perry, A. (1996) Supporting children when parents separate: a neglected family, justice or mental health issue? *Child and Family Law Quarterly*, **8**(2), 121–35.

Dowler, E. & Calvert, C. (1995) *Nutrition and Diet in Lone-parent Families in London*. Family Policy Studies Centre, London.

Dunn, J. (1988) *The Beginnings of Social Understanding*. Basil Blackwell, Oxford.

Dunn, J. (1993) *Young Children's Close Relationships: Beyond Attachment*. Sage, London.

Dunn, J. (1996) Children's relationships: bridging the divide between cognitive and social development. *Journal of Child Psychology and Psychiatry*, **37**, 507–18.

Dunn, J. & Kendrick, C. (1982) *Siblings, Love, Envy and Understanding*. Harvard University Press, London.

Dunn, J. & McGuire, S. (1992) Sibling and peer relationships in childhood. *Journal of Child Psychology and Psychiatry*, **33**(1), 67–105.

Dunn, J., Deater-Deckard, K., Pickering, K., O'Connor, T.G. & Golding, J. (1998) Children's adjustment and prosocial behaviour in step-, single-parent and non-stepfamily settings. *Journal of Child Psychology and Psychiatry*, **39**, 1083–95.

Dweck, C. (1986) Motivational processes affecting learning. *American Psychologist*, October, 1040–46.

Dwork, D. (1987) *War is Good for Babies and Other Young Children: A History of the Infant and Child Welfare Movement in England 1895–1918*. Tavistock Publications, London.

Early Childhood Education Forum (1998) *Quality and Diversity in Early Learning*. National Children's Bureau, London.

Edwards, C., Gandini, L. & Forman, G. (1998) *The Hundred Languages of Children: The Reggio Emilia Approach – Advanced Reflections*. Ablex Publishing, London.

Eekelaar, J. (1996) The interests of the child and the child's wishes: the role of dynamic self-determination. In: *The Best Interests of the Child* (ed. P. Alston), pp43–61. UNICEF.

Elliot, F.R. (1996) *Gender, Family and Society*. Macmillan, Basingstoke.

Enkin, M., Keirse, M.J.M.C., Renfrew, M. & Neilson, J. (1995) *A Guide to Effective Care in Pregnancy and Childbirth*. Oxford University Press, Oxford.

Erikson, E.H. (1963) *Childhood and Society*. Penguin Books, Harmondsworth.

European Commission Network on Childcare (1996) *Quality Targets in Services for Young Children*. Thomas Coram Foundation/European Commission, London.

Evans, P. & Fuller, M. (1998) The purposes of nursery education in the UK: parent and child perspectives. *European Early Childhood Education Research Journal*, **6**(2), 35–54.

Falbo, T. (1992) Social norms and the one-child family. In: *Children's Sibling Relationships* (eds F. Boer & J. Dunn). Erlbaum, Hillsdale, NJ.

Family Policy Studies Centre (1994) *Policies for Families: Work, Poverty and Resources*. Family Policy Studies Centre, London.

Farmer, E. & Owen, M. (1995) *Child Protection Practice: Private Risks and Public Remedies*. HMSO, London.

Fawcus, M. (ed.) (1997) *Children with Learning Difficulties: A Collaborative Approach to their Education and Management*. Whurr Publishers, London.

Fergusson, D.M., Horwood, J. & Thorpe, K. (1996) Changes in depression during and following pregnancy. *Paediatric and Perinatal Epidemiology*, **10**, 279–93.

Ferri, E., Birchall, D., Gingell, V. & Gipps, C. (1981) *Combined Nursery Centres*. National Children's Bureau, London.

Ferri, E. & Smith, K. (1996) *Parenting in the 1990s*. Family Policy Studies Centre, London.

Finlayson, G. (1990) A moving frontier: voluntarism and the state in British social welfare 1911–1949. *Twentieth Century British History*, Vol. 1, pp183–286.

Fisher, M., Marsh, P., Phillips, D. with Sainsbury, E. (1986) *In and Out of Care.* Batsford, London.

Flin, R. & Spencer, J.R. (1995) Children as witnesses – legal and psychological perspectives. *Journal of Child Psychology and Psychiatry,* **36**(2), 171–89.

Fonagy, P., Steele, M., Steele, H., Higgit, A. & Target, M. (1994) The theory and practice of resilience. *Journal of Child Psychology and Psychiatry,* **35**(2), 231–57.

Fordham, K. & Stevenson-Hinde, J. (1999) Shyness, friendship quality and adjustment during middle childhood. *Journal of Child Psychology and Psychiatry,* **40**(5), 757–86.

Fortin, J. (1998a) Case Commentary Re C. A baby's right to die. *Child and Family Law Quarterly,* **10**(4), 11–416.

Fortin, J. (1998b) *Children's Rights and the Developing Law.* Butterworths, London.

Fox Harding, L. (1991) *Perspectives in Child Care Policy.* Longman, London.

Frankenburg, C. (1934) *Common Sense in the Nursery.* Cape, London.

Franklin, B. (ed.) (1995) *The Handbook of Children's Rights: Comparative Policy and Practice.* Routledge, London.

Garbarino, J. (1982) *Children and Families in the Social Environment.* Aldine De Gruyter, New York.

Garbarino, J., Kostelny, K. & Dubrow, N. (1991) *No Place to be a Child: Growing up in a War Zone.* Lexington Books, Lexington, MA.

Gardner, H., Torff, B. & Hatch, T. (1996) The age of innocence reconsidered. In: *The Handbook of Education and Human Development* (eds D.R. Olson & N. Torrance), pp28–55. Blackwell, Oxford.

Garvey, C. (1977) *Play.* Fontana/Open Books, London.

Gathorne-Hardy, J. (1972) *The Rise and Fall of the British Nanny.* Hodder & Stoughton, London.

Gibbons, J., Gallagher, B., Bell, C. & Gordon, D. (1995) *Development after Physical Abuse in Early Childhood.* HMSO, London.

Gingerbread (1999) *Glue and Glitter.* Gingerbread.

Gipps, C. (1990) *Assessment: A Teachers' Guide to the Issues.* Hodder & Stoughton, London.

Gladstone, D. (1999) *The Twentieth Century Welfare State.* Macmillan, London.

Golding, J. (1996) Short and long term associations of smoking in pregnancy. In: *Smoking and Pregnancy Conference Report,* meeting held 20/10/94 Newcastle, Co Down, N. Ireland, Belfast Health Promotion Unit, pp1–18.

Goleman, D. (1996) *Emotional Intelligence.* Bloomsbury, London.

Goldschmied, E. & Jackson, S. (1993) *People Under Three.* Routledge, London.

Goldschmied, E. & Selleck, D. (1996) *Communication between Babies in their First Year.* National Children's Bureau, London.

Gonzalez Mena, J. (1993) *Multicultural Issues in Child Care.* Mayfield Publishing Company, London.

Gordon, L. (1989) *Heroes of Their Own Lives: The Politics and History of Family Violence.* Virago, London.

Gough, D. (1993) *Child Abuse Interventions: A Review of the Research Literature.* HMSO, London.

Graham, H. (1980) Mothers' accounts of anger and aggression towards their babies. In: *Psychological Approaches to Child Abuse* (ed. N. Frude), pp39–51, Batsford, London.

Graham, H. (1993) *Hardship and Health in Women's Lives.* Harvester Wheatsheaf, London.

Green, J.M., Coupland, V.A. & Kitzinger, J.V. (1990) Expectations, experiences, and psychosocial outcomes of childbirth: a prospective study of 825 women. *Birth,* **17**(1), 15–24.

Green, J.M., Coupland, V.A. & Kitzinger, J.V. (1998) *Great Expectations. A Prospective Study of Women's Expectations and Experiences of Childbirth*, 2nd edn, Books for Midwives Press, Hale, England.

Gregg, P., Harkness, S. & Machin, S. (1999) Trends in child poverty in Britain 1968–1996. *Fiscal Studies*, **20**, 2 June.

Gregory, S. (1991) Challenging motherhood: mothers and their deaf children. In: *Motherhood: Meanings, Practices and Ideologies* (eds A. Phoenix, A. Woollett & E. Lloyd), Sage, London.

Gregson, N. & Lowe, M. (1994) *Servicing the Middle Classes: Class, Gender and Unwaged Domestic Labour in Contemporary Britain*. Routledge, London.

Guillemin, J.H. & Holstrum, L.L. (1986) *Mixed Blessings: Intensive Care for Newborns*. Oxford University Press, New York.

Gunnoe, M.L. & Mariner, C.L. (1997) Toward a developmental-contextual model of the effects of parental spanking on children's aggression. *Archives of Pediatrics and Adolescent Medicine*, **151**, 768–75.

Hackett, L. & Hackett, R. (1994) Child-rearing practices and psychiatric disorder in Gujerati and British children. *British Journal of Social Work*, **24**, 191–202.

Hainstock, E.G. (1978) *The Essential Montessori*. Mentor Books, New York.

Hall, D.M.B. (ed.) (1996) *Health for All Children: Report of Joint Working Party on Child Health Surveillance*. Oxford University Press, Oxford.

Hardiker, P., Exton, K. & Barker, M. (1995) *The Prevention of Child Abuse: A Framework for Analysing Services*. The National Commission of Inquiry into the Prevention of Child Abuse, London.

Hardyment, C. (1995) *Perfect Parents: Baby-care Advice Past and Present*. Oxford University Press, Oxford.

Harker, L (1999) Assessment of the UK's second report. *Childright*, **160**, 4–5.

Harlen, W., Gipps, C., Broadfoot, P. & Nuttall, D. (1992) Assessment and the improvement of education. *Curriculum Journal*, **3(3)**, 217–25.

Harris, P. (1989) *Children and Emotions: The Development of Psychological Understanding*. Blackwell, Oxford.

Hartcliffe and Withywood Black Support Group (1993) *Standing Out: To be Black in Hartcliffe and Withywood*. Sari/Barnardos, Bristol.

Harvey, E. (1999) Short-term and long-term effects of early parental employment on children: the National Longitudinal Survey of Youth. *Developmental Psychology*, **35(2)**, 445–59.

Haskey, J. (1996) *Population Trends*. HMSO, London.

Hazareesingh, S., Simms, K. & Anderson, P. (1989) *Educating the Whole Child*. Building Blocks/Save the Children, London.

Hendrick, H. (1999) *Child Welfare: England 1872–1989*. Routledge, London.

Hester, M. & Radford, L. (1996) *Domestic Violence and Child Contact Arrangements in England and Denmark*. Policy Press, Bristol.

Hetherington, E.M., Reiss, D. & Plomin, R. (eds) (1993). *The Separate Social Worlds of Siblings: Impact of Nonshared Environment on Development*. Erlbaum, Hillsdale, NJ.

Hill, P. (1993) Recent advances in selected aspects of adolescent development. *Journal of Child Psychology and Psychiatry*, **34(1)**, 69–99.

Hillman, M. (ed.) (1993) *Children, Transport and the Quality of Life*. Policy Studies Institute, London.

Hillman, M., Adams, J. & Whitelegg, J. (1990) *One False Move ... a Study of Children's Independent Mobility*. Policy Studies Institute, London.

Hills, J. (1995) *Joseph Rowntree Foundation Inquiry into Income and Wealth*. Joseph Rowntree Foundation, York.

Hobcraft, J. & Kiernan, K. (1999) *Childhood Poverty, Early Motherhood and Adult Social Exclusion*, Case Paper 28, London School of Economics.

Hohmann, M. & Weikart, D. (1995) *Educating Young Children*. High/Scope Educational Research Foundation.

Holland, P. (1996) I've just seen a hole in the reality barrier. In: *Thatcher's Children* (eds J. Pilcher & S. Wragg), Falmer Press, London.

Holterman, S. (1995) *All Our Futures*, Barnardo's, Barkingside.

Home Office (1989) *Report of the Advisory Group on Video Evidence* (Pigot Report). Home Office, London.

Home Office (1992) *Memorandum of good practice on video recorded interviews with child witnesses for criminal proceedings*. HMSO, London.

Home Office (1998) *Supporting Families: A Consultation Document*. Home Office, London.

Hooper, C.A. (1992) *Mothers Surviving Child Sexual Abuse*. Routledge, London.

Horn, P. (1994) *Children's Work and Welfare, 1780–1890*. Cambridge University Press, Cambridge.

Horn, P. (1995) *Women in the Twenties*. Alan Sutton Publishing, Stroud.

Horrell, S. & Humphries, J. (1995) The exploitation of little children: child labour and the family economy in the Industrial Revolution. *Explorations in Economic History*, **32**, 485–516.

Howard, S. (ed.) (1998) *Wired Up – Young People and the Electronic Media*. UCL, London.

Howarth, C., Kenway, P., Palmer, G. & Street, C. (1999) *Monitoring Poverty and Social Exclusion: Labour's Inheritance*. Joseph Rowntree Foundation, York.

INFOPEDIA (1995) *World Almanac Map*. Futura Vision.

Iwaniec, D. (1999) *The Emotionally Abused and Neglected Child*. Wiley, Chichester.

Jackson, P. (1968) *Life in Classrooms*. Holt, Rinehart & Winston, New York.

Jackson, S. (1987) *The Education of Children in Care*. University of Bristol.

Jackson, B. & Jackson, S. (1979) *Childminder*. Routledge & Kegan Paul, London.

James, A. & Prout, A. (eds) (1990, 1997) *Constructing and Reconstructing Childhood*. Falmer Press, London.

James, A., Jenks, C. & Prout, A. (1998) *Theorizing Childhood*. Polity Press, Oxford.

James, W., Nelson, M., Ralph, A. & Leather, S. (1997) Socioeconomic determinants of health: the contribution of nutrition to inequalities in health. *British Medical Journal*, **314**, 1545–57.

Jensen, J.J. (1996) *Men as Workers in Childcare Services*. European Commission Network on Child Care, Brussels.

Johnson, Z. & Molloy, B. (1995) The community mothers programme – empowerment of parents by parents. *Children and Society*, **9(2)**, 73–83.

Jones, A. (1998) The child welfare implications of UK immigration and asylum policy. *Childright*, **149**, 3–5.

Kagan, J., Kearsley, R.B. & Zelazo, P.R. (1978) *Infancy: Its Place in Human Development*. Harvard University Press, Cambridge, MA.

Kagan, J. (1998) Biology and the child. In: *Handbook of Child Psychology* (ed. N. Eisenberg), 5th edn Vol. 3, *Social, Emotional and Personality Development*. Wiley, New York.

Kağitçibaşi, C. (1989) Child rearing in Turkey: implications for immigration and intervention. In: *Different Cultures Same School: Ethnic Minority Children in Europe* (eds L. Eldering & J. Kloprogge), pp137–52. Swets, Berwyn, PA.

Kağitçibaşi, C. (1990) Women's intra-family status in Turkey: cross-cultural perspectives. In: *Women, Family and Social Change in Turkey* (ed. F. Ozbay), pp51–69. UNESCO, Bangkok.

Kağitçibaşi, C. (1996) *Family and Human Development Across Cultures: A View from the Other Side*. Lawrence Erlbaum Assoc., Mahwah, New Jersey.

Kaseras, P. & Hopkins, E. (1987) *British Asians in the Community.* Wiley, Chichester.

Kay, H. (1999) The mental health problems of children and young people. *Child-right*, April, 9–11.

Kessen, W. (1979) The American child and other cultural inventions. *American Psychologist*, **34(10)**, 815–20.

Kiernan, K., Land, H. & Lewis, J. (1998) *Lone Mothers in Twentieth Century Britain.* Oxford University Press, Oxford.

King, M. (1997) *A Better World for Children: Explorations in Morality and Authority.* Routledge, London.

King, T. & Fullard, W. (1982) Teenage mothers and their infants: new findings on the home environment. *Journal of Adolescence*, **5**, 333–46.

Kiray, M. (1990) The family of the migrant worker. In: *Women, Family and Social Change in Turkey* (ed. F. Ozbay), pp70–90. UNESCO, Bangkok.

Kovacs, M. (1997) Depressive disorders in childhood: an impressionistic landscape. *Journal of Child Psychology and Psychiatry*, **38(3)**, 287–98.

Kramer, R. (1976) *Maria Montessori: A Biography.* G.P. Putnam and Sons, New York.

Kuhl, P.K. (1991) Perception, cognition and the ontogenetic and phylogenetic emergence of human speech. In: *Plasticity of Development* (eds W. Hall & R. Dooloing), MIT Press/Bradford Books Cambridge, MA.

Kumar, V. (1993) *Poverty and Inequality in the UK: The Effects on Children.* National Children's Bureau, London.

Lamb, E.K. (1999) Dyslexia, gender and brain imaging. *Neuropsychologia*, **37(5)**, 521–36.

Lamb, M. (1997) *The Role of the Father in Child Development.* Wiley and Sons, New York.

Land, H. (1999) New labour, new families. Paper presented to Bristol International Credit-Earning Programme, 26th June, Bristol.

Lansdown, G. & Newell, P. (eds) (1994) *UK Agenda for Children.* Children's Rights Development Unit, London.

Leach, P. (1999) Physical punishment of children in the home. *Highlight*, **166**, National Children's Bureau & Barnardo's, London.

Lealand, G. (1998) Where do snails watch TV? Preschool television and New Zealand children. In: *Wired Up – Young People and the Electronic Media* (ed. S. Howard). UCL, London.

Leathard, J. (1994) *Going Interprofessional: Working Together for Health and Welfare.* Routledge, London.

Legg, C., Sherick, I. & Wadland, W. (1974) Reaction of pre-school children to the birth of a sibling. *Child Psychiatry and Human Development*, **5**, 3–39.

Lindon, J. (1999) *Too Safe For Their Own Good?* National Early Years Network, London.

Livingstone, S. & Bovill, M. (2000) *Young People New Media.* Sage, London.

Lochman, J.E., Coie, J.D., Underwood, M.K. & Terry, R. (1993) Effectiveness of a social relations, intervention programme for aggressive and non-aggressive rejected children. *Journal of Consulting and Clinical Psychology*, **61**, 1053–8.

Logan, B. (1992) Prelearning: trials and trends. *International Journal of Prenatal and Perinatal Studies*, **4**, 67–9.

London Borough of Lambeth (1987) *Whose Child? The Report of the Public Inquiry into the Death of Tyra Henry.* London.

Maccoby, E.E. (1984) Middle childhood in the context of the family. In: *Development during Middle Childhood* (ed. W.A. Collins), National Academy Press, Washington, DC.

Macdonald, G. & Roberts, H. (1995) *What Works in the Early Years.* Barnardos, Barkingside.

Machel, G. (1996) *Report on the Impact of Armed Conflict on Children.* United Nations A/51/306. 26th August.

Machin, S. (1999) Childhood disadvantage and intergenerational transmission of economic status. In: *Persistent Poverty and Lifetime Inequality.* CASE Reports, London School of Economics.

Makins, V. (1997) *Not Just a Nursery: Multi-agency Early Years Centres in Action.* National Children's Bureau, London.

Makrides, M., Neumann, M.A., Byard, R.W., Simmer, K. & Gibson, R.A. (1994) Fatty acid composition of brain, retina, and erythrocytes in breast fed and formula fed infants. *American Journal of Clinical Nutrition,* **60**, 189–94.

Malaguzzi, L. (1993) For an education based on relationships. *Young Children,* **49(1)**, 9–12.

Mama, A. (1989) *The Hidden Struggle.* Runnymede Trust/London Race and Housing Research Unit, London.

Mayall, B. (1994a) *Negotiating Health: Children at Home and Primary School.* Cassell, London.

Mayall, B. (1994b) *Children's Childhoods Observed and Explained.* Falmer, London.

Mayall, B. (1996a) The changing context of childhood: children's perspectives on health care resources including services. In: *The Health of our Children, The Registrar General's decennial supplement for England & Wales* (ed. B. Botting). HMSO, London.

Mayall, B. (1996b) *Children, Health and the Social Order.* Open University Press, Buckingham.

McCarthy, G. & Taylor, A. (1999) Avoidant/ambivalent attachment style as a mediator between abusive childhood experiences and adult relationship difficulties. *Journal of Child Psychology and Psychiatry,* **40**, 465–77.

McGlone, F., Park, A. & Roberts, C. (1996) Relative values: kinship and friendship. In: *British Social Attitudes, the 13th Report* (eds P. Jowell, J. Curtice, A. Park, L. Brook & K. Thomson). Social & Community Planning Research, Dartmouth, Aldershot.

McGurk, H. & Glachan, M. (1987) Children's conception of the continuity of parenthood following divorce. *Journal of Child Psychology and Psychiatry,* **28**, 427–35.

McGurk, H., Caplan, M., Hennessy, E. & Moss, P. (1993) Controversy, theory and social context in contemporary day care research. *Journal of Child Psychology and Psychiatry,* **34(1)**, 3–23.

Meadows, S. (1993) *The Child as Thinker: The Development and Acquisition of Cognition in Childhood.* Routledge, London.

Meltzer, H. (1994) *Day Care Services for Children.* Office of Population Censuses and Surveys, Social Survey Division. HMSO, London.

Mental Health Foundation (1999) *Bright Futures: Promoting Children and Young People's Mental Health.* Mental Health Foundation, London.

Middleton, S., Ashworth, K. & Braithwaite, I. (1997) *Small Fortunes.* Joseph Rowntree Foundation, York.

Miller, P.H. (1993) *Theories of Developmental Psychology.* W.H. Freeman & Co., New York.

Minty, B. & Patterson G. (1994) The nature of child neglect. *British Journal of Social Work,* **24**, 733–48.

Mitchell, B.R. & Deane, P. (1962) *Abstract of British Historical Statistics.* Cambridge University Press.

Moore, R. (1986) *Childhood's Domains,* Croom Helm, London.

Morley, R. (1998) Food for the infant's brain. *BNF Nutrition Bulletin,* **23**, Supplement 1.

Moss, P. & Penn, H. (1996) *Transforming Nursery Education*. Paul Chapman, London.

Mullender, A. & Morley (eds) (1994) *Living with Domestic Violence*. Whiting & Birch, London.

Murray, L. & Trevarthen, C. (1985) Emotional regulation of interactions between 2 month olds and their mothers. In: *Social Perception in Infants* (eds T. Field & N.A. Fox), Ablex, Norwood, NJ.

Murray, L., Hipwell, A. & Hooper, R. (1996) Cognitive development of 5 year old children of postnatally depressed mothers. *Journal of Child Psychology and Psychiatry*, **37(8)**, 927–35.

Nash, J. (1997) Fertile minds. *Time*, **149**, pp48–56.

Nathanielsz, P.W. (1996) *Life before Birth*. Freeman & Co, Basingstoke.

National Asthma Campaign (1998) *Information for Asthma Sufferers*. National Asthma Campaign, London.

NCH Action for Children (1991) *Poverty and Nutrition Survey*. NCH, London.

Newcomb, A.F., Bukowski, W.M. & Pattee, L. (1993) Children's peer relations: a meta-analytic review of popular, rejected, neglected, controversial and average sociometric status. *Psychological Bulletin*, **113**, 99–128.

Newell, P. (1989) *Children are People Too: The Case against Physical Punishment*. Bedford Square Press, London.

Newson, J. & Newson, E. (1989) *The Extent of Physical Punishment in the UK*. Approach, London.

Nic Ghoilla Phádraig, M. (1994) Day care – adult interests versus children's needs. In: *Childhood Matters: Social Theory, Practice and Politics* (eds J. Qvortrup, M. Bardy, G. Sgritta & H. Wintersberger), pp77–100, Avebury, Aldershot.

Nobes, G. & Smith, M. (1997) Physical punishment of children in two-parent families. *Clinical Child Psychology and Psychiatry*, **2(2)**, 271–81.

Nowicki, S. & Duke, M. (1992) *Helping the Child Who Doesn't Fit In*. Holt, Rinehart & Winston, New York.

Nunes, T. (1993) Psychology in Latin America: the case of Brazil. *Psychology and Developing Societies*, **5**, 123–34.

Nutbrown, C. (ed.)(1997) *Respectful Educators – Capable Learners: Children's Rights and Early Education*. Paul Chapman, London.

Oatley, K. (1994) *Best Laid Schemes: The Psychology of Emotions*. Cambridge University Press, Cambridge.

Oatley, K. & Nundy, S. (1996) Rethinking the role of emotions and education. In: *The Handbook of Education and Human Development* (eds D.R. Olson & N. Torrance), pp257–74, Blackwell Science, Oxford.

O'Brien, M., Alldred, P. & Jones, D. (1996) Children's constructions of family and kinship. In: *Children in Families: Research and Policy* (eds J. Brannen & M. O'Brien), pp84–100, Falmer Press, London.

O'Neill, J. (1994) *The Missing Child in Liberal Theory*. University of Toronto Press, Toronto.

Office of National Statistics (1998a) *Social Trends 28*. The Stationery Office, London.

Office of National Statistics (1998b) *Living in Britain: Results from the 1996 General Household Survey*. The Stationery Office, London.

Office of Population Censuses and Surveys (OPCS) (1991) *Adult Nutrition Survey*. HMSO, London.

Office of Population Censuses and Surveys (OPCS) (1995) *Social Trends 25*. HMSO, London.

Okagaki, L. & Sternberg, R.J. (1993) Parental belief and children's school performance. *Child Development*, **64**, 36–56.

Oliver, M. (1996a) *Understanding Disability: From Theory to Practice.* Macmillan, Basingstoke.

Oliver, M. (1996b) Defining impairment and disability. In: *Exploring the Divide: Illness and Disability* (eds C. Barnes & G. Mercer), The Disability Press, Leeds.

Olsen, J.H., Nielson, A. & Schulgen, G. (1993) Residence near high voltage facilities and the risk of cancer in children. *British Medical Journal,* **307**, 891–5.

Olson, D.R. & Bruner, J. (1996) Folk psychology and folk pedagogy. In: *The Handbook of Education and Human Development* (eds D.R. Olson & N. Torrance), Blackwell, Oxford.

Opie, I. & Opie, P. (1959) *Children's Games in Street and Playground.* Oxford University Press, Oxford.

Owen, D. (1993) *Ethnic Minorities in Great Britain: Housing and Family Characteristics.* Centre for Research in Ethnic Relations, Warwick.

Ozbay, F. (ed.) (1990) *Women, Family and Social Change in Turkey.* UNESCO, Bangkok.

Palmer, G. (1993) *The Politics of Breastfeeding.* Pandora, London.

Paradice, R. (1993) The effects of postnatal depression on child development. In: *Surviving Childhood Adversity* (eds H. Ferguson, R. Gilligan & R. Torode). Social Studies Press, Trinity College, Dublin.

Parkes, C.M., Stevenson-Hinde, J. & Marris, P. (eds) (1991) *Attachment across the Life Cycle.* Routledge, London.

Pascal, C. & Bertram, T. (1997) *Effective Early Learning.* Hodder & Stoughton, London.

Passaro, K.T., Little, R.E., Savitz, D.A., Noss, J. & the Alspac Study Team (1996) The effects of maternal drinking before conception and in early pregnancy on infant birthweight. *Epidemiology,* **7**, 377–83.

Pellegrini, A.D. & Bjorklund, D.F. (1996) The place of recess in school: issues in the role of recess in children's education. *Journal of Research in Childhood Education,* **11(1)**, 5–13.

Penn, H. (1995) The relationship of private day care and nursery education in the UK. *European Early Childhood Education Research Journal,* **3(2)**, 29–41.

Penn, H. (1996) Sizing up babies' needs. *Nursery World,* 18 January, 18–19.

Penn, H. (1997) *Comparing Nurseries.* Paul Chapman Publishing, London.

Penn, H. (1998) Facing some difficulties. In: *Training to Work in the Early Years* (eds L. Abbott and G. Pugh), Open University Press, Buckingham.

Perris, C., Arrindel, W.A. & Eisemann, M. (1994) *Parenting and Psychopathology.* Wiley, Chichester.

Pettitt, B. (ed.) (1998) *Children and Work in the UK.* Save the Children/CPAG, London.

Phillips, D. (1995) Giving voice to children. *European Early Childhood Education Research Journal,* **3(2)**, 5–14.

Phoenix, A. (1990) Black women in the maternity services. In: *The Politics of Maternity Care* (eds J. Garcia. & R. Kilpatrick). Oxford University Press, Oxford.

Phoenix, A., Woollett, A. & Lloyd, E. (1991) *Motherhood: Meanings, Practices and Ideologies.* Sage, London.

Pinchbeck, I. & Hewitt, M. (1973) *Children in English Society, Vol. II: From the Eighteenth Century to the Children Act 1948.* Routledge & Kegan Paul, London.

Pinker, S. (1994) *The Language Instinct.* Penguin, London.

Platt, L. & Noble, M. (1998) *Race, Place and Poverty: Ethnic Groups and Low Income Distributions.* Joseph Rowntree Foundation, York.

Plomin, R. (1994) *Genetics and Experience: The Interplay between Nature and Nurture.* Sage Publications, London.

Plomin, R. (1995) Genetics and children's experiences in the family. *Journal of Child Psychology and Psychiatry*, **36**, 33–68.

Plomin, R., Corley, R., DeFries, J.C. & Fulker, D.W. (1990) Individual differences in television viewing in early childhood: nature as well as nurture. *Psychological Science*, **1(6)**, 371–7.

Pollard, A. (1985) *The Social World of the Primary School*. Cassell, London.

Pollard, A. (1996) *Reflective Teaching in the Primary School*. Cassell, London.

Pollard, A., Broadfoot, P., Croll, P., Osborn, M. & Abbott, D. (1994) *Changing English Primary Schools?* Cassell, London.

Pollard, A. with Filer, A. (1996) *The Social World of Children's Learning*. Cassell, London.

Pollard, A. & Filer, A. (1999) *The Social World of Pupil Careers*. Cassell, London.

Pollard, A. & Triggs, P. (2000) *Policy, Practice and Pupil Experience*. Cassell, London.

Pollock, L. (1983) *Forgotten Children: Parent–Child Relations from 1500–1900*. Cambridge University Press.

Pollock, L. (1987) *A Lasting Relationship: Parents and Children over Three Centuries*. Fourth Estate, London.

Population Trends 92 (1998) Summer. The Stationery Office, London.

Porter, R. (1982) *English Society in the Eighteenth Century*. Penguin Books, Harmondsworth.

Postman, N. (1983) *The Disappearance of Childhood*. W.H. Allen, London.

Prout, A. & James, A. (1997) *Constructing and Reconstructing Childhood: Contemporary Issues in the Sociological Study of Childhood*. Falmer Press, London.

Pugh, G. (1989) Parents and professionals in pre-school services: is partnership possible? In: *Parental Involvement* (ed. S. Wolfendale). Cassell Educational, London.

Pugh, G. (ed.) (1996) *Contemporary Issues in the Early Years*, 2nd edn. National Children's Bureau, London.

Pugh, G., De'Ath, E. & Smith, C. (1984) *Confident Parents, Confident Children*. National Children's Bureau, London.

Qualifications and Curriculum Authority (QCA) (1998) *Draft Framework for Qualifications and Training in the Early Education, Childcare and Playwork Sectors*. QCA, London.

Qualter, A., Francis, C., Boyes, E. & Stanisstreet, M. (1995) The greenhouse effect. What do primary children think? *Education*, **(3)13**, 23–8.

Quennell, P. (ed.) (1969) *Mayhew's London: Selections from London Labour and the London Poor*. Spring Books, London.

Quinton, D. & Rutter, M. (1988) *Parenting Breakdown: The Making and Breaking of Inter-generational Links*. Avebury, Aldershot.

Quinton, D., Pickles, A., Maughan, B. & Rutter, M. (1993) Partners, peers and pathways: assortative parenting and continuities in conduct disorder. *Development and Psychopathology*, **5**, 763–83.

Qvortrup, J., Bardy, M., Sgritta, G. & Wintersberger, H. (eds) (1994) *Childhood Matters: Social Theory, Practice and Politics*. Avebury, Aldershot.

Ranger, G. (1993) Kids in Cities Conference Report. *Streetwise*, **4(3&4)**, 24.

Reading, A., Cheng Li, C. & Kerin, J.F. (1989) Psychological state and coping style. *Journal of Reproductive and Infant Psychology*, **7**, 95–105.

Reggio Children (1997) *Shoe and Meter: Children and Measurement*. Reggio Children, Reggio Emilia, Italy.

Reggio Children (1998) *Children, Spaces, Relations: Metaproject for an Environment for Young Children*. Reggio Children, Reggio Emilia, Italy.

Rice, P.L. & Manderson, L. (eds) (1996) *Maternity and Reproductive Health in Asian Societies*. Harwood Academic Publishers, Amsterdam.

Richards, M. (1993) Children and parents and divorce. In: *Parenthood in Modern Society: Legal and Social Issues for the Twenty-first Century* (eds J. Eekelaar & P. Sarcevic), pp307–16. Martinus Nijhoff Publishers, Dordrecht.

Richman, N. & Stevenson, J. (1982) *Pre-school to School: A Behavioural Study*. Academic Press, London.

Roberts, H. (1995) Deaths of children in house fires – fanning the flames of child health advocacy? *British Medical Journal*, **311**, 1381–2.

Roberts, H., Smith, S. & Bryce, C. (1995) *Children at Risk? Safety as a Social Value*. Open University Press, Bucks.

Robinson, C. & Stalker, K. (eds) (1998) *Growing up with Disability*. Jessica Kingsley, London.

Rodgers, B. & Pryor, J. (1998) *Divorce and Separation: The Outcomes for Children*. Joseph Rowntree Foundation, York.

Rogan, W.J. & Gladen, B.C. (1993) Breastfeeding and cognitive development. *Early Human Development*, **31**, 181–93.

Rogoff, B. (1990) *Apprenticeship in Thinking*. Oxford University Press, Oxford.

Rose, L. (1991) *The Erosion of Childhood, 1860–1918*. Routledge, London.

Rosenbaum, M. (1993) *Children and the Environment*. National Children's Bureau, London.

Rowling, J.K. (1998) *Harry Potter and the Philosopher's Stone*. Bloomsbury, London.

Royal College of Physicians (1992) *Smoking and the Young*. Royal College of Physicians, London.

Rustin, M. & Rustin, M. (1987) *Narratives of Love and Loss*. Verso, London.

Rutter, M. (1981) *Maternal Deprivation Reassessed*, 2nd edn. Penguin, Harmondsworth.

Rutter, M. (1985) Resilience in the face of adversity: protective factors and resistance to psychiatric disorder. *British Journal of Psychiatry*, **147**, 598–611.

Rutter, M. (1989) Pathways from childhood to adult life. *Journal of Child Psychology and Psychiatry*, **30(1)**, 23–51.

Rutter, M. (1995) Clinical implications of attachment concepts. *Journal of Child Psychology and Psychiatry*, **36**, 549–71.

Rutter, M., Quinton, D. & Hill, J. (1990) Adult outcomes of institution-reared children: males and females compared. In: *Straight and Devious Pathways from Childhood to Adulthood* (eds L. Robins & M. Rutter). Cambridge University Press, Cambridge.

Rutter, M. & Rutter, M. (1993) *Developing Minds*. Penguin, Harmondsworth.

Rutter, M. and the ERA team (1998) Developmental catch up and deficit following adoption. *Journal of Child Psychology and Psychiatry*, **39(4)**, 465–76.

Ruxton, S. (1999) *A Children's Policy for 21st Century Europe: First Steps*. Euronet, Brussels.

Sanderson, M. (1983) *Education, Economic Change and Society in England, 1780–1870*. Cambridge University Press, Cambridge.

Saporiti, A. (1994) A methodology for making children count. In: *Childhood Matters* (eds J. Qvortrup, M. Bardy, G. Sgritta & H. Wintersberger), pp189–210. Avebury, Aldershot.

Sawyer, C. (1999) One step forward, two steps back – the European Convention on the Exercise of Children's Rights. *Child and Family Law Quarterly*, **11(2)**, 151–70.

Sayer, A., Cooper, C. & Barker, D.J.P. (1997) Is lifespan determined in utero? *Archives of Disease in Childhood*, **77**, F162–4.

Schaffer, H.R. (1977) *Mothering*. Open Books, London.

Schweinhart, L. & Weikart, D. (1997) The High/Scope Preschool Curriculum Comparison Study Through Age 23: Executive Summary. OMEP *Update Number 87*. OMEP, London.

Scott-Heyes, G. (1983) Marital adaptation during pregnancy and after childbirth. *Journal of Reproductive and Infant Psychology*, **1**, 18–29.

Seiter, E. (1995) Toy based video for girls: My Little Pony. In: *In Front of the Children*. (eds C. Bazalgette & D. Buckingham). British Film Institute, London.

Selleck, R.J.W. (1972) *English Primary Education and the Progressives 1914–1939*. Routledge, London.

Seltzer, J.A. (1991) Relationships between fathers and children who live apart: the father's role after separation. *Journal of Marriage and the Family*, **53**, 79–101.

Selwyn, J. (1996) Mirror, mirror on the wall: identity and childlessness. In: *A Case of Neglect: A Sociology of Childhood* (ed. I. Shaw). Avebury, Aldershot.

Sharland, E.D., Jones, J., Aldgate, J., Seal, M. & Croucher, M. (1995) *Professional Interventions in Child Sexual Abuse*. HMSO, London.

Sheridan, M. (1973) *Children's Developmental Progress from Birth to Five Years*. National Foundation for Educational Research, London.

Sinclair, R., Hern, B. & Pugh, G. (1997) *Preventive Work with Families: The Role of Mainstream Services*. National Children's Bureau, London.

Shropshire, J. & Middleton, S. (1999) *Small Expectations: Learning to be Poor*. Joseph Rowntree Foundation, York.

Smiley, P.A. & Dweck, C.S. (1994) Individual differences in achievement goals among young children. *Child Development*, **65**, 1723–43.

Smith, T. (1996) *Family Centres and Bringing up Young Children*. HMSO, London.

Smith, J.R. & Brooks-Gunn, J. (1997) Correlates and consequences of harsh discipline for young children. *Archives of Pediatrics and Adolescent Medicine*, **151**, 777–86.

Society of Teachers Opposed to Physical Punishment (STOPP) (1979) *The European Example: The Abolition of Corporal Punishment in European Schools*. STOPP, Croydon.

Soloman, M. (1995) *Mozart: A Life*. Hutchinson, London.

Southworth, M. (1993) City learning: children, maps and travel. *Streetwise*, Issue 15/16, **4(3&4)**, 13–20.

Spencer, C., Blades, M. & Morsley, K. (1989) *The Child in the Physical Environment*. Wiley, Chichester.

Spodek, B. (1973) *Early Childhood Education*. Prentice-Hall, New Jersey.

Springer, S.P. & Deutsch, G. (1993) *Left Brain Right Brain*. Freeman & Co., New York.

Spring-Rice, M. (1981) *Working-Class Wives: Their Health and Conditions*. Virago, London.

Steedman, C. (1990) *Childhood, Culture and Class in Britain: Margaret McMillan, 1860–1931*. Virago, London.

Steedman, C. (1992) Bodies, figure and physiology: Margaret McMillan and the late nineteenth century remaking of working class childhood. In: *In the Name of the Child: Health and Welfare 1880–1940* (ed. R. Cooter), pp19–44. Routledge, London.

Stevenson, O. (1998) *Neglected Children: Issues and Dilemmas*. Blackwell Science, Oxford.

Stevenson-Hinde, J. & Glover, A. (1996) Shy girls and boys: a new look. *Journal of Child Psychology and Psychiatry*, **37**, 181–7.

Steward, J.C. (1995) *The New Child: British Art and the Origins of Modern Childhood, 1730–1830*. University of California, Berkeley.

Stone, L. (1977) *The Family, Sex and Marriage in England 1500–1800*. Penguin Books, Harmondsworth.

Stott, F. & Bowman, B. (1996) Child development knowledge: a slippery base for practice. *Early Childhood Research Quarterly*, **11**, 169–83.

Straus, M., Sugarman, D. & Giles-Sims, J. (1997) Spanking by parents and subsequent antisocial behaviour of children. *Archives of Pediatrics and Adolescent Medicine*, **151**, 761–7.

Strongman, K.T. (1996) *The Psychology of Emotion*, 4th edn. Wiley, Chichester.

Sudbury, J. (1998) Black voluntary organisations working with children: surviving the nineties. In: *Children's Services: Shaping up for the Millennium* (eds B. Cohen and U. Hagen), Children in Scotland/Stationery Office.

Super, C.M. & Harkness, S. (1986) The developmental niche: a conceptualization at the interface of child and culture. *International Journal of Behavioural Development*, **9**, 545–69.

Sutton, A. (1995) The new gene technology and the difference between getting rid of illness and altering people. *European Journal of Genetics in Society*, **1(1)**, 12–20.

Tekeli, S. (1990) The meaning and limits of feminist ideology in Turkey. In: *Women, Family and Social Change in Turkey* (ed. F. Ozbay), pp139–59, UNESCO, Bangkok.

Tekeli, S. (ed.) (1995) *Women in Modern Turkish Society*. Zed Books, London.

Tharp, R. & Gallimore, R. (1988) *Rousing Minds to Life*. Cambridge University Press, New York.

Thom, D. (1992) Wishes, anxieties, play and gestures: child guidance in inter-war England. In: *In the Name of the Child: Health and Welfare 1880–1940* (ed. R. Cooter), pp200–219. Routledge, London.

Thompson, R.A. (1994) Emotion regulation: a theme in search of definition. *Monograph of the Society for Research in Child Development*, **59** (2–3, Serial No. 240).

Tilly, L.A. & Scott, J.W. (1987) *Women, Work and Family*. Methuen, London.

Timberlake, L. & Thomas, L. (1990) *When the Bough Breaks ...* Earthscan, London.

Titman, W. (1991) Children set aside. *Streetwise*, Summer Issue, **7**, 5–7.

Tizard, B., Blatchford, P., Burke, J., Farquhar, C. & Plewis, I. (1988) *Young Children at School in the Inner City*. Erlbaum, Hove.

Tizard, B. & Phoenix, A. (1993) *Black, White or Mixed Race: Race and Racism in the Lives of Young People of Mixed Parentage*. Routledge, London.

Trevarthen, C. (1987) Brain development. In: *The Oxford Companion to the Mind* (ed. R. Gregory), pp101–10. Oxford University Press, Oxford.

Triseliotis, J., Shireman, J. & Hundelby, M. (1997) *Adoption Theory, Policy and Practice*. Cassell, London.

Tronick, E. & Gianino, A. (1986) The transmission of maternal disturbance to the infant. In: *New Directions for Child Development* (eds Z. Edward, E. Tronick & T. Field). Jossey Bass, San Francisco, CA.

Tronick, E., Morelli, G. & Winn, S. (1987) Multiple caretaking of Efe (Pygmy) infants. *American Anthropologist*, **89**, 96–106.

Troyna, B., & Hatcher, R. (1992) *Racism in Children's Lives*. National Children's Bureau, London.

Tuan, Y.F. (1978) Children and the natural environment. In: *Children and the Environment* (eds I. Altman & J.F. Wohlwill). Plenum Press, New York.

UNICEF (1998) *State of the World's Children* , Unicef, New York.

United Nations (1989) *The Convention on the Rights of the Child*. United Nations, New York.

Urwin, C. & Sharland, E. (1992) From bodies to minds in childcare literature: advice to parents in inter-war Britain. In: *In the Name of the Child: Health and Welfare 1880–1940* (ed. R. Cooter), pp174–99. Routledge, London.

van Montfoort, A. (1993) The protection of children in the Netherlands: between justice and welfare. In: *Surviving Childhood Adversity: Issues for Policy and Practice* (eds H. Ferguson, R. Gilligan & R. Torode), pp27–37. Social Studies Press, Trinity College, Dublin.

Vygotsky, L. (1978) *Mind in Society: The Development of Higher Psychological Processes.* Harvard University Press, Cambridge, MA.

Wadsworth, M.E.J. (1991) *The Imprint of Time: Childhood, History and Adult Life.* Oxford University Press, Oxford.

Walczak, Y. & Burns, S. (1984) *Divorce: The Child's Point of View.* Harper & Row, London.

Walvin, J. (1982) *A Child's World: A Social History of English Childhood 1800–1914.* Penguin Books, Harmondsworth.

Ward, C. (1978) *The Child in the City.* Architectural Press Ltd, London.

Ward, S. (1997) Turned on and switched. *Times Educational Supplement,* April 18, p11.

Wardle, D. (1976) *English Popular Education, 1780–1975.* Cambridge University Press, Cambridge.

Warner, M. (1989) *Into the Dangerous World.* Chatto, London.

Webster-Stratton, C. & Herbert, M. (1994) *Troubled Families: Problem Children.* Wiley, Chichester.

Wells, G. (1985) Pre-school literacy-related activities and success in school. In: *Literacy, Language and Learning: The Nature and Consequences of Reading and Writing* (eds D.G. Olson, N. Torrance & A. Hildyard), pp229–55. Cambridge University Press, Cambridge.

Werner, E. (1979) *Crosscultural Childhood Development: A View from Planet Earth,* p270. Brooks/Cole, Monterey, CA.

Werner, E. (1990) Protective factors and individual resilience. In: *Handbook of Early Childhood Intervention* (eds S. Meissels & J. Shonkoff). Cambridge University Press, Cambridge.

Westlake, D. & Pearson, M. (1997) Child protection and health promotion: whose responsibility? *Journal of Social Welfare and Family Law,* **19(2)**, 139–58.

Wheway, R. & Millward, A. (1997) *Child's Play: Facilitating Play on Housing Estates.* (Rowntree Foundation Report) Coventry Chartered Institute of Housing.

Whitbread, N. (1975) *The Evolution of the Nursery-Infant School.* Routledge & Kegan Paul, London.

White, A., Freeth, S. & O'Brien, M. (1992) *Infant Feeding 1990.* HMSO, London.

Whitebook, M., Howes, C. & Phillips, D. (1989) *Who Cares? Child Care Teachers and the Quality of Care in America.* Child Care Employee Project, Oakland, CA.

Whitehead, M. (1992) The health divide. In: *Inequalities in Health: the Black Report and the Health Divide* (eds P. Townsend, M. Whitehead & N. Davidson). Penguin, London.

Whiting, B.B. & Edwards, C.P. (1988) *Children of Different Worlds: The Formation of Social Behaviour.* Harvard University Press, Cambridge, MA.

Whiting, B.B. & Whiting, J.W.M. (1975) *Children of Six Cultures: A Psycho-Cultural Analysis.* Harvard University Press, Cambridge, MA.

Willow, C. & Hyder, T. (1999) *It Hurts You Inside: Children Talking about Smacking.* National Children's Bureau, London.

Wilson, A. (1987) *Mixed Race Children: A Study of Identity.* Allen & Unwin, London.

Wolf, A.W., Lozoff, B., Latz, S. & Paludetto, R. (1996) Parental theories in the management of young children's sleep in Japan, Italy, and the United States. In: *Parental Cultural Belief Systems: Their Origins, Expressions and Consequences* (eds S. Harkness & C.M. Super), pp364–8. Guilford Press, New York.

Wolkind, S. & Zajicek, E. (1981) *Pregnancy: A Psychological and Social Study.* Academic Press, London.

Wollstonecraft, M. (1792) *A Vindication of the Rights of Men and A Vindication of the Rights of Women.* Cambridge Texts in the History of Political Thought, 1995. Cambridge University Press.

Women's Indicators and Statistics (1999) http://www.die.gov.tr/toyak/hhturkey/index.html.

Woodhead, M. (1996) *In Search of the Rainbow.* Bernard van Leer Foundation, The Hague.

Woodhead, M. (1997) Psychology and the cultural construction of children's needs. In: *Constructing and Reconstructing Childhood* (eds A. James & A. Prout), pp63–85. Falmer Press, London.

Woodhead, M. (1999) Towards a global paradigm for research into early childhood education. *European Early Childhood Education Research Journal,* **7(1)**, 5–22.

Woodhead, M., Faulkner, D. & Littleton, K. (eds) (1998) *Cultural Worlds of Early Childhood.* Routledge, London.

Woodroffe, C., Glickman, M., Barker, M. & Power, C. (1993) *Children, Teenagers and Health: The Key Data.* Open University Press, Buckingham.

Wordsworth, W. *Ode: Intimations of Mortality.*

Wright, P. (1990) Psychological insights into early feeding experience. In: *Excellence in Nursing: The Research Route* (eds A. Faulkner & T. Murphy-Black). Scutari Press Midwifery, London.

Wynn, D. (1992) Addition and subtraction by human infants. *Nature,* **358(6389)**, 749–50.

de Young, M. (1994) Women as mothers and wives in paternally incestuous families: coping with role conflict. *Child Abuse and Neglect,* **18**, 73–83.

Statutes and conventions

Children and Young Persons Act 1933

Children (England and Wales) Act 1989

Children (Scotland) Act 1995

Criminal Justice Act 1991

Family Law Act 1996

Human Rights Act 1998

African Charter on the Rights and Welfare of the Child 1990, Organisation for African Unity

European Convention on the Exercise of Children's Rights 1995

European Convention on Human Rights 1959, 1996

United Nations Convention on the Rights of the Child 1989 (ratified by the UK in 1991)

Landmark legal cases

A v. *United Kingdom Application no. 25599/94* (Eu Comm Report 18-9-97).

Campbell and Cosans v. *United Kingdom* (1982) 4 EHRR 293.

Costello-Roberts v. *UK* (1994) ELR 1

R v. *Hopley* (1Russ.Cr.751) 1860

Sutton London Borough Council v. *Davis* (1994) 1 FLR

Tyrer v. *United Kingdom* (1978) 2 EHRR 1

Web addresses

General

http://childhouse.uio.no:80/index.html   A site dedicated to information on children, including health, lists of resources, access to data and to online journals. The site on early childhood is very good.

http://www.cybereditions.com/aldaily   A daily digest of the best writing on the web. Links to international newspapers and magazines.

Charities and voluntary organisations

http://www.unicef.org/sowc96pk/mainmenu.htm   The Unicef site which includes the State of the World's Children.

http://www.vois.org.uk   Links to most voluntary and charity organisations.

Law and policy

http://www2.essex.ac.uk/clc   The Children's Legal Centre. The site is concerned with law and policy affecting children and young people.

http://webjcli.ncl.ac.uk   A good general law resource.

http://www.itsofficial.net   Access to legislation, offical government publications and information affecting government at a regional and national level.

http://www.parliament.uk   The House of Commons web site.

http://www.audit-commission.gov.uk   Concerned with statistical information and best value in health and social care.

http://www.carelaw.org.uk   Guide to the law for young people in care.

http://www.open.gov.uk   Entry point for all government papers.

http://www.doh.gov.uk   Includes current policy documents and links to SSI publications and national statistics.

Health

http://www.bmj.com   The British Medical Journal on line, also has a very good search engine.

http://www.healthfinder.gov   General health site run by the US government. It has lots of useful links.

History

http://landow.stg.brown.edu/victorian/victov.html   Concentrates on Victorian Britain, includes child labour, education and public health.

Journals

There are more and more full text electronic journals coming on line. Here are a few:

http://www.futureofchildren.org

http://www.childwelfare.com

http://www.pgi.edu

Psychology

http://www.worthpublishers.com/thedevelopmentofchildren   This site is linked to the text Cole, M. & Cole, S. (1996) *The Development of Children*. Freeman, New York. It has good education web links to other sites related to child development.

Research findings

http://www.jrf.org.uk   The summaries of research findings funded by the Joseph Rowntree Foundation.

http://www.regard.ac.uk   Searchable bibliographic database containing information on UK social science research.

http://www.soton.ac.uk/~chst/   UK data and reference source, in particular children and families and child and family law.

Index